MW00356106

# DEVIL'S GATE

The middle of nowhere. Looking up the Sweetwater toward Split Rock, 1870, tents of the Hayden Survey in the middle distance. Photograph by W. H. Jackson, courtesy of USGS photo archive.

# Devil's Gate

## Owning the Land,
## Owning the Story

Tom Rea

UNIVERSITY OF OKLAHOMA PRESS : NORMAN

Also by Tom Rea

*Man in a Rowboat* (Copper Canyon Press, 1977)
*Smith and Other Poems* (Dooryard Press, 1985)
*Bone Wars: The Excavation and Celebrity of Andrew Carnegie's Dinosaur*
  (Pittsburgh, 2001)

Library of Congress Cataloging-in-Publication Data

Rea, Tom, 1950–
    Devil's Gate : owning the land, owning the story / Tom Rea.
       p.   cm.
    Includes bibliographical references and index.
    ISBN 0–8061–3792–4 (alk. paper)
  1. Sweetwater River Valley (Wyo.)—History.  2. Sweetwater River Valley
(Wyo.)—Biography.  3. Oregon National Historic Trail—History, Local.
4. Devil's Gate (Wyo.)—History.  I. Title.
    F767.S92R43 2006
    978.7'85—dc22                                    2006040258

The paper in this book meets the guidelines for permanence and durability of
the Committee on Production Guidelines for Book Longevity of the Council on
Library Resources, Inc. ∞

Copyright © 2006 by the University of Oklahoma Press, Norman, Publishing
Division of the University. All rights reserved. Manufactured in the U.S.A.

1 2 3 4 5 6 7 8 9 10

for Max

# Contents

# Illustrations

## Photographs

## Maps

# Acknowledgments

Many people helped me think about, research, and better understand this book. Among those at the Casper College Library, I need to thank Laurie Lye and her assistant Ami Dyrek on the interlibrary loan desk, and Kevin Anderson of special collections, for many cheerful and tireless efforts on my behalf. The Wyoming State Historical Society granted me generous assistance from its Homsher endowment, which financed research trips to Denver and Oshkosh, Nebraska. Dan Whipple, Geoff O'Gara, Paul Hannan, Dan Neal, and Anne MacKinnon read parts of the book in manuscript and offered many useful suggestions. Candy Moulton gave me good ideas on where to look for material when I was just starting out. Beth Southwell, my fellow Billy Owen fan, led me to Daniel Meschter's extraordinary *Carbon County Chronology*. Berthenia Crocker, attorney for the Arapaho Tribe in Wyoming, tipped me off to Loretta Fowler's *Arapahoe Politics,* which opened so many routes for me to pursue in my understanding of the tribes in the nineteenth century.

Gaynell and Norman Park of the Dumbell Ranch, and Ruth Stevenson of the Pathfinder Ranch cheerfully answered many questions and allowed me to explore on foot and by car some places important to the book. Elder Bryce Christiansen at the Mormon Handcart Visitors' Center was kind enough to share his thoughts with me early on and cleared up some of my early confusions among the Lajeunesses. Much later in the process, Scott Lorimer, former president of the Riverton Stake, gave me crucial insights—both to the nature of the Mormon attachment to Martin's Cove and to his own role in securing the Sun Ranch for the Church.

Among the Suns, I need especially to thank Dennis, Steve, Kathleen, Adelaide Sun Reinholtz, Tena, and Noeline, for taking many hours to talk with me. Among local historians, Lee Underbrink, Randy Brown, and Pinky and Jackie Ellis deeply enriched my understanding of the Oregon-California Trail over the course of many conversations and field trips. For helping me understand John C. Frémont's various scientific instruments and how they worked, I'm grateful to Bob Graham and his excellent Frémont website at www.longcamp.com. I also need to thank Rick Young and his staff at the Fort Caspar Museum, the historian Jack McDermott, who steered me to the Guinard depredation claims; and Jefferson Glass, who steered me to the Magloire Mosseau interviews. And I'd particularly like to thank Ellie Hufsmith, for turning over a variety of Watson-Averell material from her husband's collection to the special collections at the Casper College Library, including two photos of Ella Watson, one of which I've used in the book. The historian Lyndia Carter of Springville, Utah, gave me important help on my handcart chapter, particularly on the questions of resupply and the subsequent evolution of Mormon attitudes toward the event. She and her co-author, Gary Long of the Bureau of Land Management, have books on the day-to-day progress of the Willie and Martin companies due out soon from the University of Utah Press. Among other historians, I'm especially grateful to Phil Roberts of the University of Wyoming and Will Bagley of Salt Lake City, who read my first draft for the publisher, and were so positive in their support and specific in their suggested improvements.

Next to last, I'd like to thank Chuck Rankin, my editor at the University of Oklahoma Press, who liked this idea and somehow seemed to understand it better than I did the first time I described it to him three years ago. And finally, I need to thank Barb, lover of the truth, my wife, my best reader, and my best friend.

# DEVIL'S GATE

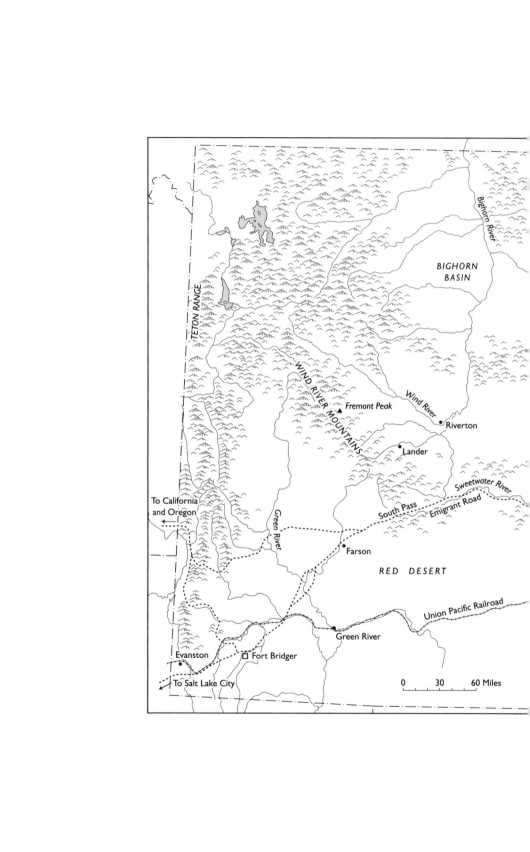

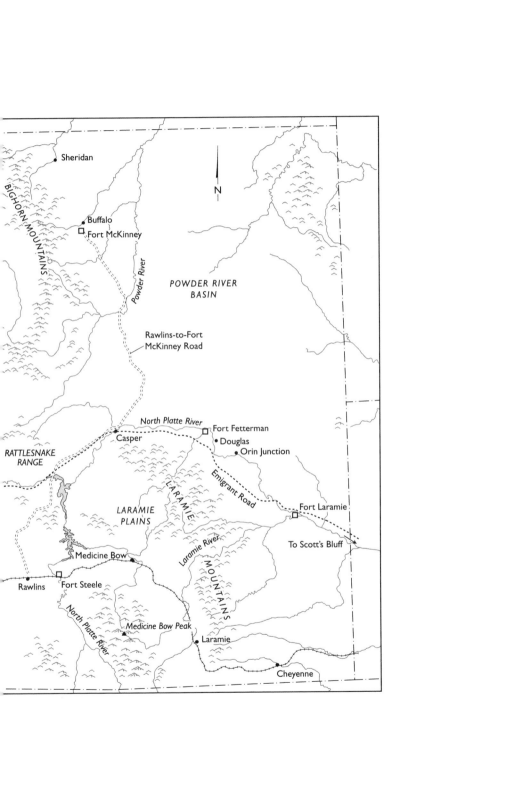

# The Middle of Nowhere

In school we learned that North America was nowhere until Europeans arrived and its history began. Columbus, the first explorer, discovered America; the Pilgrims, the first settlers, landed at Plymouth Rock. And so on, from right to left, east to west across the continent, the pattern continued. Nowhere gradually became somewhere; an unknown landscape became known, then owned. First it was explored, and then it was taken up. When the taking got violent, the newcomers used the word "conquer"—a word that implies a superior right on the part of the conquistadors, the conquering ones.

In a human sense, nowhere had been somewhere all along. The land the Europeans stumbled on was full of human occupants, alive with their civilizations, their commerce and economies, their contending empires. The newcomers, with their more advanced weapons and their diseases, laid waste to these things. Conquest meant holocaust, devastation, an end to nearly everything for the original inhabitants. Conquest turned a vibrant somewhere into nowhere.

These two versions of the story—the victors' version, and the survivors'—seem at first to pass completely through each other, untouched, as though they were opposite doctrines and only one could be true. The first gained an initial power that has lasted centuries. The second, because it is truer, may in the long run prove equally resilient.

I first entered Wyoming from Pittsburgh decades ago, carried here by the east-to-west vectors of version one. The horizon, the rising and setting sun, the space, the startling clarity all seemed to confirm an essentially book-born sense of romance I'd carried with me. Since then, for more than thirty years, the West has been entering me, instead of the opposite. Version two, in small increments, has been gaining on me ever since.

What I find before me now is a place where the two opposite versions of the truth are mingling with and soaking into one another. One way to better understand it, I thought, would be to look at a small part of the West where many interesting things have happened: the country in the middle of Wyoming around Independence Rock and Devil's Gate. From the start, without knowing quite what I was looking for, I kept finding middle ground.

I found middle ground, literally, between Bird Island and the former shore of Pathfinder Reservoir, the ground whose drouthy existence threatens those elegant pelicans' future a little more each year. I found middle ground between what the Boston historian Francis Parkman wanted Indians to be in the 1840s and the ways he found his Oglala hosts surviving. I found middle ground among Lieutenant John C. Frémont's ambitions, skills, and heedless incompetencies, and middle ground between peace and war in the trading cabins kept by the French Indians along the North Platte and the Sweetwater. The emigrant road itself came to seem a long, thin middle ground between home and exile, or old homes and new, its landmarks simply landmarks to the travelers, not places with pasts or futures. When the war did come, I found U.S. Army Private Hervey Johnson discovering wide stretches of uneasy middle ground between himself, his neighbors, and his foes.

Everything seemed ambiguous. William Henry Jackson's photos crystallized the ambiguity: he caught the Sweetwater just before so many decisions were made, with the country's exploit-or-preserve-it questions yet unasked. Billy Owens's surveying work, by contrast, was unequivocal. He was all about exploitation, bursting with eagerness to grid the country with township and range. He seems never to have given his surveys' meaning a second thought. They altered the place profoundly, if invisibly at first; they made private land ownership possible. Billy's understanding may have been simple, but ownership was not; it was complicated by a thousand years of European custom and a hundred years of a simple Enlightenment idea, Jefferson's plan of the six-mile square.

Neither concept ever imagined such a dry, treeless place as the country along the Sweetwater, let alone how people might best live in it. It was as if the survivors' version of the North American past was starting to take revenge on the victors' version. The system for taking up land was wrong for the place from the start. It rewarded scofflaws like the ranching Durbins and Bothwells, and punished the middling classes who tried, more or less, to abide by its rules. The punishment we remember is an infamous lynching; but many, many more people just left. This took a long time, and, but for the trailer village of Mormon missionaries a few miles south of Devil's Gate, the country again is nearly as empty as when Tom Sun first brought in his shorthorned Oregon Durhams.

Things might have turned out differently if John Wesley Powell had been as skilled a politician as he was explorer and bureaucrat. He might have been able to persuade one or two key senators that it was not too late to change U.S. land law. Under their influence, Congress might have enacted something close to his idea of four-section grazing homesteads for the arid West. By 1889, the grazing homesteads plus Powell's idea of a larger grazing commons on the uplands away from the streams, managed jointly by the ranchers using them, would have meant harmony on the Sweetwater, so the daydream goes. All the ranches would have been roughly the same size and quality. There would have been no hatred of newcomers by first-comers, no backlash or thievery among later arrivals, no lynching, and no bitterness down through the years in its wake.

All that is just a daydream, of course. Conflicts between native and newcomer were built into every equation in North America from Columbus and the Pilgrims onward; they probably were unavoidable. Each group of newcomers aspired to the status of native, seeking a power base on which to turn and protect itself against the next incoming group. Mormonism grew strong out of a disciplined reaction to exactly those forces: the self-exile to Deseret was meant to be a journey away from conflict, a journey to a place where Brigham Young and his followers could rule unmolested. By the time the handcart companies came along, the discipline was so strong it could overrule common sense, and so the Willie and Martin companies were caught in the snow.

That, too, might have turned out differently. Levi Savage, who spoke up against the plan to continue on to Salt Lake so late in the year, might have had one good friend, one influential supporter among the elders in the room. One more eloquent, high-status, well-informed voice at the right moment, advising caution, not zeal, might have persuaded the Willie and Martin companies to winter at Winter Quarters on the Missouri River, scrounging what food they could, instead of starting on those last thousand miles with such high hopes and bad equipment. There would have been no long string of deaths over the 150 miles from the North Platte to South Pass in 1856, and thus no reason, as the years went by, for the faithful to focus all that sorrow on a single place, Martin's Cove.

Nearly a century and a half later, there would have been no Mormon market for the Sun Ranch when finally it was divided. The Mormon urge to own the land to control the story would have been irrelevant here. The Sun Ranch would have been no more nor less important than any other big single-family ranch in the West. The many, many stories of people and land at Devil's Gate and Independence Rock, with all they have to tell us about ambiguity, about the middle ground between nowhere and somewhere, would have survived on an equal footing.

Instead, Levi Savage went unheeded and now the Mormons are interested in only one story at Devil's Gate. It's the simple, inspiring story of suffering and faith, shorn of its confusions and contradictions, shorn even of many of its facts. The little People of the Sweetwater Museum is there, with Indian backrests, irrelevant pistols, and pictures of Tom Sun and Boney Earnest, and in the Suns' old front room the Buffalo Bill carbine still hangs over the river-rock fireplace. Without asking, anyone can scramble all over the rocks and the country to his heart's content, as I have—something the Suns did not generally allow. I'm deeply grateful to the Mormons for that. But we part ways on the storytelling. The truth is, it's become largely a one-story place. The Sun Ranch is a parking lot for Martin's Cove.

Left this way, it will be the greatest tragedy of all: the victory, at Devil's Gate, of the one story over the many. Martin's Cove is now a Mormon somewhere, and will remain so; faith appears to have tricked history off the land. This book is an attempt to tell the land's other stories, too.

# CHAPTER 1

# Pelicans on the Sweetwater

The Casper Tribune said not long ago, if one saw a man coming down the street, with a cowboy hat on, wearing a business suit, and a pair of bright red boots, it surely was Bill Grieve. His brand was the Sunset.

—*Ruth Beebe, 1973*

Pelicans are fishing birds, and in the West they generally fly along rivers. Among those rivers is the Sweetwater, flowing down off the Continental Divide in Wyoming to join the North Platte about 100 miles to the east. The river got its name when some trader's sugar-laden pack mule, on fording, lost its footing and its load and sweetened the water for miles downstream. Or it got its name from the sweetish taste that the alkaline soil roundabout imparted to the water, or it got its name because the water *wasn't* alkaline and bitter but, rather, sweet, fresh, and pure. In any case, white travelers when they reached it from the east had just crossed fifty-five dust-dry miles of sagebrush steppe, with scarcely any water at all—and after a month or more following the brown and silty Platte. By then, any water would have seemed sweet, simply by being there.

But we were speaking of pelicans. In Wyoming we have the American white pelican, *Pelecanus erythrorhynchos*, and white they are, blazing white, with black wing tips and great orange-yellow bills. They are enormous, much bigger than the bald eagles that also coast our rivers, hunting fish; the pelicans' wings spread sometimes to nine and a half feet. Their grace, however, and their unanimity are more startling even than their size. They fly in flocks of two or three to fifteen or twenty. Like many species of smaller birds, but few of large ones, they can move in unison. Eagles fly mostly alone and, individualists that we think we are, we enjoy them for that. Pelicans fly together. They soar together, bank together, slide sideways and then spiral together up the thermals—so high sometimes they disappear. They never stray far from water, though. If a person has time and stays near the water, the pelicans will be back. They are common in central Wyoming along the North Platte and Sweetwater rivers, spring through fall. In winter, sensibly, they go south.

One place surpasses all others for pelican watching. Ten miles upstream from its mouth, the Sweetwater swings around a last meander, passes the corrals of the old Sun Ranch, and then abruptly cuts through a wall of granite. Just two hundred yards later, the river emerges again onto the sagebrush plain, meanders through the Dumbell Ranch, past Independence Rock and on east through sagebrush and alkali flats to a long arm of Pathfinder Reservoir. There, the Sweetwater's water first mingles with the waters of the North Platte.

Back where it flows through the granite, however, the river leaves a notch 360 feet high, a gunsight, a steep-sided, counterintuitive vee. For why wouldn't the river go *around* the granite wall? The wall ends only half a mile farther east. Surely so irresolute a stream, with its constant meanders and oxbows, its springtime sloughs and year-round willow thickets, would, when faced with an obstacle, choose detour over frontal assault?

Time is the answer; time, which feels no more constant in its flow than a western river in drought, still alters everything. It changes rocks, climate, birds, and people. It changes memory, and sooner or later it changes historical meaning. Seventy million years ago, near the end of dinosaur times, what's now Wyoming was low and flat, bordering a shallow sea that bisected North America from the Gulf of Mexico to the Arctic Ocean.[1] Then the older granite underneath Wyoming began to be stressed from below. The North American land plate, floating then as now on the hot mantle underneath it, was moving north and west over a plate flooring the Pacific. The planet is always active where such plates grind and bump against each other; similar forces are pushing the Andes up today and threw up the terrible tsunami of Christmas 2004. Wyoming and the Rocky Mountains began to rise, oddly, when the pressure at one point released a little, allowing the rocks to bob upward, almost like marshmallows emerging from hot cocoa. Eventually, the Rockies rose far higher than their highest peaks now. Most of Wyoming's present mountain ranges were formed at this time—the Uinta Mountains in the southwest, the Medicine Bow Mountains in the south and southeast, and the Wind Rivers along the Continental Divide in the western half of the state, where the Sweetwater begins.

As uplift increases, erosion does, too; as slopes get steeper, streams get faster. Gradually, the basins between the new mountain ranges began filling with the sediment that the water brought down off them. Huge freshwater lakes formed in some of these basins; the water in them was crystal clear and very still. The air was warm and moist, and the Florida-like forests around the lakes were thick and subtropical. Then about fifty million years ago, enormous volcanoes arose in what's now northwestern Wyoming and filled the air with ash; the ash when it fell continued filling the basins between the mountains, burying trees, burying the lakes that had formed, and eventually burying the mountains themselves. Rivers that previously had flowed into the big lakes now flowed out of the filled-up basins, often right over the tops of the buried mountains. About ten million years ago a new round of mountain building began. The rivers, meanwhile, kept right on flowing, sawing indiscriminately from above through newer sediments and older granite. The new uplift together with the faster erosion that came with it carried away the softer sediments and re-exposed the hard granite mountains, notched and canyoned now by the newer rivers. The Sweetwater and North Platte, the Bighorn and Green rivers meander lazily across wide, nearly flat basins—until they come to the cuts through the mountains. Then the rivers get rocky and fast again. The Sweetwater does so just briefly at Devil's Gate, and used to do so again nearer its mouth, before its mouth was flooded by Pathfinder Reservoir. Similarly, the North Platte cuts through Fremont Canyon, the Green River dives through Flaming Gorge, and the Wind River boils through Wind River Canyon. A river might be expected to be steep near its source, then to flatten and slow gradually on the rest of its journey. Not in Wyoming. Our rivers move fast off the mountains, then slowly across basins, fast through new canyons, then again wind slowly across more basins. Like time in anyone's life, the rivers flow unevenly. In fact, they speed up and slow down for good reason. The world, that way, is orderly. People's lives are another matter.

As the mountains rose, the land dried out to the east of them in their rain shadow. By five million years ago, after the new round of mountain building, forests were shrinking on the east of the mountains as steppes and grasslands grew. Drought-tolerant plants moved in, including sagebrush, a newcomer from Asia by way of Siberia and Alaska.

Summers in Wyoming still smell like sagebrush, especially after a rain. But we never think of it as an Asian smell. It's sharp, clear, metallic, local; it's the smell of memory in the West, and the smell has the gray-green color of the sage leaves and of the skies that make the rain. *Breeze*, we say in summer; *wind*, we call it the rest of the year.

At Devil's Gate, the wind is chronic. "A drying wind blows almost continuously," Kathleen Sun wrote in 1986, after she'd lived on the Sun Ranch for forty years.[2] And it's been doing so four million years longer than that. Not far to the west and south, the Continental Divide sags to its lowest point between Alaska and Mexico. That's why the Oregon Trail followed the Sweetwater to cross the Divide at South Pass, near the river's headwaters. South of the pass the Divide splits and is lower still—only about 7,000 feet—where I-80 and the Union Pacific Railroad now cross Wyoming. Like water, wind funnels through this low spot in the mountains. A narrow, 100-mile-long strip of sand dunes crosses the Red Desert north of and parallel to the interstate highway. If Mrs. Sun's testimony weren't enough, the dunes make it clear the wind has been blowing from the west for millions of years. The wind is still moving the dunes.

By two million years ago, the mountains and rivers in Wyoming lay about where they are now, and the plants were not so different—aspen and conifers on the mountain slopes, shrubs and grasslands in the basins and valleys, cottonwoods along the rivers. Then the world began to cool. The planet's icecaps grew enormously. The great continental ice sheets did not come as far south as Wyoming, but thick mountain glaciers came much farther down the mountainsides. Local and continental glaciers advanced and retreated many times. As they retreated, meltwater filled huge lakes. One drowned northwestern Utah; another filled the valleys of western Montana.

In Wyoming, glaciers scooped cirques in the granite walls at the head of mountain valleys and rounded the valleys themselves, from V- to U-shaped. Tundra covered the lowlands, permafrost was widespread, and the animals were arctic: lemmings, caribou, and musk ox. Mammoths roamed the intermountain basins. The ice in the mountains ground rock to dust. When the glaciers retreated, water and wind carried the dust off the mountains and out east toward the plains, where it was deposited as loess, enriching the soil and helping out the plants and animals. The richer soil makes for more grass and less sagebrush in northeastern Wyoming's Power River Basin. When the grass-rich basin became the last refuge of the great buffalo herds, it became the last refuge, too, of the people who followed the buffalo.

People had arrived in the basins and along the rivers by 11,000 years ago.[3] Like the sagebrush millions of years earlier they, too, appear to have come from Asia—either across the Bering Strait and down a corridor that had opened through the glaciers, or down along the coast from Alaska in skin boats, or both. An Arapaho story tells of the people crossing a wide stretch of ice. A little girl and her grandmother were coming along near the tail end of the group when the girl saw a horn sticking up out of the ice. The girl wanted to make a doll with the horn, and her grandmother, to oblige the child, took a stone axe and began to chop it off. Blood flowed after a few strokes, and suddenly the ice began to heave and buckle: the horn was the horn of a huge sea monster, and the monster was rising up in pain. The people fled forward, but a few, farther back still from the girl and her grandmother, were left behind. No one knows what happened to the ones we left behind, the story goes—but far to the north there must still be others like us.[4]

Their beautifully made spear points—all that survives of their intricate culture and competent lives—seem to show that people roamed the plains hunting big game on foot. The animals 11,000 years ago were enormous. Probably the people worked in small groups, ambushing prey at springs or streams, preferring the younger and smaller mammoths and butchering two or three at a time. As the people kept hunting, the world got slowly warmer and drier. Many of the big American mammals of the Pleistocene epoch—mammoths, mastodons, beavers the size of bears, giant ground sloths, rhinos, camels, cheetahs, sabertooth cats and horses—went extinct eleven or ten thousand years ago. By 9,500 years ago, lodgepole pines replaced spruce trees in the mountains. People learned to hunt the giant *Bison antiquus* in larger numbers, driving them over cliffs or into ravines or up into the ravinelike head of a parabolic sand dune, and killing them there. The warming and drying continued; drought-tolerant sagebrush, juniper, and grasses were expanding their range. Finally, the plains got so hot and dry that bison and people seem to have disappeared from them altogether. The drought began about 7,000 years ago and lasted 2,000 years.

Such an event dwarfs the seven-year, dust-bowl drought of the 1930s, or the current drought of the interior West that some now think the worst in 500 years, or the fifty-year and twenty-three-year droughts that scoured the West with cultural and biotic change in the twelfth and thirteenth centuries A.D. Climate swings are a way of life—and death—on the plains. The air that comes east over the Rockies, dry by the time it arrives, meets moist, warm air coming up from the Gulf of Mexico and cold, dry air coming south from the Arctic. These three forces never achieve a very stable equilibrium, nor, 1,200 miles from any ocean, are any moderating influences available. Sometimes, however, the normally volatile situation swings much farther out of balance. Distant changes in the regular circulation patterns of ocean and atmosphere weaken the prevailing westerlies, and result in long swings from dry to wet and back again as the northern air or southern air, for a time, dominates. The bison, during the drought, retreated far to the north. Some of the people followed them; others retreated from the plains to the coasts of the largest rivers, the Missouri and the Mississippi.

By about 4,500 years ago, people had returned, but with a new economy. Adversity appears to have made them generalists. They stayed in caves and rock shelters from time to time; they gathered plants and ground the seeds; they fished, and they hunted and ate small mammals, reptiles and amphibians. Far away to the north and east a bison economy persisted, and would eventually return. Also by that time the larger *Bison antiquus* appear to have been replaced by the modern *Bison bison*, and from now on, we will call them by their familiar name: buffalo.

The world was cooling again, and the plains were looking much as they do now. Grass and shrubs, which had advanced partway up the mountainsides during the long drought, again grew primarily in the basins, and were replaced by conifers on the slopes. Wolves and pronghorn antelope had survived the Pleistocene extinctions, and buffalo slowly returned to the plains. Some people again found the old, nomadic hunting to be the most efficient way to make a living. People left tipi rings, pictures and carvings on rocks, and much larger stone circles oriented to the sun and stars. Hundreds of miles east, semi-permanent villages grew up along the Missouri, where people grew corn, beans, and squash in the river bottoms, and learned to make pottery in which they could store the seeds. Around 500 A.D. people began using bows and arrows. Trade grew up between the plains hunters and riverside farmers. After 1700, horses began arriving from the Spanish south, and steel tools, cloth, iron pots, mirrors, glass beads, and guns began arriving from the French and British northeast. And after that, everything that had been happening to the people for 11,000 years began to happen very fast. Change sped up a hundredfold.

The most dramatic place for watching pelicans is from the top of Devil's Gate. There, 360 feet above the river level, you could feel like a pelican yourself if able to leave the rocks and fly. You can see downstream past Independence Rock to the reservoir, and upstream to another granite landmark, Split Rock—thirty miles or more of the Sweetwater valley. Pelicans are most common along here in May. After the first of June, for some reason, they confine their foraging to the reservoir and to the Platte valley north and south of the reservoir. Home base is Bird Island, a narrow thirty-acre sage- and rabbitbrush-covered mound in what used to be a bay of the reservoir where Sand Creek flows into it from the southwest. There, chicks before they can fly are safe from foxes, coyotes, skunks, and people. Gulls, terns, cormorants, and a few black-crowned night herons nest

Devil's Gate, looking north. The corrals of the former Sun Ranch are in the foreground. Photograph by the author.

on the island, too—but pelicans are by far the most numerous citizens. A state biologist counted 245 active nests on the island in 1984 and 384 nests in 1985; by the end of the 1990s, the annual census topped 1,200.[5] In dry years, the U.S. Bureau of Reclamation allows the reservoir to fall very low, as its first job is to protect not the birds but the Nebraska irrigators 350 miles away who own the rights to the water. Bird Island then becomes a peninsula, or lately more like a part of the mainland. Most of the former bay is filled with dirt flats. Before the young pelicans can fly, coyotes, foxes and badgers can trot out there and eat their fill. But the pelicans are long-lived birds, and the colony can survive at least a season or two—perhaps more, perhaps not—when all their young are eaten.

The same biologist noted in his report that, despite their local success, white pelicans are declining. There may be as few as twenty colonies left throughout the West, down from perhaps three times that number. But they are newcomers in central Wyoming; as far as anyone seems to know, none nested on Bird Island before 1983. They like remote places where they can breed and nest undisturbed, and so perhaps they came here because they were crowded out of somewhere else.

Devil's Gate, therefore, is not the place to see the *most* pelicans. That would be from the shore of the reservoir, before the chicks have fledged, when the enormous adults come and go all day from the island. But the adults, flying up the Sweetwater in May, seem to like the Gate because the wind plays tricks there. On top of the Gate, pools of clear water lie in pockets in the granite. Wind ruffles the pools. Far below, the river boils its way through the notch, while the plains are still visible to the north and east. Pelicans are likely to rise off the river out beyond the Dumbell's ranch buildings. They aren't hunting, or foraging. Lazily, they loaf higher, bank and float, then flap directly overhead. Each wingbeat gains them ten yards. Wind blows hard all the time.

From the air, the sage-steppes must look like a sea to the pelicans, and these big granite outcrops like islands. Emigrants who came this way in their covered wagons used the word *cove* to describe a place where the steppes lap up into a sheltered place in

the rocks. Many such coves would easily be visible to a pelican flying up the Sweetwater from Bird Island. In one of those coves, on
the south side of the river halfway between where the reservoir is
now and Devil's Gate, six men hanged a woman and a man, without
first binding their hands or feet, from a pitch-pine tree barely tall
enough to keep their feet off the ground while they kicked and
slowly strangled. In another cove a few miles upstream from Devil's
Gate, fifty, thirty, or more likely only twenty people—the number
these days is a political sore spot—died when the scant shelter it
offered proved insufficient to protect them from bad weather, bad
planning, starvation, and their own religious zeal. To the pelicans,
of course, neither of the coves looks remarkable, for the pelicans
have better things to do than worry over who owns the land and, by
owning it, owns the past.

# Tenantless and Forlorn

We encamped close to the river. The night was dark, and as we lay down we could hear, mingled with the howlings of wolves the hoarse bellowing of the buffalo, like the ocean beating upon a distant coast.

—*Francis Parkman, 1846.*

Buffalo were still numerous on the plains when the first people began to exist not only in their own stories, but in stories over which they had no control—the stories of the arriving whites. In those years, everyone depended on the buffalo. Indians needed them for livelihood; traders needed them for business. Life for people wasn't so much about following the buffalo, as about knowing where and when to expect them. Hunters waited for the animals, and traders waited for the hunters to bring in the skins.

In the fall of 1832, many hundreds of miles to the east of the Sweetwater valley, the Brulé and Yankton Lakota people came as usual to the river bottoms around Fort Pierre on the Missouri. There they waited for the buffalo to come in off the plains, down to the river for shelter from winter storms. When the first snows fell, the old cows would come in first, and the people would be careful to let them pass. Later, if the people's ceremonial invitations were effective, the rest of the buffalo would follow. After a full summer and fall on good grass, the younger cows were at their fattest now. Their meat would be packed with calories, and could be eaten on the spot or dried, pounded with tallow and berries, and stored against hard times. Sometimes the fall hunt was so good that the people built wooden houses along the river and stopped wandering for an entire season.

But the fall of 1832 was oddly warm. Week after week, no snow fell; frost on the riverbank grasses was gone by midmorning. Still the people waited, yet the buffalo remained scattered far from the river on distant grasslands. Other tribes—Oglala, Hunkpapa, and Blackfeet Lakota camps 100 miles west near the forks of the Cheyenne River, Yankton on the Little Cheyenne to the east and north—reported some success. But elsewhere, people were hungry. So they ate stored provisions and hunted small game, neither providing nearly what they needed. A month went by, then another. It was a risk to stay and wait; it was a risk to leave and hunt. A family could lose more energy wandering than it would gain from a single isolated kill. Some stayed, some left; many starved.

The buffalo never did come to the river that year—nor the next, equally warm. In the spring of 1834, when Prince Maximilian of Wied passed up the Missouri, he reported everyone at the fort "in great want of fresh provisions, no buffalo having been seen during the whole winter." Finally, in the fall of 1834, the weather turned cold at the right time and the buffalo, their numbers swollen from two warm winters and very little hunting, returned to the river in their enormous, comforting patterns: the old cows first, then the young cows, calves, and bulls. So many were they, the people said, that all the dead buffalo must have come back to life. The people butchered and feasted, feasted and butchered, dried the meat, made pemmican and tanned the hides into robes, gear, moccasins, clothing, and lodge covers. The traders feasted too, and took in pack after pack after ten-robe pack to ship downriver in spring. Everything seemed to have regained its balance.[1]

When he was an old man, the naturalist John Muir recalled a conversation his father, Daniel Muir, had one day at a store in a hamlet near the Muirs' farm in the big oak openings of Wisconsin. This would have been in the 1850s. Daniel Muir argued that as settlers were using only ten or at most forty acres to feed a family, they were making far better use of the land than were the Ojibwa Indians in the district, who needed a thousand acres, or many thousands for the same purpose. Settlers, the old Scot argued, naturally had a superior claim; Indians, he said, only leave the land in "unproductive wildness."

Then another neighbor, George Mair, pointed out that the pioneers they knew had left lives as servants, shopkeepers, or tradesmen in the British Isles, to take up free land in America. As a result, most of them—present company included, he seemed to imply— were bad farmers. They were ignorant, wasteful, and uncertain of the causes of their poor crops. How would Mr. Muir feel, Mr. Mair asked politely, if scientific farmers, who could raise five or ten times as much per acre, came in and claimed their skills alone gave them rights to the land? Would that not amount to the same claim Mr. Muir was making against the Ojibwas? Would Mr. Muir be willing peacefully to relinquish his land to such newcomers? Would he continue to argue that God must have meant for the land to belong to the user who used it the most efficiently? Muir does not give his father's answer, but the old man's ideas were common.[2]

Land going unplowed, ungrazed, with its timber unharvested, had no real value in the minds of the arriving Euro-Americans. Even Francis Parkman, a young Harvard graduate who scorned farms, farmers, and more or less all English-speaking people of the lower and middle classes, didn't have much use for it. He found only melancholy in the sight of uncultivated land when, in 1846, he came up through the canyon of the Laramie River onto the Laramie Plains from the east:

> First, we saw a long dark line of ragged clouds upon the horizon, while above them rose the peak of the Medicine-Bow, the vanguard of the Rocky Mountains; then little by little the plain came into view, a vast green uniformity, forlorn and tenantless, though Laramie Creek glistened in a waving line over its surface, without a bush or tree upon its banks.[3]

*Forlorn and tenantless* Parkman scribbled, back in a Boston jostling with tenants and ruled by landlords. Or one of his two editors wrote the words, as he was too flattened by depression to work the book into shape on his own. To someone so divorced by class from agriculture, unused land wasn't exactly a tragedy. Still, the great historian seems to be saying, it was kind of a shame. Beautiful, said the Romantic in him, and lonely. But not worth much, said the part of him that was a prince of New England's merchant class.

The Indians of the northern plains, meanwhile, who had quickly become mobile in the previous century as horses came up from the south, now were traveling even faster. Now they were riding on a five-thousand-year journey in about fifty years, from the Stone Age to the heart of the Industrial Revolution.

Visiting, trading, making war, gathering prairie turnips or chokecherries, waiting for buffalo at the appointed times and places, they were always on the move. In 1795, the Arapahos, for example, were reported on the branches of the Cheyenne River in what's now western South Dakota. In the next ten years they roamed northwestern and central Montana, northeastern Wyoming, western south Dakota again, western Nebraska, the country along the South Platte in central Colorado, and by 1806 were even farther south, on the Arkansas. They had crossed the Missouri in the mid-1700s, and allied with the Cheyennes against the power of the Teton Lakotas when the latter crossed the river some years later. The Cheyennes then became middlemen in the Missouri river trade, while the Arapahos ranged south for horses. They traded horses to the Cheyennes, who in turn swapped them to the upper Missouri river tribes—Arikara, Mandan, Hidatsa—for the European pots, knives, hatchets, blankets, guns and beaver traps that proved so useful, and for the mirrors, cloth, beads, paint, whiskey, sugar, and tobacco that proved so enticing. By the 18-teens, one group of Arapahos was regularly ranging north from the mountain parks of Colorado. The other congregated to the southeast out on the plains, between the South Platte and the Arkansas.[4]

In 1829, the secretary of war received reports of around six thousand "Arripahas" in what are now Wyoming and Colorado, with the Arapahos relying on the Cheyennes to help hold their hunting grounds against Crows to the north and Lakota power to the north and east. In the 1830s, the lives of the Plains tribes began orbiting the new fur-trade forts along the front of the Rockies—Bent's Fort on the Arkansas, Fort St. Vrain on the South Platte, Fort Laramie on the North Platte. Trade with Indians meant big money for a few white partners and a risky life on wages for engagés of all races; trade with whites tangled the lives of Indians with manufactured goods, and the complicated loyalties they commanded.

Though the Sweetwater was only on the margins of these ranges, its valley was the route to the mountains where the beaver trade took a different turn. In the years before the fur forts were built along the Front Range, competitors had begun packing goods up the Sweetwater each summer by mule and two-wheeled carts to various well-watered spots straddling the Continental Divide, where they set up big trade fairs. White and mixed-race trappers brought their year's take from all over the Rockies. Indians showed up to trade, drink, make love, sing, talk, gamble, and race with the white men.

Suddenly, the Shoshones, who lived in those high valleys, found themselves in a prime business location. Like their Ute and Paiute relatives of the dry Great Basin west and south, the Shoshones for centuries had gathered more than they hunted, living largely on grass seeds, piñon nuts and camas roots, following the times and places of the ripenings. But by now they were buffalo Indians, too. Like their Flathead and Nez Perce relatives along the Divide farther north, some Shoshone bands rode east every fall to make meat on the buffalo plains. There they met the Lakotas, Crows, and Blackfeet—always far more numerous and, until now, better armed because they were closer to British traders from the north and Americans from the east. Beginning in 1825, however, traders began appearing every summer in the Shoshones' midst, for rendezvous. The next step was obvious; the Shoshones made friends with the white men. Trade flourished. Traders brought goods and guns to the fairs; the Shoshones brought skins and horses. Trappers and traders took Shoshone wives and began Shoshone families with names still common in Wyoming. The Shoshones resisted the Blackfeet at last and hunted each summer and fall in peace. For a short time the Shoshones were as wealthy as any tribe in the interior of North America. Briefly, again, it felt as if some kind of balance had been restored.

Then, supply and demand in the beaver trade disappeared at about the same time; just as beaver hats lost out to silk, the beaver themselves were gone. They were trapped out, rubbed out, killed off and banished, so it seemed, to memory. Their dams got old and broke and spongy mountain meadows grew dry and hard. The last mountain rendezvous was held in 1840. Everyone knew the institution had outlived its usefulness. The fur trade became the buffalo-robe trade, the mountain men found other ways to make a living, and the Shoshones began to feel the squeeze.

First, the seed-gathering half of their economy crashed. The traders' route to the Divide became the first half of the emigrants' route to Oregon. Traffic swelled from a trickle in 1843 to a river of people by 1846; in 1847 the first Mormons arrived in the Salt Lake Valley and in 1848 gold was discovered in California. The river became a flood. By the peak years of the early 1850s, as many as 70,000 emigrants were making the trip annually. Many brought enormous herds of livestock. The grass began to suffer, the game to go elsewhere. It hardly mattered to the emigrants. They didn't think of themselves as using the land; they were just crossing with their herds. But they were using it up in any case, and that began to make the tribes very nervous.

As late as the 1830s, small game and even buffalo, dependent on many of the same food sources as the Shoshones, were still plentiful west of the Divide. By the 1850s, emigrant livestock herds and Mormon farms had changed all that. In taking up the best bottom land in the drainages around the Great Salt Lake, the Mormons blocked Indian access to the seeds that once had grown there, and to the game, which always seeks cover near water.[5] This left only buffalo. But buffalo, too, dwindled fast west of the Divide. And as Plains Indians to the east were themselves pushed west, Shoshone chances in their traditional buffalo grounds east of the Divide shrank each year.

Meanwhile, the mountain man Jim Bridger and his partner, Louis Vasquez, built a fort in 1843—really a store and blacksmith shop—on Black's Fork of the Green River, on the southern edge of the rendezvous country. The store lay where the route to Salt Lake would split off from the main Oregon-California road, and the former trappers were soon getting rich off emigrants of all kinds. For Indian business, the two trappers relied on their old friends, the Shoshones, and the eastern bands of the Shoshones established a more or less permanent presence there. Bridger cemented his friendship by marrying Little Fawn, daughter of Washakie, an old trapping companion.[6]

But while the Shoshones settled in, the Arapahos kept moving. They had to, if they wanted to eat. As buffalo numbers dwindled during the 1840s, the herds' arrivals and departures became less reliable. And like other tribes, the Arapahos were alarmed by the devastation on the trails—doubly alarmed, as they regularly ranged between two trails, from the Santa Fe on the south to the Oregon on the north. Travelers along the northern route in the 1830s generally found buffalo plentiful all the way to the Divide. But by the mid-1840s, buffalo were already spottier: along the Sweetwater, the hunters who did find them were often five or ten miles from the trail.[7]

The first large party of Oregon-bound emigrants—1,000 pioneers led by Marcus Whitman—came along the northern trail in 1843. Just two years later the tribes were edgy enough that the army chose to make a show of force. In 1845, Colonel Stephen Watts Kearny led 250 dragoons—a large force for the time—up to South Pass, back to Fort Laramie, south across the plains to Bent's Fort on the Arkansas, and back to Fort Leavenworth. At Fort Laramie—still a trading post and not yet an army fort—he shot off his mountain howitzer and, after dark, some rockets, to impress the Arapahos and other assembled tribes. Kearny's column may have been impressive, but it didn't change matters much.[8] The tribes began complaining to traders, Indian agents, and anyone else who would listen that emigrants were responsible for the disappearing game. Some Arapahos demanded tolls for passage through their lands. Others sought letters from the emigrants, telling of their assistance or kindness, which they would then show to Indian agents in hopes of more reward.[9]

When Parkman arrived at Fort Laramie in 1846, he stepped into this unease without understanding it. He and his friend Quincy Adams Shaw learned that the Sioux (the Lakotas) were about to make war on the Snakes (the Shoshones) to avenge nine deaths

Francis Parkman, about 1844, the year the young historian graduated from Harvard and two years before his trip on the Oregon Trail. From Farnham, *A Life of Francis Parkman.*

in war the summer before. The Oglala Lakota war parties would leave as soon as Minniconjou Lakota parties arrived to reinforce them, better news than the adventure-seeking Parkman had dared hope for. Soon, however, the effort fell apart, though not before much riding around on the part of Parkman, Shaw, and their hired mountain man Henry Chatillon, chasing lost horses and trying to find out what was up. Parkman eventually left Shaw at the fort with a bad case of poison ivy and, though debilitated himself by depression and dysentery, hired two French traders, Raymond and Reynal, to guide him to an Oglala village. But then Chatillon and Reynal had to leave when they learned that Chatillon's wife Bear Robe—traveling with a different Oglala band—was very sick. That left Parkman and Raymond to travel alone to the village, on the move somewhere on the Laramie Plains, beyond the Laramie Mountains from the fort. Parkman and Raymond knew that once they found the village they would be welcome there, as Bear Robe was the daughter of the charismatic Oglala chief Bull Bear, dead a few years earlier. Any friends of Chatillon could still count on status and safety among the Oglalas. But Raymond was nervous about other tribes. "[We] were fast approaching a region quite dangerous on acct. of Snakes, Gros Ventres and Arapahoes. Raymond advised return," Parkman wrote in his notebook that night.[10]

The Oglalas, when Parkman and Raymond caught up with them shortly afterward, were equally ill at ease. They had never hunted west and south of these mountains before; in the past, there had always been sufficient buffalo closer to home. They knew they were well into Shoshone summer territory, and they posted sentinels on every hilltop. When at first they found only herds of bulls, their hides too stiff and thick for tipi covers, the Oglala kept traveling both morning and afternoon, contrary to custom on a hunt. Finally they found a herd of cows, made the kill, butchered and dried the meat, tanned the hides, and, relieved, headed out through the mountains again to cut lodgepoles on their way back to familiar territory.

The nervousness spread outward, like rings on a pond. Two hundred fifty miles away, over on the far side of the Divide, five hundred

Shoshones were camped at Fort Bridger. When an emigrant named Edwin C. Bryant arrived with news of all the war excitement among the Oglalas and Minniconjous around Fort Laramie, most of the Shoshones packed up and left. Bryant assumed they'd gone off to raise war parties of their own.[11] On his hunt for scenery and romance, Parkman traveled blithely through a scary, fluid time. Everything was changing—who used the land, who therefore felt they owned it, and what they used it for.

As the 1840s drew to a close and the buffalo continued to dwindle, the Arapaho resistance advanced from seeking tolls and letters of recommendation to stealing horses and goods. Fewer buffalo meant the tribes needed more horses, as they had to travel more often for food. And horses themselves were usefully portable wealth; they could be swapped, like buffalo robes, for ammunition and trade goods.[12] Some Arapaho men began raiding for horses on the Santa Fe Trail and into the New Mexico settlements.

By 1849, government officials in the U.S. Indian Office knew the long trains of emigrants and their stock were destabilizing everything. Bridger's old trapping comrade Tom Fitzpatrick, now Indian agent for the northern plains, noted that it wouldn't be long before the Indians couldn't even find food and clothing. His boss in St. Louis, D. D. Mitchell, reported that the tribes on the upper Platte considered raids on travelers a fair consequence for the destruction of grass, timber, and buffalo they caused by passing through Indian country—without Indian consent. The solution would be to get that consent, and at the same time, to get the tribes to ignore all these unfamiliar pressures and leave each other alone. Mitchell sent Fitzpatrick out with presents for the plains tribes, to ask them all to come in and sign a treaty of peace and friendship.

In the summer of 1851, about 9,000 Indians traveled to Horse Creek, east of Fort Laramie near the present Wyoming-Nebraska line. The tribes were asked to keep peace with each other and with whites, to allow the government to establish posts in Indian lands and roads through them, to pay restitution if Indians preyed on whites, and to accept government protection if whites preyed on Indians. The tribes also—and this would get tricky later—were asked to select principal chiefs through whom all business with the U.S. government would be conducted. In return, the combined tribes that signed were to receive a total payment of $50,000 worth of provisions per year, to be divided proportionally among the tribes.

And the tribes were asked to stay mostly on their own lands. So those lands had to be, for the first time, defined. Mitchell and Fitzpatrick had Father Pierre-Jean De Smet, well known in the plains and mountains for his missionary work, draw a map of the new Indian fiefs. The Lakota, most populous of the tribes, would get the biggest chunk. It included land bound by a line running north up the Missouri, west along the Yellowstone, south along the crest of the Bighorn Mountains, east along the North Platte, then northeast across country from the forks of the Platte back to the Missouri. Mandan, Arikara, Assiniboine and Gros Ventre Indians were to stay on their traditional lands north and west of the Lakota heartland, and the Crows were to stay west of the Bighorns.

Finally, the Arapahos, jointly with their relatives the Cheyennes, were offered the territory bound by a line beginning at Red Buttes, near present-day Casper, Wyoming, and running upstream—that is, south—up the North Platte, past the unmentioned mouth of the Sweetwater and all the way to the Platte's source in Colorado, then farther south along the crest of the Continental Divide, past the source of the South Platte to the headwaters of the Arkansas, down the Arkansas to its junction with the Santa Fe Trail near present Dodge City, Kansas, back north to the forks of the Platte, and back up the North Platte, to Red Buttes.[13]

The Shoshones are not mentioned at all in the treaty. They were not, in the minds of the Indian Bureau, plains Indians, and therefore had no interests there. But the Shoshones knew better. A handful, including Washakie, went anyway, and took Bridger along to help them figure out what was happening.[14]

At least one Oglala, when the dust settled, was disgusted with the outcome. Black Hawk was angry that the Lakotas, accustomed to roaming so far, would now be confined north of the Platte even though they had suffered no apparent defeat:

These lands once belonged to the Kiowas and the Crows, but we whipped those nations out of them, and in this we did what the white men do when they want the lands of the Indians. We met the Kiowas and the Crows and whipped them at Kiowa Creek, just below where we are now. We met them and whipped them again, and the last time at Crow Creek. This last battle was fought by the Cheyennes, Arapahoes and Oglalas combined, and the Oglalas claim their share of the country.[15]

As the years went by, the search for buffalo pushed the tribes farther into each other's lands than any of them liked. They were alert to the old boundaries, and newcomers feared those boundaries' defenders. But everyone moved around so much that the defenders could as easily be behind the next outcrop as hundreds of miles away—and because of white pressure from the east, the boundaries kept shifting. The lands that Parkman saw as tenantless were anything but; despite their apparent emptiness, they were full of jostling people. Yet Fitzpatrick and Mitchell, who probably knew better, and their superiors in Washington, who probably did not, thought they could impose a European order on the West by having a priest draw lines on a map.

Already in their minds, the government was landlord and the tribes were tenants, subject to eviction on short notice, no matter how well their territory was defined. For their part the tribes were on a learning curve that would continue getting steeper and more slippery. No longer were the plains, rivers, mountains, and scattered forests parts of a whole world, connected seamlessly with the air a person breathed and the stories a person lived in and moved through. Something new was happening. The tribes had ideas of ownership, but especially for an element as large as land, the ownership was communal. For whites, land was an object. Once mapped by the government as tribal territory, land became just another possession, like a tribe's horses, its lodges, its pemmican stored against an uncertain future. The whites were making Indian land a thing, a chattel. Now it could be swapped or stolen away.

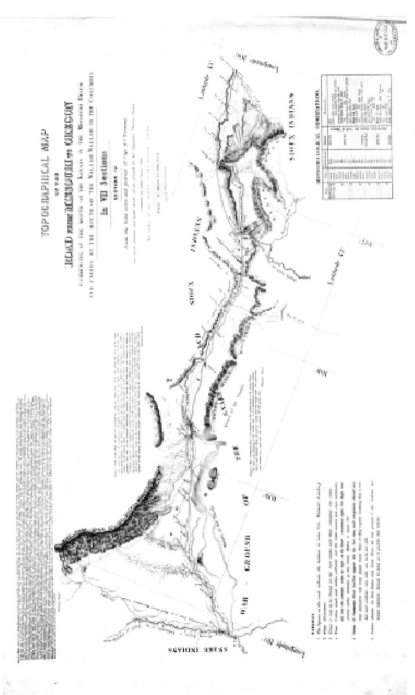

The Pathfinder's maps were his greatest achievement. An 1846 map of the road from Missouri to Oregon, all at an easy-to-use ten miles to the inch, included this section along the Sweetwater. Courtesy of Library of Congress.

# CHAPTER 3

# The Pathfinder's
# Lost Instruments

I had remarked that the noise produced by the explosion of
our pistols had the usual degree of loudness, but was not in the
least prolonged, expiring almost instantaneously. Having now
made what observations our means afforded, we proceeded to
descend.

—*J. C. Frémont, 1842*

July 28, 1842, was a hot day along the North Platte River, and
when John C. Frémont's voyageurs pitched his tipi, they raised
the lodge skins slightly around the bottom edge, hoping to let a
breeze blow through. Inside, Frémont's cartographer, the phleg-
matic Charles Preuss, started a fire under a pot of water. Outside
the tipi, Frémont himself erected a tripod. From a leather case
he withdrew a brass tube with a glass tube inside it, and hung the
apparatus from the tripod's apex. At the bottom of the tube was
attached a small glass canister, about the size of a modern soup
can, sealed at its top around the tube. The bottom of the canister
was leather, through which protruded the head of a screw that a
person could loosen or tighten with thumb and forefinger. The
whole instrument was less than a yard long.

This was a cistern barometer, a key tool for making maps and
as such a key tool for objectifying the landscape, then fragmenting

the West. Barometers measured elevation, chronometers measured longitude, and various kinds of sextants measured latitude. Frémont was fascinated by all of them. He has often been called Pathfinder, but a more accurate nickname would be Pathmapper, for his maps are his true legacy. They were commissioned, first, to aid travelers, but would soon be used for politics. The maps on which Father De Smet divided the tribes' lands one from another were based on Frémont's maps. Maps allowed land to be understood in pieces, a Cartesian, European understanding. If land was to be property, you had to be able to map out which pieces belonged to whom.

The day was calm, and the barometer hung straight and still. Though it was the only one the expedition had left, it looked safe enough. To read it, Frémont would have had to put his hands on his knees and peer at a place near the top of the tube where the brass was cut away, and the height of the column of mercury inside the glass could be read on a measured scale. But first, he had to make some adjustments.

They were now forty-eight days out from the Missouri settlements and were near present-day Casper, Wyoming, approaching Red Buttes, soon to become a well-known landmark. Though his orders were simply to travel up the North Platte as far the Sweetwater, Frémont seems from the beginning to have planned to lead his men to the mountains beyond South Pass.[1] This was the first of his five exploring expeditions to the trans-Missouri West, expeditions that would make him, briefly, as famous as any man in America. Later, an eagerness for fame would drive him into otherwise inexplicable risks. But for now, he was just curious. He wanted to know his elevation above sea level at the moment, and he planned soon to measure the true altitude of the Rocky Mountains.

Barometers measure the pressure of the column of air reaching upward into space, where there is no longer any air at all. The greater the observer's elevation, the shorter and less dense the column of air above, and therefore the less it weighs. In Frémont's time the connection between weather events and changes in local air pressure were not well understood; barometers were rare and used primarily to measure elevation. In this case, measuring the height of the mountains would mean getting the instrument safely to the top of a peak still 200 miles off. They had already left one barometer behind at Fort Laramie for safekeeping, and since then, trail travel had broken another.

Earlier in the day, the expedition had crossed the braided channels of the North Platte River and camped on the river's north side. They were two dozen men, most mounted on mules and the others driving two-wheeled carts. They took the wheels and canvas covers off the carts and concealed them in dense brush in a cottonwood grove. In sand drifts nearby, they buried everything else they felt they could do without for a few weeks. They would be traveling light now, carrying fewer provisions, and they would have to hunt more often. This was a risk; they had been warned that morning by some very thin-looking Indians that they soon would enter a landscape ravaged by drought and skinned by grasshoppers. Without the wheeled vehicles they could leave the established trail, perhaps find more game for themselves and grass for their animals, and see country seldom or never seen before by whites.

First, however, elevation, latitude, and longitude must be measured, for Frémont was first of all a geographer. In 1842 he was twenty-nine, a second lieutenant in the Corps of Topographical Engineers, a semi-autonomous branch of the U.S. Army in which he was one of only thirty-six officers. Financing for the trip had been quietly engineered by Senator Thomas Hart Benton of Missouri, who also happened to be Frémont's father-in-law. An expansionist, Benton had his eye on Oregon, which at the time meant all the country west of the Continental Divide and north of the forty-second parallel, now the northern border of California, Nevada, and Utah. South of that line was still Mexico. Oregon was claimed jointly by Britain and the United States; Benton wanted to see it filling up with U.S. settlers as soon as possible. And though much of the information on how to get to Oregon was sound, it was available only from word of mouth and a few maps that mixed guesswork and fable with fact. Frémont, Benton knew, would return with good information, and afterward the government could issue thousands of reliable maps. Then, given the right publicity, Benton could turn the politics over to a fast-growing, land-hungry public, and count on a reliable outcome.

Frémont was well equipped for his tasks. To measure latitude, he had two sextants and a reflecting circle. These were sophisticated protractors; they were used to measure the angle of the sun or the polestar above the horizon.[2] A sextant was useful up to an angle of 60 degrees; at higher angles he could use his reflecting circle, which could measure a full circle of angles if necessary. Among trees or in the mountains, however, it was impossible to locate the horizon, and so Frémont also carried with him a couple of so-called artificial horizons. These were flat boxes, each filled with a shallow puddle of mercury. They provided a level, still, bright silver surface in which the heavenly object would be clearly reflected. The geographer could use his sextant to measure the apparent angle between the object and its reflection and divide the result by two, thus doubling the accuracy of his observation.

Measuring longitude was trickier. Ancient geographers divided the round earth into 360 degrees of longitude, which corresponded nicely with a twenty-four-hour day, with fifteen degrees of longitude corresponding to one hour, or one twenty-fourth, of the globe's daily rotation. With a reliable clock that told the time at a distant, fixed spot on the globe, a person could, by noting the time difference between actual noon and when the clock read noon, figure the number of degrees he was east or west of the spot. By Frémont's time, the spot had been established for 150 years in Greenwich, England. Accurate, spring-driven clocks that would keep reliable time on board ship or on a long journey overland—chronometers, they are called—had been available for about sixty years.

At first, chronometers were expensive and rare; Lewis and Clark didn't have one. By 1842, Frémont felt able to afford three, a big one in a box, suspended with gimbals like a ship's compass, and two smaller, pocket-sized ones. The big one was already useless by the time they reached Fort Laramie. Frémont got it running again, but it was off by one hour in twenty-four and they left it and one other behind at the fort. They took the best one with them but it, too, did not keep perfect time. For that reason, it was standard practice to use a backup system of astronomical observations. By noting, on a clear night, the exact moments when the moons of Jupiter disappeared behind the planet and then reappeared, and comparing the times of these occultations against tables that predicted precisely when they would occur, they could work out an accurate longitude. The observations required a powerful telescope; Frémont's was 120 power, fifteen times as strong as a pair of modern binoculars. He used the method primarily as a way to keep tabs on how fast or slow his clocks were running. The method demanded good weather, a lot of math, a time of the month when Jupiter was in the sky, and lengthy nighttime observations. The clocks, of course, could be read at a glance and worked about the same night or day in all weather. But they were fragile. They would not work again if they were dropped, or if they got wet.

At Cache Camp on the North Platte, where they hid the carts, Frémont's astronomical and chronometric observations worked out to a longitude of 106 degrees, 38 minutes, 26 seconds west of the Greenwich meridian, and a latitude of 42 degrees, 50 minutes, 53 seconds north of the Equator. This is reasonably accurate for the time; as might be expected, it is better in its latitude than in its longitude.

That still left the matter of elevations, which is what both Frémont and Preuss were trying to measure—by different methods—once the tipi was pitched. While Frémont unpacked and hung the barometer, Preuss, seeking a second opinion, started the fire. Water boils at 212 degrees Fahrenheit at sea level, and boils at lower temperatures—because of the lower air pressure—at higher elevations. The difference between 212 degrees and the actual boiling point gives an indication of the actual elevation. But as with the chronometers, the expedition was having trouble keeping the thermometers safe from damage. Already they were down to just one with a scale that went high enough to measure water's boiling point. This was the one Preuss was using, even though it was too small to allow for graduations of much accuracy.

In any case, it's possible to imagine him, tall and red-faced, thermometer in hand, watching closely as the water came to a boil, while Frémont, slight and dark-eyed, adjusted the screw on the bottom of the barometer. By turning the screw he could bring the level of mercury inside the glass beaker up just high enough to touch the point of an ivory pin set there to mark zero on the scale, allowing, each time, an accurate reading at the top.

Perhaps Preuss said something from inside the tipi about the water starting to boil. Perhaps Frémont answered him absently. Suddenly, a gust of wind slammed the lodge and blew it over—Preuss, fire, water pot and all, along with, Frémont wrote later, "about a dozen men, who had attempted to keep it from being carried away." In the confusion Frémont managed to save the barometer, "which the lodge was carrying away with itself," but the thermometer broke. They had no others that would measure above 135 degrees, so from now on, elevation data would depend on the barometer alone.

The tipi blew over through no fault of its own, however. It was a good-sized lodge, eighteen feet across and twenty feet high, of that wonderful conical design which keeps a person warm in winter, cool and mosquito-free in summer.[3] Frémont had bought it at Fort Laramie a week before. There, he had hired the trader Joseph Bissonette as an interpreter, and Bissonette had brought along his Lakota wife. Tipis were women's work; when the men had tried to set up the tipi the first night out from Fort Laramie, she had laughed at their clumsiness and since then had often helped, probably supervised, in setting it up every evening. But Bissonette had agreed to accompany the expedition only as far as the Red Buttes, now just miles away. That afternoon at Cache Camp, he and his wife would have been preparing to leave, and so the voyageurs must have set up the tipi on their own for the first time. They had done a poor job.

As the tipi toppled, and the men struggled with poles and flapping lodgeskins, Frémont would have unhooked the barometer from its tripod and then tilted it very carefully to allow the mercury to flow slowly to the top of the tube, preserving the vacuum inside the tube and allowing for accurate pressure readings in the future. Next, he would have had to screw up the screw at the bottom of the cistern, sealing the leather against the bottom of the tube and sealing the mercury into the column. It would have been a delicate moment, between wind gusts. If the instrument was tilted too fast, the mercury could slam into the top end of the tube and break it. If the bottom wasn't securely sealed, the mercury could slosh and air would get into the tube, ruining the vacuum. Then, very carefully, the barometer would be slid back into its leather case and slung from a strap over the geographer's shoulder, upside down with the cistern at the top, ensuring that the mercury filled the tube and the vacuum stayed safely protected.[4]

Geographer that he was, Frémont chose to follow the North Platte instead of the trail. They headed south now, upriver past Red Buttes, and camped at a grassy spot a few miles above the mouth of what's now called Bates Creek. Another day's journey brought them to Goat Island, which they named for some bighorn sheep they found there and killed. The island lay a short distance downstream from a narrows they named Hot Spring Gate—the site of the present Alcova Dam—where the river cut through a ridge between high walls near a hot spring. Upstream from there, canyon walls closed in completely, and so the next day the men left the river, climbed over steep, barren hills and fifteen miles later descended more gradually back down to the Sweetwater, flowing in from the west. Turning right, up the Sweetwater, they headed for the Continental Divide.

Frémont reported the stream to be sixty feet across, twelve to eighteen inches deep, flowing moderately—much the same as it would appear now, at the end of a modern July. But then, buffalo grazed near the river. The men camped in a cold rain, and the hunters killed some cows; the next day they moved seven miles farther up to camp a mile below Independence Rock. Here they spent two nights, the hunters killed more buffalo, and everyone pitched in to cut the meat in strips and hang it on racks to dry in the sun. An extra day by the stream must have been a welcome respite from traveling.

By now it was August, and the weather was changing as they steadily gained altitude. At Devil's Gate, Frémont noticed the dike of volcanic rock that makes a dark stripe in the granite of the right side as a person faces downstream. Again it rained. No one had any tents; they seem to have left them behind with the carts. Some nights, big sagebrush was their only shelter. There were no trees along the river, but driftwood lay scattered along its banks. With this, and what the voyageurs called *bois de vache*—buffalo chips—they made cheerful fires, Frémont reported.

A day and a half beyond Devil's Gate, they got their first view of the Wind River Mountains, looking low and dark; these marked the Continental Divide and beyond them lay Oregon. On up the Sweetwater they progressed, timbered mountains miles off on their left, bare-granite rocks rising close and steep on their right. They passed buffalo, antelope, spied the only grizzly bear of the trip, found an abandoned dog and a sore-footed horse, and now and then unpacked their instruments to take more readings.

Toward the head of the valley, they came to the place where the Sweetwater, now a rocky creek, foamed out of a canyon in "wildness and disorder," Frémont wrote later. The route got steeper and the trail again left the river for easier going. As he had on the North Platte, Frémont stayed with the river. They found traces of old beaver dams, falling apart for lack of tenants to keep them up. Finally, the rock walls came too close. They followed a ravine up to a high prairie and camped by a tributary. Here, Indians had left some poles, and so Frémont, Preuss, and some of the men were able to spend a night in the tipi, which they had brought along. The next night, just a few miles from South Pass and the Continental Divide, they again took longitude and latitude, but, for some reason, no barometer readings for altitude.

Instead, Frémont estimated the pass's elevation at 7,000 feet. It was a good guess, though the following year when he again came through the pass and used a barometer, his calculation of 7,490 was far better. Like so many travelers before them and since, the men were hard-pressed to tell exactly when they crossed the height of land. The place is open and undramatic. The Wind River Mountains rise off to the northwest, isolated buttes show on the southern horizon, sagebrush stretches in all directions and because everything else is so dry and windy people seldom choose to linger.

The men had come 120 miles from the mouth of the Sweetwater, Frémont reported, 320 miles from Fort Laramie, 950 miles from the settlements on the Missouri. Now they had gone far beyond Frémont's orders to explore up the North Platte only as far as the Sweetwater. Crossing South Pass, they were leaving the drainage of the Mississippi and Missouri rivers. They were leaving the United States and entering Oregon.

Frémont now led the party northwest up the west side—the Oregon side—of the Wind River range. Off the established trail now, he relied more heavily on the wilderness skills of his best men. These were Kit Carson, a Taos-based former fur trapper who would be made famous by Frémont's reports, and Basil Lajeunesse and Clément Lambert, the most competent of the St. Louis–based voyageurs. From the west side, the mountains rose more steeply and appeared more dramatic. Frémont admitted they were beginning to appeal to his ideas of alpine beauty. Preuss remained skeptical. Soon they turned their mules east and headed into the mountains. More than anything, it seems—certainly more than he wanted to follow orders—Frémont wanted to know how tall these mountains were.

His desire is a mix of old-fashioned pride and a mechanistic passion for fact. He wanted to be the first to top what he thought was the highest mountain in the Rockies, and at the same time he wanted to know exactly how tall it was. Frémont was not the first scientist to come up the North Platte and Sweetwater valleys; the botanist Thomas Nuttall and the ornithologist John Kirk Townsend had collected along the same route in 1834. But he was by far the best equipped up to that time. His up-to-date instruments were a few of many that allowed nineteenth-century science to move from qualitative descriptions of the world to accurate, quantitative ones. He wanted to measure the true height because he knew the barometer would allow him to do so.[5]

Then, near the end of a day, they broke the barometer—Frémont does not say exactly how—while crossing a stream at the outlet of a lake. The entire party, he would announce later in his published report, felt the loss. Trappers, travelers, hunters, and traders had been arguing so long about the mountains' true height that "all had looked forward with pleasure to the moment when the instrument, which they believed to be true as the sun, should stand upon their summits, and decide their disputes." They camped on the north shore of the narrow lake. Frémont took latitude and longitude readings—the western- and northernmost readings of the trip—and took compass bearings to the various mountain peaks. Then he settled in to fix the barometer.

The main tube was still intact, but the glass cistern had broken. To replace it, he tried to cut the bottom out of an extra glass vial he had of the correct size, but he had only a rough file to cut with. The first vial broke; then two more. Giving up temporarily, he stored the barometer for the night in a groove the men cut in a tree trunk, and in the morning he began again. He commandeered a powder horn, worn thin by years of use and nearly transparent. Frémont boiled it to make it soft and workable, scraped it thinner for greater transparency, stretched its wide end on a piece of wood to exactly the diameter he needed, bound it to the bottom of the instrument with stout thread, and sealed it snug with buffalo glue. A piece of leather that had served as a cover for one of the glass vials made a good adjustable pocket for the bottom of the powder horn cistern. He next took mercury from one of his artificial horizons, heated it to drive off any excess moisture, and filled the cistern with the bright, heavy, liquid metal. Then he left the instrument upside down for several hours while the glue dried. Finally came the moment of truth. Carefully, he turned the barometer right side up. Everything held, nothing leaked, the vacuum stayed intact.

Time to climb the mountain. Leaving eleven men and twenty or so mules in a little fort-corral they built by the lake, the other fourteen men took fifteen of the best mules, and headed out.

The climb eventually cost them six days and a sharp quarrel between Carson and Frémont over the fact that Carson was walking too fast, and Frémont and the rest couldn't keep up. Eventually, Frémont sent Carson back to the base camp and it was Lajeunesse who found the route. Six men made it to the summit: Frémont, Preuss, Lajeunesse, Lambert, a voyageur named Descoteaux, and

Lieutenant John C. Frémont, about 1843, shortly after the first of his five expeditions to the Rocky Mountains made him famous. Portrait by George Peter Alexander Healy (1813–1894), courtesy of the Union League Club of Chicago.

Auguste Janisse, called by the men Johnny, a mulatto and the only African-American in the group. Descoteaux and Lambert at one point extended a ramrod from above to help the others over a steep, slick slab. Janisse carried the barometer.[6]

At the top, large enough for only one person to stand at a time, they unfurled an American flag, fired off pistols and cheered. Then someone set up the tripod and hung the precious barometer. Preuss took two readings: 18.320 inches of mercury and 18.293. Later computations produced an estimated altitude of 13,570 feet, only 160 feet below the true height of the mountain, subsequently named Frémont Peak. Frémont was elated, and convinced that he'd climbed the highest peak of the Rocky Mountains. Preuss, as often before, felt rushed and underappreciated. "As on the entire journey" he wrote later, "Frémont allowed me only a few minutes for my work."[7]

The barometer broke for a final time on the last afternoon of their march out of the mountains, before they'd even returned to their camp by the lake. Frémont was chagrined, as he'd hoped to be able to compare the instrument's readings with those of another scientist's barometer back in St. Louis, for a better read on his accuracy. He doesn't say whether he decided to leave his broken barometer behind. His other instruments still worked fine—sextants, reflecting circle, artificial horizon, telescope, chronometer, several compasses, and probably a couple of thermometers—and he continued recording latitudes and longitudes.

On August 22, they again reached Independence Rock. Hoping for the best, Frémont unpacked yet another piece of remarkable equipment—an India rubber boat. It was twenty feet long and five wide, Frémont tells us, and appears to have had separate compartments, each inflatable with a bellows. He had ordered it the previous March, and it was delivered a few weeks later to the household of Senator Benton, in Washington, where Frémont lived then with Jessie Benton Frémont, his bride of a few months. Its maker, a Mr. Horace Day of New York, uncrated it on a broad gallery that opened off the Benton dining room, apparently for the admiration of friends and family, warning everyone as he did so that the chemicals might give off a strong odor.

It was so bad everyone at the party had to leave, and the boat—still uninflated, apparently—was hustled out to the barn. Servants hurried among the rooms and hallways, carrying ground coffee on hot shovels to cut the stench with something more pleasant. Sixty years later, Jessie told her biographer that though she barely remembered the boat, she clearly recalled its smell; she was newly pregnant at the time and the odor brought on an oceanic nausea.[8]

Frémont says he brought the boat along specifically to survey the Platte, but its purchase really shows his affection for everything newfangled. The men had used it first to cross the swollen Kansas River in early June. The boat was so large that it could easily carry a cart with the wheels removed, and still provide room for three men to paddle. On the Kansas, the resourceful Basil Lajeunesse swam out ahead, bow rope in his teeth, until his feet touched bottom toward the far shore and he could stand, grab the rope taut and pull in the boat. Six carts and their contents, including all the valuable instruments, were carried safely across. But by dusk, two carts were still unferried. In a hurry, Frémont told the men to load both on at the same time. Unfortunately, the carts slid off and the boat capsized. With the help of some Indians hired as divers, Frémont's men recovered nearly everything, including guns and bullet lead, but they lost a lot of sugar and nearly all the coffee. And two men had nearly drowned. Frémont blamed the man who was steering the boat for being "timid on the water." A wiser leader might have learned not to risk his men's lives in haste.[9]

Now Frémont was eager to try the boat again—and this time for a voyage, not just a crossing. Remarkably, they tried to launch at Independence Rock, still nine winding miles upstream from the Sweetwater's mouth. Packed with gear and four or five men, the boat drew too much water, however, so they dragged it for two miles along the sand and pebble river bottom before giving up and deflating it. After waiting for the rest of the party to arrive, they repacked boat and gear onto the mules, and headed down along the south bank—again, with no trail—toward the North Platte. They had to scramble up and over some big rocks before coming down finally to a small open place near where the Sweetwater rushed into the bigger stream, which was running swollen and smooth. They camped for the night. From this distance, they could not yet hear the roar of rapids below.

Next morning they started before sunrise, expecting to reach Goat Island, thirteen or fourteen river miles away, for breakfast. Seven men climbed aboard—Frémont, Preuss, Lambert, Lajeunesse,

Descoteaux, and two more voyageurs, Honoré Ayot and Leonard Benoît. The boat had already been loaded with all the instruments, with their trail journals, their notebooks of data, their guns, personal baggage, and food for ten days.

"In short," Preuss wrote, "since we now live separate from 'the common crowd,' all the good things were retained for us"—sugar, chocolate, macaroni, the best meat of three recently killed buffalo cows and some recently smoked buffalo sausage—"and only the ordinary left for the others."[10] The rest of the men and all the mules were dispatched overland, under the leadership of Baptiste Bernier, another of the voyageur lieutenants. Frémont may have taken far more food than they needed on the boat with the intention of easing the mules' burdens, floating all the way to Fort Laramie and letting the others pick up the carts at Cache Camp. But the fact that they also took the *best* food, that Carson was not put in charge of the overland contingent, and that Preuss hints at some kind of rift also may reveal that Frémont and Carson had not entirely patched up their earlier quarrel.

Frémont's motives are unclear. He made a career of rash decisions; this was the first notorious one. Perhaps he was so eager to know what his new rubber boat could do that he didn't think of much else. He had a keen mind for mathematics, for cartography, and geography, and understood thoroughly all the processes of measurement that would get him the best data possible. At the same time, he risked the notebooks that contained all the information he'd gathered so far and, worse, he risked his men's lives unnecessarily. "We paddled down the river rapidly," he reported later, "for our little craft was as light as a duck on the water."[11]

The sun was well up when they came to the river's first cut through a ridge, a mile and a half downstream from the present Pathfinder Dam. They stopped on a point on the right, just inside the first steep curve where the river was starting to move fast. They got out, scrambled up the ridge for a better look, and saw rapids but no falls that looked too large to navigate. Looking at the broken ridges around them, Frémont was sure it would have been too much trouble to carry the boat and all their stuff around the fast water, "and I determined to run the cañon," he wrote. It was narrow and high; back down at the water level they saw where big logs from spring floods lay stranded on walls twenty or thirty feet above their heads. Preuss pocketed the chronometer and clutched his notebook. They made it safely through three rapids in quick succession, emerged into an open place where the river slowed and, exhilarated, pulled over for breakfast—some of that good sausage and a swallow of brandy.

After an hour they embarked again. Twenty minutes of smooth water brought them to a much larger, darker canyon, ominous in its height. They stopped again, Frémont wrote, and climbed to a spot where they could see the river winding seven or eight miles through walls 200 to 300 feet high on the near end, 500 feet high farther down. These vertical distances are about right, but there is no view of the entire canyon from the hill they most likely climbed, or from anywhere near its upper entrance. Though both men would remember they were now bold from their earlier success, Preuss noted specifically that they did *not* reconnoiter. Hoping to protect the chronometer, he got out to walk the shore, but soon found the shore gone and rock walls running straight into the water. Meanwhile, the other men tried lining the boat; Lajeunesse and two others got out and walked the shore, holding one end of a fifty-foot rope attached to the stern. Then the boat stuck between two rocks. Water swept over the sides and began carrying away a sextant and a pair of saddlebags; Frémont grabbed the sextant but the saddlebags flowed away. Next, the boat unstuck and came up to where Preuss was standing. With the chronometer in a bag around his neck, he climbed aboard—the roar of the water now deafening—while the men with the rope made it to a big rock twelve feet above the level of the river. But the force of the water proved too great. Two of the men let go. Lajeunesse kept holding, and the line jerked him headfirst into the water. The boat shot on and, remarkably, he appeared again behind them in the current, disappeared, reappeared, his head a black speck in the white, white foam.

At last they turned the boat into an eddy. Lajeunesse caught up, swearing he'd swum half a mile. All three rope men climbed aboard yet again. Everyone knelt now in the boat, took up a short paddle and on they went, finally so exhilarated they shouted "hurrah," as Preuss has it, or, as Frémont has it, joined in a French-Canadian boat song just when the boat careened down a fall, struck a hidden rock, and flipped. Frémont and Preuss found themselves on the left-hand shore, the other men with the turtled boat on the right. Lambert was holding Descoteaux, who could not swim, by the hair. "Lâche pas," cried Descoteaux, "lâche pas, cher frère" (Don't let go, brother!) "Crains pas," came the reply, "Je m'en vais mourir avant de te lâcher" (Fear not! I'll die before I let go of you!)

At least, that's how Frémont wrote the story.[12] Lajeunesse, meanwhile, righted the boat and with one or two of the others, managed to paddle some ways farther before a rock tore a hole in a second compartment and the boat slowly deflated into uselessness.

There is only one route by which any of them could have climbed the four or five hundred feet up out of the canyon, and it leads up from the west, that is, left-hand side of the river. Frémont and Preuss appear to have taken this; how the others made it out is less clear. Preuss managed to hang on to the chronometer, but the water had stopped it. He also saved his detailed, melancholic diary—which did not turn up for more than a century, and which provides such a valuable anchor to Frémont's buoyant optimism.

It was a long, hungry walk to Goat Island. Frémont had lost one moccasin and had to pick his way among rocks and cactus on one sock foot. After several more miles the canyon ended; then it was another five miles along braided river meanders now drowned under Alcova Reservoir. Then Hot Spring Gate, a final scramble over a sharp, red-rock ridge, and finally, below them, they saw Goat Island, waved to their friends, and smelled buffalo ribs roasting on the fire. That night it rained, but they slept right through. Early next morning, Frémont sent the tireless Lajeunesse and a mule or two back to the canyon to recover whatever he could. They made Cache camp the following day, exhumed the stuff and re-rigged the carts, and camped the following night at the ford on the North Platte.

When they finally sorted everything out, they'd lost many of the notebooks, though not all. Descoteaux had happened to have Frémont's double-barreled rifle between his legs when the boat flipped and so it, too, was saved. Most of the scientific instruments were lost: the sextants, the big telescope, the five compasses, the artificial horizons, even the thermometers. The chronometer was ruined, and the one they'd left at Fort Laramie ran poorly, so Frémont got no more reliable longitudes for the rest of the trip. He did save the reflecting circle, and kept measuring his latitudes.

That winter Frémont wrote his report, or rather, dictated it to Jessie, who almost certainly added color and pace to the account. The document, including a detailed map of the corridor the expedition had traveled from the Missouri River to South Pass, was delivered to the Senate in March 1843. The Senate immediately ordered 1,000 copies printed for sale to the general public. Benton's propaganda plans were working; that summer saw the first really large emigrant party—a thousand people—heading out for Oregon. Frémont, too, set out again. His orders were to travel to Oregon and come back the same way. But again, he followed his own wishes and took a much longer side trip, this time to California. An ill-advised crossing of the Sierras in midwinter cost him the lives of two of his men and could easily have cost many more. The trip also made clear to him and Preuss the nature and existence of the Great Basin, that enormous, counterintuitive sink east of the Sierras and west of the Green and Colorado drainages, where rivers flow out of mountains and simply disappear. When, in 1845 and 1846 Frémont traveled again to California to—accidentally on purpose—get the California end of the Mexican War started, Preuss stayed behind in Washington to keep working on the maps.

In the shadow of America's and Frémont's reckless imperialism in those years, of Frémont's growing incompetence and despair, and finally in our pity for his obscure decline and poverty-ridden death, it's easy to forget those maps. They're wonderful. The Senate published the first in 1845. It covers most of the trans-Missouri

West, but Frémont and Preuss, to their great credit, mapped, with one or two exceptions, only the places they'd seen. Good scientists, unwilling to vouch for what they didn't know for sure, they left the rest blank. In 1846, they published a user-friendly, seven-part map of the road from the mouth of the Kansas on the Missouri to the mouth of the Walla Walla on the Columbia. Tens of thousands were published. No one needed a Kit Carson, Jim Bridger, or Tom Fitzpatrick any longer to lead the wagons over plains and deserts. One had only to follow the map—with landmarks, water sources and dates keyed to the descriptions in Frémont's reports—all at an easy-to-read ten miles to the inch.[13]

Similar to what Captain Cook's maps of the Pacific had done sixty-five years earlier, Frémont's maps allowed for a new objectification of the West. Here was information from good scientific instruments, graphically presented by men who knew what they were doing. It was reliable; it was separate from the vagaries of memory and passion—yet it came, ironically, from the mind of a reckless man willing to inflate stories and risk men's lives more and more as time went on. But finally, his skill made his failings and fame irrelevant. The West as a whole could now become an object for admiration and exchange. Soon enough, land law and commerce would combine for its fragmentation into property.

"War—Ground of Snake and Sioux Indians" says the map, in elegant capitals that curve two hundred miles from the Green River to the hills north of Red Buttes. True. "Ridges and masses of naked Granite destitute [*sic*] of vegetation," it says in smaller letters the length of the Sweetwater Rocks, just north of the river of the same name. Also true. Under "Remarks" in the lower left-hand corner it lists "Fuel," then adds, "Cotton wood and willow sufficient near the water courses and sage (artemisia) all over the country ... often as high as the head ... sometimes eight feet high, and several inches in diameter in the stalk. Makes a quick fire." True again. "Game. At Sweetwater River buffalo appear for the last time, and emigrants should provide themselves well with dried meat. West of that region nothing but a few deer and antelope, very wild, are to be met with." True, though within a year or two, buffalo would be scarce on the Sweetwater. "Water," it reads. "Abundant." True, if a traveler kept close to the rivers. Otherwise, false, false, false.

When he got back to Washington, Frémont made Jessie a present of the flag flown from the top of the peak, unfurling it across their bed. The report in its various editions contains several illustrations of the Pathfinder on top of the mountain, hand on the pole, flag whipping in the wind while the others gaze up admiringly from below.

But an equally true picture would have shown Preuss on the peak, hands on his knees, notebook under his armpit and pencil behind his ear, peering through the wind at the top end of the barometer while Janisse or Lajeunesse steadies one of the tripod legs from below. Frémont, meanwhile, already headed downward, shouts back over his shoulder for them to hurry up, get a move on; one reading was good enough. The Pathfinder's haste, his well-equipped sloppiness may have been the most American thing about him. He was too busy to think too hard about what he was doing. They had a lot more ground to cover, and time was getting short.

# CHAPTER 4

# A Road to Somewhere Else

Wednesday, June 15th—Came 19 miles today; passed Independence Rock this afternoon, and crossed Sweetwater River on a bridge. Paid 3 dollars a wagon and swam the stock across. The river is very high and swift. There are cattle and horses drowned there every day; there was one cow went under the bridge and was drowned, while we were crossing, belonging to another company. The bridge is very rickety and must soon break down. We are camped 2 miles this side of the bridge, near the river.

*—Amelia Stewart Knight, 1853.*

The road left the river at Red Buttes, crossed sagebrush flats, passed white-rimmed alkaline swamps, and then wound fifteen miles through waterless hills to Willow Springs, where the emigrants generally camped. At first, they called it an oasis. Sheltered by cottonwoods, they remarked on the pleasures of clear water and birdsong in the rustling shade. Within a few years, however, the trees were chopped down and diarists noted only stumps. Still, the water in the two springs—one by the trail and the second some ways up a draw—stayed good and reasonably plentiful. For water was what mattered on the trail, water and a steady grade. People could carry enough water for two or three days in an eight-gallon keg, but the stock needed long drinks daily, and would not discriminate between good water and bad. An ox that drank from an alkali spring would be dead by morning. Where the soil was alkaline it was white, yet the poison grass came up through it a dark, deceptive green. For days after leaving the river, there was enough bad water along the road that travelers often found it littered with carcasses of oxen and mules. Stock traveling unyoked or unharnessed required extra care and protection. But at Willow Springs they could drink their fill. Cold, clear water bubbled up among the rocks.

Leaving Willow Springs, the trail climbed four hundred feet in the steepest mile on the journey so far. Often the emigrants would double-team the oxen at this point, taking a team from one wagon to hitch to the one before it for the climb, and then walking both teams back down the hill to bring up the second wagon. This might leave some in a party with time to enjoy the view from the top. People called it Prospect Hill. "We could see a great ways," wrote Anna Maria Goodell. Sarah Mariah Mouseley noted three years later: "[R]eally a beautiful spot we beheld the . . . mountains in the distance."[1] The plateau before them looked like desert. The West already was changing them, if they were ready to call beautiful a landscape so dry.

The land rose gradually to their right; not much to see in that direction. Ahead, far to the south and southwest, a flank of blue mountains made the horizon. These mountains had no name yet; later they would be called, from east to west, Seminoe, Ferris, and Green mountains. If the emigrants were early and it was still June, the tops might be snowed. Some miles closer, a jumbled series of rocks rose from the sagebrush plateau. On a windless day the rocks showed bare and untimbered, and looked tan instead of blue. Some of the rocks were attached to longer spurs leading off to the west. Others were isolated.

The air was drier. If a breeze was blowing, and it hadn't just rained, there would be dust in the breeze and alkali in the dust. It stung the throat and made the skin feel rashy. After a few miles travelers noticed a new redness at their neighbors' eyes and nostrils, new cracks in their lips. The land rolled away toward the rocks. The road followed the land. As they often had along the Platte, the wagons, after coming over the brow of the hill onto the high pla-teau, would spread out and roll abreast, a major chord of advancement now instead of a melody. Emigrants felt powerful when they didn't have to spend the day in a neighbor's dust. Walking beside their oxen, watching the wagon jolt crazily over the sagebrush, they could see where they were going and breathe better air.

Ten miles beyond Prospect Hill, Horse Creek trickled in from the right. Though the water was satisfactory, the grass was unpredictable, there was only sagebrush for campfires, and of course there was no shade. One early group had to chop the sage stalks out of the ground to make space for their tents.[2] A party that camped at Horse Creek could make it to the Sweetwater by noon the next day. Though no wider than a good-sized creek to eastern eyes,[3] the Sweetwater meant water worries were over for a while at least, and the party would reach the Continental Divide in less than a week.

When they approached the Sweetwater, one branch of the road forked to the left, dipped down to the river and crossed it. In the early 1850s, traders built a bridge here and began charging emigrants to cross. A second branch of the trail kept to the near side of the river for another mile, until it reached alluvial meadows at the base of a remarkably large rock. Here in most years there was enough grass even for the largest herds; it was where Frémont stopped to make meat. But even after buffalo became scarce, emigrants continued to stop here, attracted by the grass, the water, and the rock.

Higher at one end than the other, grayish-tan, humped and folded deeply, smooth yet seamed, the rock looked fleshy; it looked "more like a big elephant to his sides in the mud than any thing else," a cavalry soldier wrote in the 1860s.[4] It rose 160 feet from the plains around it. Because it was noticeable, separated from other rocks nearby, because the grass and water made it such a good place to stop, people gave it a name early on. And they began to carve their names on it. It became a landmark.

Rock Independence, the trappers called it, probably to commemorate a riotous Fourth of July that eighty of them spent there in 1830. Within fifteen years the Oregon-bound emigrants had flipped the name to Independence Rock, and continued to honor the Fourth at the site, for there was more than one reason to celebrate. Arrival by early July left time to reach Oregon or California before fall snows filled the passes in the Cascades or the Sierras. On the first of July, 1853, Virginia Ivins found strangers "hard at work hoisting a deserted wagon to the top, intending to roll it off to celebrate Independence day, so near at hand."[5] As the nation stretched toward civil war in those years, it's easy to imagine a patriotism that would torch a decrepit wagon and roll it off the rock after dark. Passing the rock a year later, however, Anna Maria Gooddell also noticed a wagon on top:

> July 3rd. We have got to Independence Rock about noon. William and I went around it. Lib and Lucretia and the rest of the girls went over it. There is a wagon and tent on top of it. I do not see any names on it that I know.[6]

Maybe it was the same wagon. Maybe the wagon hoist and fiery roll-off was by then a tradition—along with the more mundane activities most travelers report: rest, a good meal, and time to gather gooseberries and check out the names.

People all over the world mark rocks. In the North American West, the first people had been marking rocks with signs and pictures for millennia. But they left their art in out-of-the way places, on rock walls protected from weather by an overhang, with lots of cover and a clear creek nearby. They left their art where there was game and shelter, in places where a family might want to winter for a thousand years. They assumed they'd be coming back.

When white trappers and fur traders first arrived in the country in an organized way in 1825, they began leaving their names for other reasons—ego, mostly. Religion and politics quickly followed, and over the inscriptions there began to float a whiff of propaganda. The Jesuit Father De Smet, on his way to the Salish people in what's now western Montana in 1841, left the sacred initials I.H.S, a derivative of an ancient Greek acronym for Christ by now long associated with his order. The same day he launched his rubber boat in 1842, Frémont carved a large cross on the rock, and

Independence Rock, looking northeast. Early travelers sometimes compared the Rock to an elephant, up to its sides in the mud. Photograph by the author.

then filled in the carving with black India rubber, boat-patching material "calculated to resist the influence of wind and rain."[7] He would regret it fourteen years later when he ran for president and opponents claimed he was under the thumb of the Pope. In July of 1843, *New Orleans Picayune* reporter Matthew Field and his friends enthusiastically wrote HENRY CLAY in large capitals. On their return a month later, they found that William Gilpin, editor of the *St. Louis Argus* and later the first territorial governor of Colorado, had written MARTIN VAN BUREN over the top in letters three times as large—and signed his inscription. Indians, who appear to have mostly ignored the rock heretofore, caught the inscription bug that year from the whites. Field carefully copied into his diary some inscriptions they had left in a vermilion paint so fresh it was still wet. "Our Scioux squaw gave us the explanation," he writes, but doesn't pass the explanation along.[8] Inscribers, he tells us, often made paint by heating buffalo grease and mixing it with gunpowder and glue. Those with more time used a cold chisel, and theirs are the names that have lasted.

Use of the trail by emigrants had at that time barely begun. ("The female names," Field speculated, "are, many of them, sweethearts of the wanderers, except some of the newest, which may have been left by the ladies of the Oregon party.") But the emigrants, unlike the trappers, did not expect to return. They knew they were changing their lives, that it was a one-way journey,[9] that it was dangerous,[10] and that despite their risks the world was likely to forget them. Having left wives, husbands, customers, creditors, lovers, enemies, even children behind in the settlements, they must often have wondered, as they walked, about those people and lives whose stories they would never know. So the names they carved were their declaration, for good or ill, of independence from the past. The act announced their loneliness, but wouldn't have assuaged it. Free land and new families, they hoped, would take care of that.

Turning up the Sweetwater, they saw now that the granite outcrops had consolidated into a spur of bare rock running east-west. Many, like Ohio-born Sarah Sutton, now admitted to themselves a difficult, new fact. The Rocky Mountains are "made of soled rock, and heaps upon heaps of rocks, and not earth as the mountains are in our own land."

They could make out a vertical gap in the spur, six miles away. The trail detoured through a pass near the east end of the spur and came at last to a close view of Devil's Gate from the far side, that is, from the southwest. There everyone stopped again, to look northward through the opening to the faint plains beyond, to scramble up the rocks and look down into the chasm, to leave more names.

Some called the opening Hell's Gate. A few speculated in their diaries about its wild connections with the underworld. But all were impressed. They layered its rocky facts with their fearful longing for God in nature. They called it *sublime*.

In the 1830s, a Scottish tourist named William Drummond Stewart began making annual trips to the Rocky Mountains to fish, hunt buffalo, and hang out with mountain men.[11] His party included Antoine Clément, a mixed-blood Delaware hunter, at least two other hunters, a cook, and probably some muleteers and stock tenders to look after the teams and the two-wheeled wagons called charettes. The party of a dozen or so traveled up the Platte and Sweetwater with the larger trade-goods caravan headed for the trappers' yearly rendezvous. A nobleman and army officer on leave—he was a veteran of Waterloo—with time and money to spare, Stewart ran his vacations like campaigns and demanded a military respect that members of his party were sometimes reluctant to grant him. In 1837, when he passed through New Orleans, he hired a Baltimore painter named Alfred Jacob Miller to come to the mountains and record their magnificence. Miller, only twenty-six, had already trained in Paris and Rome. He made watercolor sketches on the trail and at rendezvous; he was the first artist to paint the trail's landmarks and the only artist to paint trapper life first-hand. Later, back at his studio in Baltimore and during two years in Scotland in Stewart's employ, he worked the sketches into big dark oils to hang on Murthly Castle's drafty walls.

The watercolors, however, are fresh and immediate. Miller painted the packtrain caravan. He painted Stewart at a distance, well mounted and wearing a flat-crowned sombrero. At least two of his sketches include a mounted Jim Bridger, wearing an odd gift Stewart brought him that year—a suit of armor, with casque, cuirass, and greaves (helmet, breastplate, and shinguards)—that make the mountain man a conquistador. Miller painted portraits of Clément; he painted important Lakota and Kansas men he met on the trail and important Shoshone and Nez Perce men he met at rendezvous. He painted young Shoshone girls swimming, one swinging dreamily from a tree branch. He worked up a picture of a languid trapper taking a Shoshone girl for a bride, which was later to become extremely popular. He painted trappers, tipis, horse herds from a distance, and all kinds of buffalo hunts; he painted rocks and sky and mountains. Despite all the portrait work, it is the scenery for which he is best remembered. All is hazed by an aesthetic as plain as a trapper's name on a rock: he thought his subjects exotic and picturesque—closely related qualities—and expected his viewers to feel the same.[12]

In its proportions of width to height, the Devil's Gate of Miller's watercolor is faithful to the facts. At the same time the light is yellow, the shadows velvety, the trees look more like eastern white pines than the pitch pines and junipers that are really there, and the river has a coppery color one might more likely find in tributaries of the Hudson or the Delaware than in a high-plains river of the West. Only after a moment does a viewer notice a deer, with antlers, standing in the water in the middle foreground. And only a person who has been to the site will realize that the deer is the size of a muskrat. Relative to the only item that provides any scale, Miller has painted Devil's Gate three or four times its actual size. Grandeur was what his patron wanted, and grandeur he got.

Stewart made his last trip to the mountains in 1843. Again he passed through New Orleans on his way to St. Louis, but this time hired a writer instead of a painter to record the trip. Matthew Field was a hack at the *New Orleans Picayune* who, fancying himself the next Washington Irving or James Fenimore Cooper, jumped at the job. He kept diaries on the trail, and later expanded his notes into longer pieces for the *Picayune*. Like Miller's oils, the newspaper pieces Field wrote later seem strained and overdone. He wanted to entertain, and entertainments demanded hyperbole. At the Rock that day in 1843, Field and his friends drank toasts once they finished inscribing Henry Clay's name. Field got drunk, and took a nap on the Rock in the sun.

When the party reaches its next stop, Field relates a long tale about the origins of "the Portico of Pandemonium"—Devil's Gate—which, he says, was told to him by one of the Delawares.[13] An enormous beast with tusks and four legs was terrorizing the country, gorging itself on game, drinking streams dry, tearing up trees and devouring them. Local tribes had to bury their chronic hostilities. For three days, they danced and fasted. Finally a prophet came out of a trance, "arose slowly, erect as a medicine pole, and lifted his arms and eyes to the sun," and told them they'd have to work together. "The next day," as the Delaware hunter supposedly told it, "the combined forces of the red men set forward upon their crusade against the Evil Spirit, and it was not long before they found him in the valley of the Sweetwater, which is nearly surrounded by mighty mountains." Keeping a safe distance, the people shot the beast full of arrows until he looked like a huge porcupine. Enraged, he roared, plowed into the mountain, threw rocks around like a volcano and finally, with his great tusks, opened the "frightful gap," through which he galloped away and never was seen again.

The story was told, Field says, by "a rude and unintelligent half-breed known as 'Delaware John' . . . and there seems to us a sort of semi-Indian, semi-Saxon attraction about [the tale] that ought to awaken as wide attention in print as at the campfire."[14] And Field implies that the narrator had learned the story from local Indians, or that being part-Indian means the man simply knows all Indian tales. He names "Crows, Arrapahos, Sioux, Chayenne and other tribes" as the ones who teamed up against the tusked beast. But there are no tusked beasts native to the Rocky Mountains; the tale sounds weirdly un-local. A Delaware narrator, or Field himself, might well have seen a circus elephant by 1843. But it seems unlikely that any Crow, Arapaho, Lakota, or Cheyenne people at the time would ever have seen an elephant, a walrus, or even a wild hog. Delaware John might have made up the story to please the campfire circle; more likely, Field made it up to please his readers. It's not a local story.

Aside from the mention of Indian families living with white traders, local Indians are, for a time, absent from emigrant diaries along these stretches of the trail. For one thing, the Sweetwater Valley in the early 1840s was far from any of the centers of tribal power.[15] The tribes of the northern plains were not yet feeling the threat to their lands and livelihood that soon would become clear.

Even the mixed-race traders, well established at Devil's Gate by 1854 when Oregon-bound Sarah Sutton passed through with her family, seemed to her to be living a useless, out-of-the-way life on poor land. Just upstream from the gate she found two Indians Lodges, and 7 or 8 little cabins of traders, and numbers of half Indian children . . . in some places the pines and cedars grew large enough to build there little cabins that these french and indians traders reside in. these settlers do not pretend to raise a thing, not even a garden. one thing the land seems too poor to support any growth. Another one the gentleman told us, it was useless to try, as there would be an hundred red Indians to every ear of corn, and they would sit down by it until it got into roasting ears, and then fight who should have it. here they depend on the buffalo and bear, and what is wagond here A 1000 miles or more.

That was no life, without raising crops, living on game, and depending on a supply of goods from far away. She was as impressed as anyone by the scenery at Devil's Gate, but made it clear the glory was God's. Her mind was on higher things:

the high mountains like the Red Sea, had fled back, not to let the Isrealites pass through, but to let sweet water river run through. the high wall on each side were strait down as the side of a stone house and the river took such a horse shoe turn that the visiter could not get within 100 yards of it, without ascending the mountain and looking down, or crossing the river, and looking through the sides there is more to be seen on this wide road, to remind us of the mysteries of providenc than in all our lives before. God moves in A mysterious way His wonders to perform. He plants his footsteps in the sea. He rides upon the storm.[16]

There was no value in land so useless. The valley ran between the steep granite ridge that rose above the river on their right, and the higher, timbered mountain that paralleled their route several miles away to the left. The trail followed the south side of the river now, and was often sandy. Mostly, though, the grass was good and the feel of the mountains closing in kept everyone refreshed and eager. West of Devil's Gate, another spur came south out of the granite ridge, and it, too, was notched, though only on the top: Split Rock was clearly visible in front of and then behind the emigrants for three days or more. A person with her mind on higher things had many hours, while walking, to stare at the bite-shaped gap and wonder about the Creator's mouth and the Creator's teeth, about crops and water and life and death, and to imagine for the ten-thousandth time a good farm at the end of the journey, a piece of real and useful property, quite unlike the huts she had just passed. The Oregon soil in the Willamette Valley was so rich, people said, that you could toss seeds over a shoulder and the corn would sprout behind you.

It would be a farm you could own debt-free and unmolested, its title secured by government survey and courthouse records, and in so doing you could own your own life and the lives of your descendants as they arrived in the world and made the future real. A person whose luck so far had held—no sickness on the trail, no accident—could feel the future moving toward her faster now and passing under her feet as she walked, then stretching out behind like memory. The names of these places—Red Buttes, Willow Springs, Horse Creek, Independence Rock, Devil's Gate and now Split Rock—would stay with her.

Still, this was not land worth owning. It wouldn't support a living for a family. Its landmarks were simply that—spots to show the travelers how far they had come and how far yet they had to go. Few stories, and no one's family stories, as far as most emigrants knew, were anchored to the spots. Yet the travelers did leave a kind of story as they passed. Like wagon ruts, it was evidence more of their surprising numbers than of any single family's experience. The land that was important to them was still a thousand miles off. The Sweetwater and its rocks were only halfway along. For now there was only movement.

# CHAPTER 5

# Burning Bridges

. . . and the men owning and working about the post including the proprietors and Charles Lajeunesse, August Archambeaut and his two brothers, Moses Perat and a brother of him and Charley, some Indians and others, all of whom were from the Green River country which belonged to the Shoshones, except Mr. M., and the raiders regarded them as Shoshones, which Indians always had good horses.
  –*Judge Ricker's interview notes with Magloire Mosseau, 1906.*

By the 1850s, a third group had arrived on the North Platte and Sweetwater and was trying to make a living. These were neither one-way emigrants nor wide-ranging tribes. They were French-speaking traders with Indian wives and families. The men provided the business links, back to French St. Louis. Their Indian brides provided security, as a tribe was unlikely to harm a trader if he was married to a prominent man's daughter, or sister, or mother. As such they imported the social and commercial patterns of the mixed-race, French-and-Indian-speaking people who had been hunting, trapping, trading, and living along the rivers of North America for 250 years. But these families on the high plains were primarily traders. They were storekeepers. Like merchants any-where, they prospered as long as they could charge the prices they needed to cover their risks and costs, and as long as they could command a good location. They kept control of these spots, often at river crossings, as long as possible, accumulating families and family stories along the way. For ten or fifteen years, these people and their stories offered a bridge between Indians and whites.

By this time the fur trade had dwindled, and there was only one reason to build a post at Devil's Gate or Independence Rock: to sell supplies to emigrants. Briefly, the trading families prospered; the ruthless ones grew rich. Even the descendants of the moderately successful families, however, would remember the years when their fathers took their pay in gold.[1] Then war came, ruining business, and finally the railroad came farther south, and removed any reason for travel at all on the emigrant road.

Sarah Sutton had a sharp eye for the exotic when she first began to encounter traders and their families on the Platte, not yet as scornful as she would be by the time she reached Devil's Gate. By 1854, the route up the North Platte had become a road, and traders sought the emigrants' business at nearly every stop. Sutton and her Oregon-bound wagon train—her husband, their eleven children and various in-laws, grandchildren and friends—encountered at least seventeen different trading establishments on the seventeen days from Chimney Rock, in what's now western Nebraska, to Devil's Gate, a distance of 260 miles.

And the races, Sutton kept noticing, were sleeping together. Apparently, they were unconcerned with the racial hierarchy of beauty that was so clear in her mind. At Chimney Rock on May 28: "here is a french traders tent, and an indian wigwam with a good looking white man, and an ugly black squaw for a wife and two children." The woman wore a blue calico dress and a blue blanket. Soon they were joined by "another young squaw" whose "fair skinn'd husband sat down with her and the yellow babes played on both of them." On the North Platte near Scott's Bluff on May 31, Sutton found "a traders tent of french an[d] indians, a good looking white man with A black squaw for a bosom companion," and at one of the posts near Fort Laramie, she found "7 or 8 log huts. bakery and store, and whites and indians all together."

Soon, the sight of mixed-race families became routine. At a post the next night she noticed only that there were twenty tipis around the store. Two nights later she described another establishment as "a town of indians and whites"—this would have been Bissonette's post on LaBonte Creek. At Deer Creek, the next night, she found just one tipi at the post, but the trader was doing a brisk business in livestock. The emigrants sold him two lame cows for fifteen dollars each, and bought a grass-fattened pony for forty. Fifty ponies grazed nearby.

Many of these posts were sizable, and would have included a store, storehouse, trader's house, blacksmith shop and sheds, and corrals for the animals. And all included anywhere from one to dozens of tipis filled with relatives and customers. Smaller arrangements of a trader's tent and a tipi or two were also located at strategic spots, and some of the businesses were mobile—peddlers with wagons who moved as often as the emigrants did.[2] Nearly all were run by traders with French names: Bordeaux, Gratiot, the same Joseph Bissonette seen on the day Frémont's tipi blew down, and, most notorious in the 1850s, John Baptiste Richard.

Richard—Anglos spelled his name Reshaw—ran the trading post and big new bridge over the North Platte, near the ford where Frémont had crossed twelve years earlier. Sutton counted several log buildings and six tipis at the bridgehead when she crossed. Like other traders downstream, Richard had a Lakota wife and family; he was still east of Red Buttes, just inside the western extremity of Lakota power. This was the second or third bridge he had owned. He knew exactly what the market would bear. Because the Suttons were early—it was still only the 11th of June—the river was running high and Richard, with no competition, could charge an astronomical five dollars per wagon and five cents per head of stock. Sutton's family paid the price, and her opinion of traders began to worsen.

At Red Buttes the wagon train passed two traders' tents and a tipi. At Willow Springs they camped with another train, this one driving 1,000 head of cattle, and shot the first buffalo they'd seen the entire trip—the cause and the result of devastation exemplified in a single spot. On June 14, they passed three traders on the road and reached "Independent Rock . . . standing out by itself and independent of all others," Sutton wrote. Here they found a small bridge over the Sweetwater, a tipi, and a smooth-talking bridge-toll taker.[3]

He was probably a trader named Alfred Archambault, though he may have been any of several men. By 1854 there had been a bridge at Independence Rock and posts there and at Devil's Gate for at least a year and perhaps two.[4] Something like a village of French-Shoshone families stretched over both locations, including the families of Hubert Papin; Charles and Moses Perat and a third Perat brother; Auguste and Alfred Archambault and a third Archambault brother; Magloire Mosseau; and, best known of all of them and generally thought of as bourgeois or boss, Charles Lajeunesse.

Lajeunesse, Papin, and the Perats seem to have been the principal partners. Lajeunesse and various Papins had been important men in the American Fur Company; Pierre Didier Papin had served as bourgeois at Fort Laramie during the 1840s when the company owned the fort. Lajeunesse, a brother of Frémont's protector Basil Lajeunesse, started his career as *hivernant*, a lowly winterer, for the fur company at its forts on the Missouri, then in the 1830s came to the Platte. Francis Parkman met Pierre Papin in 1846, when Papin was trying to float the Platte with eleven bullboats full of buffalo robes and a mixed-race crew. A few weeks later, Parkman met Lajeunesse shouting greetings from the parapet at Fort Laramie, when the historian arrived there with his friends.

"Lajeunesse, Charles, *dit* [called] Simond (Simono)," he is listed in the records of the Missouri Historical Society; the nickname may actually have been Simonot—little Simon. It came down through various orthographies as Seminoe, eventually becoming an extra surname for his children and grandchildren. Parkman tried to Frenchify it even more: "This Cimoneau was [Henry Chatillon's] fast friend," Parkman explained, "and the only man in the country who could rival him in hunting."[5]

A few years after Parkman met him, Lajeunesse moved over the Continental Divide and started a little trading post of his own near Fort Bridger. Now in Shoshone country, he married a Shoshone woman. She bore him at least two sons: Mitchell (Michel) and Noel Seminoe, who would in time become well known along the Platte and Sweetwater. Jim Bridger bought them out in 1852 for $400,[6] and that money appears to have been some or all of the capital that went to start up the posts at Devil's Gate and Independence Rock.

All these traders except for Mosseau and Archambault appear to have had Shoshone wives; Devil's Gate marked the eastern edge of reliable Shoshone power. The post was substantial. Mosseau later recalled as many as fourteen different buildings at Devil's Gate. They were built on three sides of a square, with hewn logs, well-laid floors, windows and board-and-dirt roofs. The buildings clustered about half a mile south of where the Sweetwater swung through the gate, where there were good meadows along the river and the wind was deflected slightly by ground that rose gently to the south and west.[7] Business was good—many tens of thousands of emigrants were traveling the road each year—and the merchant families prospered. Half a century later, Aurelia Archambault still recalled her father's partners filling her little-girl apron with gold nuggets. Then the cloth tore, and the nuggets spilled on the ground.

Still smarting from the high prices they'd paid to cross Richard's bridge, Sarah Sutton and her family were surprised to find the trader at the Sweetwater asking only fifty cents per wagon, and offering to let one of the wagons pass for free. He said he felt generous because he could tell Mr. Sutton was a lodge brother—both were brethren of the International Order of Odd Fellows. Further, he promised to "furnish us wood to burn so according to his kind directions we drove acrosst the bridge and pitched our tents, where there was much sweet water, and was all rejoicing at the kindness of the stranger," Sarah Sutton wrote. But when a dozen of the emigrants walked back across the bridge for wood, the trader charged them twenty-five cents an armload. The men realized they'd been tricked, gamely paid the money and returned in "a high gale of laughter," she reported.

Later, however, the Odd Fellows in the train returned once again to the trader to "try his grit, and found out he did not know the mystery." Suddenly, Sutton turned judgmental. Only at this point did a trader's decision to marry into a tribe become in her eyes a symptom of moral failure: "I don't beleive any man of A good principle will live here with the indians, and their smoky Buffalo skin wigwams with a slick greasy hole to slip in at, like a wolf, . . . " Next morning, the emigrants were happy to start early, Sutton reported, and get away from "the hospitable stranger, and his venomous looking Snake indians."

The Shoshones, however, appear to have been neither as numerous along the road nor as poor as the Lakota people that Sutton and her family had encountered earlier. For days, it had seemed as if hungry Indians were everywhere. At Ash Hollow in what is now western Nebraska, Sutton and her train met a large village of 600 Lakota in fifty lodges, on the move like themselves. The village stayed with the train two or three days, dogs and horses pulling travois and scratching up the road, swapping, begging Indians mingling with the emigrants as they moved: "some of the children got a streing of beads for A biscuit, and got a pair of mockesons for an ox bow they got a little something to eat among us, but we cant afford to feed them much." Sutton admitted to her journal she felt "pesterd" but was still, at this point, cautious about judging the mendicants: "they are an innocent harmless being, and wont touch a thing that dont belong to them. all they want is something to eat." But the next day four or five Lakota left with her frying pan after they had stayed for supper.[8]

By now the emigrants and their herds were decimating the buffalo economy, and this constant, confusing back-pressure was the result. Indians were hungry, whites uneasy; before long both sides were angry. June rolled into July of 1854, and with July came the peak of the emigration season. By August, a variety of Lakota people were camped near Fort Laramie, waiting for their annuities yet angry at chronic government failure to honor the Treaty of 1851, when the northern plains were first divided into tribal territories. Then one day, east of the fort, a Minniconjou Lakota warrior killed a lame Mormon ox.

Lieutenant John Grattan, a year out of West Point and eager to prove himself, marched twenty-six soldiers and Antoine Lucien, a drunken interpreter, out of Fort Laramie to a nearby Brûlé Lakota village where the Minniconjou warrior was staying—to arrest the thief, they thought, and recover the ox. But the ox had been eaten, the Brûlés were reluctant to surrender their friend, and the interpreter loaded extra insults into the remarks of both sides. Grattan, all of his soldiers, and at least one Indian, the Brûlé chief Conquering Bear, were killed. [9] The Lakotas gave in to rage that had been building for years, and looted and burned all the posts around Fort Laramie—Bordeaux's, Gratiot's, Bissonette's. Richard's, way up by Red Buttes, was spared, perhaps because his Oglala Lakota relatives had good connections, perhaps just because he was farther away.

That fall, the Brûlés raided a coach or two carrying the new transcontinental mail, but most of their tribe, unaware that the Indian wars had entered a new phase, stuck to old ways and headed north into the Powder River Basin for buffalo. Raids also increased at Devil's Gate and Independence Rock, with Lakota, Cheyenne, and Arapaho warriors frequently running off Shoshone and Archambault horses and killing Archambault cattle.[10] The following summer, General William S. Harney caught up with the Brûlés on Blue Water Creek near Ash Hollow. Eighty-five Indians were killed; seventy-five women and children captured. This was war on a new scale. Still, the Lakotas and their allies continued raiding along the road through the fall of 1855, and finally the army decided all trade with Indians had to stop. Traders, angry about the lost business, reluctantly agreed to go to Fort Laramie or Fort Bridger for safety. Most of the Devil's Gate traders headed for Fort Bridger to spend the winter among their Shoshone relatives. Mosseau, who had a Lakota wife, went to Fort Laramie.

Last to leave the Sweetwater was Alfred Archambault, whose wife was neither Shoshone nor Lakota but Philadelphian, of German extraction. They loaded up their children and what trade goods they could carry, cached the rest, and departed for the Missouri on October 2, 1856. Fifty years later Aurelia Archambault would remember Indians excavating their buried goods before the family was even out of sight.

Suddenly, however, Indian troubles along the North Platte and Sweetwater were eclipsed by Mormon disasters. Emigrants in two ill-prepared handcart companies died in droves in the snow from Red Buttes to South Pass. By the following summer, a Mormon war seemed certain; President Buchanan sent an army of 2,500 troops to chastise the Saints and enforce the appointment of federal officers in Utah. Mormon guerillas burned trading posts and army supply trains before the little shadow-war passed on westward.[11] The army failed to reach Salt Lake, instead going into winter quarters near Fort Bridger. And behind them, the troops left a commercial vacuum, into which stepped another French-speaking trader, the enterprising Louis Guinard.

Guinard came from Quebec to the Sweetwater by way of New Orleans, California and what's now Idaho, a journey that lasted a decade and left him ready to settle down when he finally arrived. He may have repaired the bridge at Independence Rock, or he may have built a new one. Eventually, his bridge was a stout 100 feet long, ramping up over one pier in the middle of the river from abutments at both ends. He also built an L-shaped log building, 100 feet long counting both limbs of the L, with a stockade enclosing the rest of the rectangle. By late fall 1857, he was well enough established to offer to sell mules and beef cattle to the army, if the soldiers would pay his prices.[12] Guinard had a Shoshone wife, and by now they had at least one son.

In 1858, the Mormons and the federal government settled their differences short of bloodshed. As emigration tapered off, commercial traffic grew along the road. More and more goods were needed for the pilgrims already landed in the basins of Utah, the valleys of Oregon, and the gold gulches and fruit ranches of California.[13] Then gold turned up in Colorado, and Mormons began shipping vegetables and trailing cattle from the Salt Lake Valley all the way to Pike's Peak—by way of the Sweetwater and the Platte—to feed the inrushing miner hordes. All of it made for more bridge tolls for Louis Guinard. By staying in one place, he was getting rich. Perhaps he thought his family had a real future. Their stories would survive some substantial dislocations.

Getting far richer, however, was John Richard. Where Guinard's bridge over the Sweetwater was 100 feet long, Richard's at the Platte was ten times as long and sometimes commanded tolls ten times as high. Yet where Guinard's business was local, Richard was building a regional empire. For more than a decade, he had been running whiskey—Taos lightning, it was called—from New Mexico up to the Platte River road, where he probably wholesaled it to other traders and certainly retailed it to customers of all stripes. The whiskey route took him right past the new Pike's Peak gold diggings, and Richard and his brothers were soon running Denver's first store and saloon. Next they began buying worn-out cattle from arriving miners, trailing them up to the North Platte, fattening them there and selling them to emigrants. And by now, John Richard had started the West's first sweatshop at his bridge. Twenty Indian women, probably his Oglala relatives, worked full time making beaded moccasins and fancy deerskin clothing for emigrants, occasional tourists, and especially the miners in Colorado who had money to spend. Now the whiskey wagons had cargo for the return trip south.[14]

As a result, Richard was often absent in 1858 and '59. The bridge business may have suffered, and the bridge itself appears to have been falling into disrepair. His behavior became more erratic. Drunk, he drove a carriage into an emigrant train. Two men were killed when the stock stampeded. He became so angry when another party chose a ferry instead of his bridge that his reluctant non-customers had to place the muzzle of a cocked rifle behind his ear before he would calm down.[15] Guinard decided it was time to move against his competitor.

In the fall of 1859, Guinard hired twenty, perhaps fifty, men to build a new bridge on the North Platte that would compete directly with Richard's, selecting a site six miles upstream. The crew cut trees on the mountain seven miles away, hauled them, and squared them into timbers. To anchor the piers, they quarried and hauled tons of rock two and a half miles. Lacking a sawmill, they whipsawed other logs in pits, cutting them into three-inch planks for the deck. The bridge was completed by the summer of 1860. It was 1,100 feet long, stretching across columns anchored in twenty-eight piers each forty feet apart, with a plank deck eighteen feet wide from railing to railing. The piers were diamond-shaped log cribs filled with rocks, with the long ends of the diamonds pointing up- and downstream. A relative of Guinard's testified decades later that the bridge had cost $64,000 to build, and took in $10,000 to $15,000 per year in tolls.[16] But he had reason to inflate the cost; it may have cost less and taken in a good deal more.

Still, it was a substantial piece of public work in a land mostly empty of such things. Guinard was careful to keep his tolls below Richard's; that, plus its stronger appearance, diverted most traffic to the newer bridge. One of Guinard's first customers was the world-famous Englishman, Sir Richard Burton, working on a travel book.

Burton, ex-British intelligence officer, linguist, explorer of East Africa, travel writer, and infiltrator of the Muslim holy places, was dashing by stagecoach across the plains late in the summer of 1860 to meet Brigham Young and write a book on the prophet and the Mecca of the Mormons. He was eager for local color; he was a vivid writer and his book, *The City of the Saints,* is devastatingly accurate about food, manners, dress, landscape, equipment, commerce, politics, and all the other details of travel. When, for example, Burton spends a night at a post near Fort Laramie, he quickly grasps from the trader's stories how the whiskey politics of fur-trade competition leads to blood feuds in Indian families.[17] But he also thinks of himself as a disinterested observer. He finds it his duty to divide people into categories—honest traders and greedy ones, chivalrous westerners and slum rejects, pretty mixed-blood girls (part French) and ugly ones (part Anglo). He thinks he is interested in science, but the "science" that absorbs him is race.

At Guinard's bridge, Burton finds the proprietor "very downcast about his temporal prospects, and [he] handed us over, with the *insouciance* of his race, to the tender mercies of his venerable squaw." Her cooking is terrible, her tin-can coffee cups "slippery with grease," so Burton dodges the meal and goes out for a smoke and a look at the mountain. Some Arapaho men stop by. Burton decides their temper is sour because they are heading home without any Ute scalps, and declares they look more like horse thieves than warriors. Then he ranks the local tribes: Sioux the most admirable, Cheyenne in the middle, Arapaho the most degenerate.

A day later, at Devil's Gate, he again finds the food inedible and heads outdoors to reflect. "They are a queer lot these French Canadians who have 'located' themselves in the Far West," he begins. Past travel writers, he notes, may have described them as d'Artagnans in buckskin—"sashed, knived," tough, merry, generous, and handsome, relishing "the envy of every Indian 'brave,' and the admiration of every Indian belle." But, Burton says, he found them shy, proud, and very lazy. "Probably [their] good qualities lie below the surface . . . I will answer, however, for the fact, that the bad points are painfully prominent."

All peoples in the West are ranked, both within their race and their race within a larger scheme. Burton fits every individual he meets smoothly into one stratum or another. Old Indian women are so ugly they resemble gorillas; middle-aged women are broad and squat, with big hands and feet from years of work. The young women are briefly desirable, with black eyes, glittering teeth and "long black hair like the ears of a Blenheim spaniel, justifying a natural instinct to stroke or pat it, drawn straight over a low, broad Quadroon-like brow." Whites are at the top rank of the races, blacks at the bottom, Indians between, with any mixed-bloods landing tidily between their absolutes.

In these years, phrenology and its newborn cousin, anthropology, were the so-called sciences that upheld the stratification of the races. Scientists measured the skulls of the living and the dead by the thousands, then manipulated their results to keep the races in place. Among Indians, Burton notes, "the transverse diameter of the rounded skull between the parietal bones, where Destructiveness and Secretiveness are placed, is enormous, sometimes exceeding the longitudinal line from sinciput to occiput, the direct opposite of the African Negro's organization." The "projecting lower brow," similarly, comes from heightened perceptions after years of "minute observation of a limited number of objects"—the quality, he notes, that makes Indians good trackers.

Such attitudes were common; they were behind the Supreme Court's decision in the Dred Scott case just three years before that "the Negro might justly and lawfully be reduced to slavery for his benefit." Indians and blacks were each, Burton writes, a species, subspecies, or variety—the reader is invited to choose—but in any case different enough from whites to be morally and physically inferior. Then he goes even further. When the "species"—the races—mix, sterile offspring often result, he claims with a straight face. "These halfbreeds are, therefore, like the mulatto, quasi-mules." He's right that the English word for mixed-race comes from the Spanish word for mule. But that the derivation should so affect his ability to see his surroundings is remarkable. He had spent decades among races mixing in India, Africa, and the Middle East; had mastered dozens of languages and donned dozens of disguises to observe them closely. If that wasn't enough, at stop after stagecoach stop he'd been surprised to find so many mixed-blood children—"a multitude of whitey-reds," he called them. That he could convince himself they would grow up sterile, and that none of the children had mixed-blood parents themselves, testifies volumes to Burton's ability to see, after all, only what he wanted to see. It's no wonder the Richards, Guinards, and Lajeunesses of the trail are so often unnamed and invisible in white accounts. It wasn't just the Sarah Suttons of the trail who couldn't see them. It was the Burtons as well, the literate observers, the writers who told the nation and the world what the West was like.[18]

The race wars came in earnest in the 1860s. Nearly all trade stopped, except for bridge tolls. In October 1860, Louis Guinard's half-Shoshone son, whose name appears not to have survived, was out herding his father's horses and cattle near Red Buttes when a passing war party of Hunkpapa and Sans Arc Lakotas killed the boy with arrows, and left his body mangled in the sagebrush. Ambushes and killings steadily increased. The army pulled precious troops out of the Civil War to garrison the little posts along the North Platte and Sweetwater: Deer Creek, Platte Bridge, Sweetwater Station at Independence Rock, and three more on the way up to South Pass. Troops sometimes numbered as many as two dozen at the smaller posts. The post at Guinard's bridge on the North Platte became quite large, with up to a hundred soldiers there by 1865, the bloodiest year of all in that country. That July, young Lieutenant Caspar Collins and twenty-six other soldiers were killed nearby in a fight with at least fifteen hundred Cheyenne, Lakota, and Arapaho warriors. The bridge and post near Independence Rock were burned and a telegrapher killed in January 1866, probably by a band of Cheyenne and Arapaho Indians.[19] In 1867 the army pulled all troops back from the upper North Platte and Sweetwater to the new Fort Fetterman, on high ground near the confluence of La Prele Creek and the North Platte, fifty miles east of Platte Bridge. Louis Phillip Guinard, the first Louis Guinard's nephew, would remember years later the column of smoke rising from his family's once-profitable bridge as he headed east to safety.

By then, his uncle had already been dead for two years. War left no middle ground on the North Platte and Sweetwater. Commerce between Indians and whites had become nearly impossible. The burnt bridges mark an end in the district to mixed-blood trading. The stories of victors and vanquished would remain, and stories of loss and survival on both sides. But the mixed-blood stories would retreat into places much harder to find.

In 1873, Louis Phillip Guinard, who as a young man had clerked at his uncle's store at the bridge, filed an Indian Depredation Claim for reimbursement of his uncle's losses. He swore that his uncle had died June 6, 1865, but not before leaving to his nephew both bridges and all their related outbuildings, to a total value of around $75,000. Louis Guinard died when he fell off his bridge into the Platte River, Louis Phillip Guinard testified. But the nephew could not produce the will.[20]

In 1923, when white people in the West were beginning to colorize a past that often seemed too drab to them, a local newspaper editor brought out a book of local history. Alfred James Mokler liked a good story, and when he published his *History of Natrona County*, he included two stories about Guinard.

In the first, Mokler tells how an unnamed Guinard relative worked on a ranch in Bates Park, south of Casper, the town that had grown up along the river between the sites of the long-gone

Richard and Guinard bridges. This relative told Mokler that Louis Guinard had been his uncle. The relative said that his uncle and father had gone out together on the bridge for a talk one night, and the uncle fell into the river and drowned. The ranch hand's father then took over the business, married an Indian woman and had several children, including the storyteller, who was lawless and unreliable, Mokler points out.

Mokler goes on to say that most of Louis Guinard's body was never found. But a familiar high-topped boot turned up in the river, with part of the foot and leg inside. These remains were given to Louis Guinard's widow, who, Mokler writes, "hung the boot and its contents in one of the rooms of her cabin and for many months mourned over it in the regular Indian fashion."

In Mokler's second Guinard story, he tells us that John Richard's daughter, Josephine, visited Casper in 1918. She and Mokler and another history buff, James Bury, drove together to the spot where her father's bridge had crossed the river, and she showed the white men where the house, blacksmith shop, and other buildings had been located. Then Mokler asked her about a local legend, as he called it, that a French-speaking bridge owner became mentally unbalanced one year after a lucrative season of bridge tolls, filled his pockets with gold dust on a moonlit night, and walked to the center of the bridge. "You have given me all my wealth," the man cried. "I now give back to you a tithe!" So saying, he cast handful after handful of gold dust into the water. Josephine Richard Pourier was certain her hardheaded father would never have done such a thing. For Mokler, that cinched it. The payer of tithes was Guinard.[21]

A moccasin sweatshop near one end of a bridge, an apronful of nuggets spilled on the ground, a frantic man throwing gold into a river, the rescue from the same river of part of a leg still stuck in a boot: these are ambiguous stories, in-between stories, stories neither of victor nor vanquished but of people uncomfortable in either camp. Once the bridges burned, their landless owners left the country and took their stories with them. Middle ground between white and Indian would be harder and harder to find.

# CHAPTER 6

# Brigham's Curse

The clouds of war have continued to gather thicker and darker over the horizon of nations. . . . Famine has stared multitudes in the face during the past winter. . . . The present is full of calamity and evil. At this moment thousands are anxiously inquiring in their hearts, 'Is there no way of escaping from these evils?' . . . There is beyond the sea a haven of peace, and a refuge from the impending storms.
—*Editorial*, The Millennial Star, *Liverpool, April 21, 1855*

Brigham Young stood in the pulpit in the Tabernacle in Salt Lake City, and he was angry. Such public displays happened from time to time; much of his charisma came from a skill at scolding, combined with personal charm and a powerful physical presence. His portly figure was familiar to his flock; his face—broad, mobile, and clean-shaven—was well known too. This day it was red, and grew redder as he spoke.

For Young, president, prophet, seer and revelator of the Church of Jesus Christ of Latter-day Saints, governor and Indian superintendent of Utah Territory, had discovered that his solution to a difficult problem now threatened disaster. Worse, rank-and-file Mormons had lately been whispering that it was his fault, when the real fault, he knew, lay with men who had taken him too literally and allowed their zeal to trump good sense. The 1,400 Mormons coming across the plains to the Salt Lake Valley were in trouble,

Brigham Young, about 1857, a dark and disastrous time in Utah. Courtesy of Special Collections Department, Marriott Library, University of Utah.

traveling so late in the year. In fact, they were worse off than he knew. It was November 1856. The last of them had gotten only as far as Devil's Gate, and were dying daily in the snow.

It was now nine years since Young had led the first small party of Mormons to the Salt Lake Valley. Converts had been arriving every summer since, each time adding more road stories to the earlier tales of Mormon troubles and pilgrimages. Stories of the difficulties of 1856 along the North Platte and Sweetwater, however, would overtake the rest. The travelers who survived would carry the story in with them. But in their minds the story remained behind them as well, on the land where it happened. Unlike the Sarah Suttons who scattered with their stories to Oregon and California, and unlike the Guinards, Richards, and Seminoes, whose stories melted away when war burnt their bridges and businesses, the Mormons and their stories gathered into a single place—a desert they named Deseret and thought no one else wanted. In that place the faithful would continue telling the stories to each other, smoothing, streamlining, and simplifying them until much, much later they would feel compelled to return to the Sweetwater and claim the spots where they believed the stories began.

Brigham Young's problem that year was transport. Mormon missionaries had been working hard overseas. By 1856, tens of thousands more converts in Britain and Scandinavia still longed to come to the Salt Lake Valley—to gather, as the missionaries put it, to Zion. But the valley was in the midst of two years of drought, grasshopper plagues, and near famine. Contributions from the faithful to church coffers had dwindled, and Brigham and his counselors had been forced to devise a way for newcomers to travel at lower cost. A thousand or so of those 1,400 emigrants now coming across the plains were financed by the church, and traveling on the cheap. They were pulling handcarts, two-wheeled half-wagons, each equipped with a transverse bar across two shafts in the front so that a person or two could pull it, with perhaps a third pushing from behind on the hills, and two small children riding on top of the load. With the right support and supply, the carts offered a fast and inexpensive way to travel because they did away with time-consuming, slow-grazing livestock.

But though three handcart companies had come easily across the plains, the logistics of equipment and supply had faltered for the last two. Still, their leaders had persuaded their members to come ahead, late as it was. This, Brigham made clear, was not his fault. In his sermon in the Tabernacle that November Sunday, he reminded his people that they knew him well, that he was as good an organizer and manager as had ever existed on earth. "[T]herefore there is no ground or room," he scolded, "for suspecting that my mismanagement caused the present suffering on the plains."[1]

The Mormon Church is an American success, its history a long ramp up from obscurity to power, with, at present, something approaching twelve million members worldwide and new converts daily on every continent. In March 1830, six people who believed Joseph Smith gathered in a room in upstate New York and formed the new sect. They believed he had been led by Moroni, an angel, to golden plates inscribed with hieroglyphics on a hill named Cumorah in upstate New York. And they believed his translation from the plates, a book tying the Israelite tribes of Ephraim and Manasseh and Christ himself to the Americas. Lehi led his people from Jerusalem to the New World, where they split into the virtuous, fair-skinned Nephites, and the dark-skinned Lamanites. Centuries of war followed, interrupted by a visit from Christ after the Resurrection. The Lamanites were finally victorious, however; 230,000 Nephites were slain near the hill Cumorah, and the Nephites as a people destroyed. But now, before Christ's re-arrival and the final end of the world, new saints would be called to play out the rest of the drama in these latter days.

What came to be called the Church of Jesus Christ of Latter-day Saints grew quickly. The Mormons were tight-knit, socialist in their division of labor and distribution of goods, paternalistic and hierarchical in their power structure—not just members of the same denomination in their own minds but a people chosen of God. Their cohesion brought quick prosperity, which brought envy and resentment among their neighbors, which the Mormons met with stubborn belligerence and inflammatory rhetoric. Tar and feathering was followed by raids—mobbings, the Mormons called them—and counterraids, murders and countermurders. The violence persisted as the church moved from New York, to Ohio, to western Missouri, then back to the east shore of the Mississippi. There the people built Nauvoo, a city of twelve thousand in its prime and the largest in Illinois. In 1844, a Mormon apostate started the *Nauvoo Expositor*, and got out one edition aimed calmly at exposing the prophet as polygamist and fraud. Joseph Smith's Nauvoo Legion wrecked the print shop, smashed the press, and pied the type. Fearing the worst, Joseph and his brother Hyrum reluctantly abandoned an attempt to flee and surrendered themselves in nearby Carthage, Illinois, to charges already outstanding. Joseph, Hyrum, and two other supporters were attacked in the upstairs chamber of the Carthage jail by militiamen in warpaint. Hyrum was killed in the first exchange of shots. Joseph fell or leapt, wounded, from the window. The mob propped him up against a well curb, and finished him with a volley. The faith had its martyr.

From early on, however, the faith also had its church historian, for tales of persecution and martyrdom must be carefully told if good is to be kept separate from bad, right from wrong, faith from apostasy. Even before the Mormons left Illinois for their Canaan in the mountains, the church historian carefully collected documents and accounts with an eye toward the future. This instinct for narrative control—spin control, a later century would call it—was bound up with the forces that made the Mormons unlike any other people in the West. Long afterwards, the need to control the story would continue to parallel the growth of Mormon power. It would play out in a need to control a few pieces of land that history had sanctified.

Despite growing attacks from the mobbers, the Mormons stayed in Nauvoo long enough to finish the temple, consecrate it, and quickly unjam a long backlog of postponed washings, anointings, baptisms and marriages—sealings, they were called—of the living faithful and their dead ancestors. Brigham Young emerged as leader, every bit as charismatic as Joseph Smith but opposite in everything else. Where Joseph was handsome, Brigham was plain. Where Joseph had visions, Brigham fixed problems; he was the financier, logistician, trek leader, kingdom founder. And always, he was a firebrand preacher who never flinched from affixing blame. Where apostates had called Joseph quack and charlatan, they would call Brigham accessory to murder.

The Saints began to leave Nauvoo in February 1846, crossing an icy Mississippi to the Iowa side and continuing west with only a vague destination. Mud and poverty slowed them; it took a year to get across Iowa to the Missouri, where they wintered at Winter Quarters, near present Omaha. In 1847 Brigham led an advance party of 147 pioneers toward the mountains. Following Frémont's maps and reports, they took the well-known wagon route as far as Fort Bridger, then continued west over a rocky and difficult trail followed by wagons only once before. When at last they came in sight of the Salt Lake Valley, Brigham rose from a sickbed in Wilford Woodruff's wagon and said, "This is the place." Or, more accurately, he said, "It is enough. This is the right place. Drive on." Or, more accurately still, he may not have said it at all, as any record of his having done so did not appear until thirty-three years later, on the fiftieth anniversary of the church.[2] The church and the state of Utah have commemorated the spot with a massive monument at This Is the Place Heritage Park. The Mormon hierarchy, all along, has continued to care for its stories.

The saints began irrigating, plowing, and planting the day they arrived. Thousands more arrived before winter, and thousands more each year. By the early 1850s, nearly all the Mormons from the old frontiers had come to the valley. After 1852, the attention shifted overseas. Mormon missionaries chartered entire ships and accompanied the converts to Zion; travelers were in the hands of experts all the way. The standard route was by steamer from Liverpool to New Orleans, by riverboat to St. Louis, then up the Missouri to Florence, the former Winter Quarters, and by ox train to the inland empire. But these emigrants brought cholera and malaria with them out of the river valleys, and before long, expanding railroads allowed a more direct route. Beginning in 1854, the converts disembarked at Boston, New York, or Philadelphia and took the cars to the end of the line at Iowa City, where Mormon agents helped them outfit and sorted them into wagon companies. The trail hardened and unified the families of artisans, farm laborers, and factory hands into a single people. They organized for travel into groups of ten, the tens into hundreds, the hundreds into companies of three to six hundred. Authority was obeyed and progress was smooth.

Given such a well-oiled transport machine, it's hard to understand how the missionary leaders, in 1856, could have made such drastic mistakes. But Young and his counselors had taken personally the recent troubles in the Promised Land. Despite their sufferings, the Mormons had never been averse to material prosperity; in fact it was envy of the fast-growing wealth produced by their cooperation and efficiency that provoked persecutions in the first place. In the Salt Lake Valley, land no other white people wanted, they had expected to prosper without interference, and for seven years they did.[3] Then, unexpectedly, came a dry year. The withering crops were attacked by grasshoppers. In the fall of 1855, Mormon fields yielded only a third to two-thirds of the harvest of previous years. Next came the worst winter since the Saints had come to Utah. Early in 1856, Young began scolding the people for falling away from God. Certain he knew the cause of the trouble, he let them know their individual sins would come to his attention. He directed members of the church hierarchy to pry into everyone's life, and he threatened backsliders with excommunication, or worse. In the summer the grasshoppers returned, and by fall it was clear the harvest would be even more scant. Only a reformation could save the people, Brigham and his preachers thundered. Congregations submitted to mass re-baptisms. The bishops lashed their people with words and the people, feeling their sins, groaned wholeheartedly back.[4]

When other matters, involving logistics and transport, also went wrong in 1856, it was natural enough the leaders would want to show Brigham and the Lord that they could fix them by doing right. And doing right meant sacrifice.

The handcarters were constantly on his mind now, Brigham Young declared in the Tabernacle on Sunday, the second of November. He reminded the people of their present comfort, in contrast to the difficulties of their own transcontinental passage—rivers to cross, cholera, loved ones buried on the trail. And why had they suffered these trials? To get to Zion. And why were more people coming now, with handcarts, late and wading mountain snow that might be knee-deep, waist-deep, neck-deep? Also to get to Zion. But now it was a Zion devalued by the sins and backbiting of its people, a Zion needing reformation. Implying there might be some redemption in it, he added that any who still wanted to join the rescue effort begun weeks ago were welcome to do so. They would need wagons and teams, and would do well to bring along extra feed for the animals, as forage in the snows would be scarce.[5]

The winter before, Brigham and his closest counselors had decided that the church's Perpetual Emigration Fund would finance the poorest emigrants. The fund, raised from contributions at the Utah end, would advance the travel costs to the poor, who could then work off the debt once they got to the valley. The continuing influx would mean more food and shelter to find for people arriving late in the year. But to slow or stop the in-migration would be to admit doubt in the future of the faith, and that could not be permitted.

Better-off converts continued to emigrate, too; these generally paid their own way in advance and traveled in wagon companies. The people in the valley were encouraged to continue tithing and, beyond that, "consecrating" their property—turning it over free and clear—to the church. But all resources were strapped. Travel costs had to be cut to the bone.

One handcart could be counted on to carry the belongings and most of the food of a family of five, figuring just seventeen pounds of luggage per person and a pound of flour per person per day. Up to five regular wagons would travel with every hundred or so handcarts to carry extra flour and the twenty-person tents. But even that would not provide enough food for the journey, and so the system depended as well on resupply—wagons sent out from the valley to meet the newcomers at Deer Creek and South Pass with supplies for the rest of the journey. As with any relay, timing was crucial.

Three handcart companies of Europeans made it to the valley that summer with relatively little trouble. They ranged in size from 221 to 320 people; two of the companies arrived at Salt Lake City on September 26 and the third on October 2. All three traveled on short rations but still were successfully resupplied, and made it in with fewer than five percent of their members dying along the way, a respectable record. The troubles of the fourth and fifth companies, however, began in England before they even embarked.

In Liverpool, Apostle Franklin D. Richards was in charge of all overseas missions—he was the highest ranking Mormon in Europe. All through January and February, he had urged an early start, but circumstances worked against him. Wind, weather, and cargo availability delayed sailing dates. High prices and hard times led many converts, recklessly, to quit their jobs before arranging transport with church agents. The agents were then forced to choose whether to allow these people to make a late start for Utah, or stay in England and face starvation or the poorhouse. The agents acquiesced. The *Thornton*, with 764 passengers, two-thirds of them supported by the Perpetual Emigration Fund, sailed on May 4. The *Horizon*, with 856 passengers, three-fourths fund-supported, sailed May 25. Life on ship was clean, orderly, and pious, but matters in Iowa City, at the end of the rail line, proved disorderly and confused. The handcarts were not ready. The emigrants, when they arrived, were drafted to build them, saving money but spending precious time. The lumber, moreover, was green, and to economize further there was little iron for axles or tires. The wheel rims were wrapped with rawhide, or left bare. Days of delay turned into weeks while the carts were built. The fund-supported *Thornton* passengers, organized into a 500-person handcart company under James G. Willie, did not roll out from Iowa City until July 15. The fund-supported *Horizon* passengers, 576 of them under Edward Martin, did not leave there until July 28.[6] Two ox trains, each with about 200 of the better-off emigrants, left last, following close behind the Martin Company.

At Florence, on the Missouri, each company halted for another week, to ferry the river and refit. It was already August. The Willie Company met to decide whether to go all the way, or to find a spot to winter now. Out of the 500 in the company, only four had ever been to the Salt Lake Valley before: these were the ones who must have been full of the new reformation fervor, and spread it now among the incoming poor. All four spoke at the meeting, as did at least two of the most prominent missionaries returning from Britain—George

Morman missionaries in Liverpool, 1855. Franklin Richards, in charge of all LDS overseas missions at the time, is third from left in the second row. Edward Martin, captain of the last handcart company to travel to Utah in 1856, is on the extreme right of the middle row. In the back row, Joseph A. Young, second from left, was a son of Brigham Young and one of three scouts who first met the Martin Company near Red Buttes. To his immediate left are William H. Kimball and George D. Grant, who, at Florence on the Missouri in August 1856 urged the handcart emigrants to continue on despite the lateness of the year. Grant later led the rescue effort from Salt Lake. Courtesy of LDS Church archives.

D. Grant and William H. Kimball, stopping in Florence to help organize the entire effort on their way home.

Only one speaker called for caution. Disaster was certain, Levi Savage warned, if the company, with so many children, women, and old people started so late. Better to winter somewhere safe. But the other speakers scolded and ridiculed him, one even promising to eat all the snow that should fall on the party along the way, so certain was he that God would protect them. The people were persuaded, and the majority voted to go. Savage stuck by his warning, while submitting wholeheartedly to the majority. "I will go with you, . . . and, if necessary, I will die with you."[7] Plenty of others would die, though Savage did not. And not one of the deaths was necessary.

The Willie Company left Florence for Salt Lake City on August 17, the Martin Company August 27, and the two ox trains on September 2. They had a thousand miles to go.

The journeys of the Willie and Martin companies have been carefully traced elsewhere, and need not be tracked here in detail.[8] Their green-wood, iron-free handcarts had been giving trouble even in Iowa, but as the trail west grew sandier, rockier, and drier, the carts began to need nightly repair. Soon the people had to go on short rations, which further weakened everyone, slowed the pace, and meant that the flour had to stretch even further.

Last to leave Florence were Franklin Richards and a dozen other missionaries returning to the valley after two years or more overseas. They were well provisioned, traveling fast in light carriages drawn by horses and mules. Three days out they passed the last of the ox trains, the Martin Company a day later, the other ox train a day after that, and caught up with the Willie Company on September 12. They were in time to watch Willie's handcarters fording the Platte from the north to the south side. "Never was there a more soul-stirring sight than the happy passage of this company over that river," Richards reported later to Brigham Young. "Several of the carts were drawn entirely by women"—a sight that made Mormons

proud, but that other Americans found distastefully desperate—
"and every heart was glad and full of hope."

At Fort Laramie, Richards bought buffalo robes for the latecomers to pick up on their way through. In late September, west of
Willow Springs and a few days later west of South Pass, Richards and
the missionaries encountered three different parties of eastbound
Mormon supply wagons, laden with flour. The first of them—it's
not clear why—turned around with the missionaries and headed
back toward Salt Lake City; Richards directed the second two to
cache their flour and keep heading east, apparently to meet up
with the latecomers sooner than they would have otherwise.[9] These
meetings never occurred. The Willie Company and perhaps the
Martin Company, too, had been expecting resupply at Fort Laramie—perhaps from these same groups.[10] But the connection was
never made.

Richards and the other missionaries reached Salt Lake City on
October 4, having traveled the thousand miles from the Missouri
in just thirty days. He reported that the companies he had passed
three and four weeks before were in good spirits, and in a speech
the next day at the opening of the church's annual fall conference
expressed his confidence that God would "overrule the storms" and
protect the pilgrims "from suffering more than they can bear."[11]

Brigham Young, to his credit, grasped the danger immediately, and called for volunteer rescuers. Right from the start, he
threw all the power of his charisma and prestige into the request,
and the Saints were quick to respond. On October 7, twenty-seven
young men headed east, driving sixteen wagons packed with food
and warm clothes. East of Fort Bridger, they met "some teams that
had been back on the road and got tired of waiting," the rescue
leader wrote in his journal. These would have been the resupply
parties Richards had encountered in late September, who apparently decided the newcomers weren't coming this year—a reason-
able decision, but wrong.[12]

Just east of South Pass on October 20, the rescuers met Captain Willie and another man riding out of a snowstorm. Willie's

company, the men reported, was a day farther east, out of food and freezing. About half the wagons stayed to help them, while the rest pressed on to look for the Martin Company and the ox trains.

Meanwhile, at the trading post at Deer Creek, finding still no hint of any resupply, Captain Martin had ordered everyone to reduce baggage further—from seventeen to ten pounds per person, and restricted each to four ounces per day of flour—enough for two or three biscuits.[13] As the weather was still fine, most people chose to leave bedding and extra clothes behind.

On October 19 they forded the North Platte—normally a safe choice any time after mid-July—at the spot where Guinard later built his bridge. But that day the weather changed; the people hauled their carts and families through sleet and thickly falling snow. Some hitched horseback rides with the wagon companies, crossing at the same time; some waded up to their knees or thighs; many lost their footing and found themselves up to their armpits, or immersed. All were weak from their factory lives, and weaker still from twelve weeks of dwindling rations on the road. When they emerged on the far side, soaked, they walked a few miles more before camping—most with no dry clothes and no bedding. And the snow kept falling. Many froze to death that night. The next day Martin managed to get everyone moving again, ten more miles to a spot near Red Buttes. But the snow kept falling, people kept dying, and the rest, completely exhausted by now, were unable to move at all.

A full nine days later, on October 28, three scouts from the rescue party found the Martin Company still at Red Buttes. The scouts continued east to the river crossing where the ox trains had stalled, got them moving again and returned back west, to catch up for a second time with the Martin Company, toiling now up Prospect Hill. Fifty-six people had died, one of the scouts reported, just between the river crossing and Red Buttes.[14] The dying would continue, but this appears to have been where the deaths came thickest and fastest. The pilgrims made a pitiful scene walking up the hill—mud, weakness, staggering emigrants, falling snow and more mud; mud freezing in big gobs to the people's clothes and shoes. The three rescuers helped as best they could, tying their lariats to a few of the handcarts to help pull, but more important was to get news back to the main rescue party, camped now at Devil's Gate. This they did; the main party of rescuers set out and finally, on October 31, they met with the Martin handcarters at Horse Creek, halfway between Willow Springs and Independence Rock. It began snowing about noon on Saturday, November 1, and snowed far into the night. By Sunday evening, the handcarters were staggering in to camp at Devil's Gate. The rescuers had taken over the log houses abandoned a month earlier by the Archambaults, and had big fires going. People gathered around them, cheered by the warmth, and sang. "Snow deep," rescuer Robert T. Burton recorded in his journal. "Very cold."[15]

It got colder. The next morning, two riders were dispatched to the Salt Lake Valley to report and get more help. They carried a letter from George D. Grant, leader of the rescuers, detailing the suffering: snow- and mud-burdened pilgrims fainting and falling from exhaustion, children crying, many with bare and bleeding feet. "The sight is almost too much for the stoutest of us; but we go on doing all we can, not doubting nor despairing," Grant wrote.[16]

The ten wagonloads of rescue supplies at Devil's Gate were not nearly enough. In the next few days the emigrant wagon companies, too, rolled in, swelling the number of living, hungry mouths at Devil's Gate to nearly a thousand. At first no one knew quite what to do next, but then, looking at the exhausted foot travelers and the growing numbers of wagons, a logical choice revealed itself. The wagons of the Hunt and Hodgett ox trains were unloaded and the goods—nonperishable belongings of the travelers, as well as some freight under contract for customers in Salt Lake City—were stored in the log houses. Burton reports no more snow as the week crawled by, but each day colder than the one before it. We can imagine the black meanders of the Sweetwater beginning to ice along their edges, wind blowing through the pillars of the gate and roiling the leafless willows, bony stock mooing and milling, people low on food and napping much of the time in their tents. Perhaps to get out of the way as much as out of the weather, the Martin company on

Tuesday moved to a new camp. Burton noted it was three miles away, but did not locate it more specifically.

On Wednesday evening the second and last wagon train arrived; on Thursday the people began stowing its goods. The mercury dropped to 11 degrees below zero. "Remained very cold," Burton reported on Friday. "Could not travel. Stowing away goods, trying to save the people, stock, etc."—and in that brief phrase lies the only contemporary reminder that the people were continuing to die. By now, no one was bothering to count bodies.

On Saturday, the wind relented and the weather warmed. The men began hunting up scattered cattle and mules to prepare for the trail again. On Sunday, a week after the Martin Company's arrival, company members who could began walking. The rest rode in the now empty wagons of the Hodgett train, while the work caching the Hunt train's goods continued. The great majority of the handcarts were abandoned. The Hunt train rolled out about 2 p.m. on Monday, with four of the most senior men—Grant, Burton, Cyrus Wheelock, and Stephen Taylor—leaving last, an hour later. On the following Wednesday, the pilgrims met more relief wagons from the west, loaded with food and clothing. As more and more relief wagons arrived, there was room for more and more of the stricken to ride. The Martin Company reached Salt Lake about noon, November 30. The families with the ox trains kept arriving for another week or more.

Meanwhile, twenty men, including three veterans from the valley and seventeen newcomers, were left behind with twenty days' rations to guard the goods at Devil's Gate for a five-month-long winter. They were allowed some skin-and-bones cattle and a few sacks of flour. Only the good sense, good cheer and boiled-rawhide recipes of their leader, a cook and Indian trader named Daniel Webster Jones, kept them alive until spring. That, and the kindness of some passing Shoshones, whom Jones knew how to befriend.[17]

"[M]y mind is yonder in the snow, where those immigrating Saints are," Brigham Young told the people that November Sunday in the

Tabernacle, still eleven days before any update on their condition arrived. "I cannot go out or come in, but what in every minute or two minutes my mind reverts to them." Surely that was true. But when, three days earlier, he had written Orson Pratt in England that "[w]e had no idea there were any more companies upon the Plains" he was veering away toward falsehood. He had been "presuming," Brigham wrote to Pratt, that the last companies would not risk so late a start.[18] Young would have been more honest if he had said he was hoping, not presuming, the emigrants would not risk it. More honest still would have been to admit he was aware of the risk—that he was gambling they would not come so late.

For the religious wildfire he and his counselors had started now burned beyond their control. The converts felt their hearts burning powerfully enough, they thought, to melt the Rocky Mountain snows. If in fact he had "presumed" that 1,400 more hungry emigrants would not arrive in the valley that fall, Brigham's common sense had deserted him. Or perhaps it had not; perhaps he had only overridden it, and the fire of his anger was lighted by the friction of the override.

"If any man, or woman, complains of me or of my Counselors, in regard to the lateness of some of this season's immigration," he thundered that Sunday in the Tabernacle, "let the curse of God be on them and blast their substance with mildew and destruction, until their names are forgotten from the earth." The real fault, he said, lay with Franklin Richards and the others who had persuaded the people to come on through. "[T]he very spirit some have in them of pride, arrogance and self esteem, has led men and women to die on the plains by scores, at least their folly has. And if they had not have had any such spirit about them, God would have whispered to them to have held a council, and would have stopped them from rushing their brethren and sisters into such suffering."[19]

A modern historian has counted 67 deaths in the Willie Company—between thirteen and fourteen percent—and 135 to 150 in the Martin Company—a death rate of around twenty-five percent.

More members of both companies died within a short time of their arrival in the valley, and many more were maimed for life by the loss of frozen fingers, toes, and feet.[20]

If the religious reformation, his fears for the handcarters' safety, and his own reputation were the main things on Brigham's mind in the fall of 1856, the following year brought far worse trouble, a dark and bloody time in Mormon history. Brigham Young maintained order through a church-based hierarchy to which all who stayed in the valley submitted. But he also had men like Porter Rockwell and Bill Hickman, whom he could order out on rougher jobs when necessary. (Hickman later claimed to have committed a number of murders on Young's orders, and Rockwell was in jail on murder charges at the time of his death.)[21] And then there was polygamy, toward which outsiders felt a mix of shock and lurid curiosity, and which Mormons felt was a private matter on which they refused to be judged. Mormons and non-Mormons thought the worst of each other. Even though they now lived thousands of miles apart, this mattered.

Young's power and autonomy had grown steadily under the sympathetic ignorance of U.S. presidents Millard Fillmore and Franklin Pierce—to the point where federal officials were openly defied in Utah, and some fled. In 1857, the new president, James Buchanan, appointed a new slate of territorial officers, removing Young both from the governorship and the Indian superintendency. Hearing that federal troops were marching west to enforce the appointments, the Mormons mobilized the Nauvoo Legion.

As Colonel Albert Sidney Johnston and his 2,500 U.S. troops approached in the summer and fall, the militia fled ahead of the oncoming army, burning grass, stage stations, wagon trains, and Fort Bridger to slow the advance of the troops. Finally, a hundred miles short of Salt Lake City, the army went into winter quarters near Fort Bridger. Passions had cooled by spring and a compromise was arranged, but not before the Mormons briefly abandoned Salt Lake City. Finally, Buchanan offered a blanket pardon if the Saints would agree to submit to federal authority and accept the new governor, which they did, and soon returned to their capital. The army bivouacked forty miles away, improved relations with the Mormons by buying a lot of supplies at high prices, and eventually marched back to Fort Leavenworth.

The bloodiest event of 1857 in Utah wasn't part of the so-called Mormon War at all, though it happened largely as a result of a fear of outsiders that had spread throughout the territory in that panicky year. In September, at Mountain Meadows in what is now southwestern Utah, far in the opposite direction from the federal army's advance, sixty Nauvoo Legion militiamen in warpaint and a few Paiute allies laid siege to a richly equipped wagon train of 140 emigrants from Arkansas. The militiamen tricked the emigrants into a parley with a flag of truce, and then murdered everyone over seven years old.[22]

So perhaps it is not surprising that the plight of the handcarters was for a time forgotten by the Mormon culture. Traveling by wagon train was never easy, as we have seen; average death rates on the roads to Oregon, California, and Utah were perhaps as high as ten percent during the cholera years of the late forties and early fifties.[23] Everyone had a hard time getting to the valley, and once they got there, there was a lot of work to do. Group suffering and group effort were at the core of Mormon culture. It's not surprising, therefore, that handcarters would postpone recording what had happened.[24]

Aside from one remark that fifty-six members of the Martin Company died in the ten miles between fording the Platte and their discovery at Red Buttes, none of the diaries, letters, and reports written at the time bothers to note how many other people died, or where. Only after the turn of the twentieth century did the folk tradition arise that most of the dying was done at the place that came to be called Martin's Cove, two or three miles upstream and on the other side of the Sweetwater from the trading post at Devil's Gate. Here the sagebrush prairie laps up into a steep wall of granite rocks. How many people died there is still unclear, but matters because it still drives the Mormon desire to own the place.

One of the first comprehensive attempts at the handcart story came in 1873, in a skeptical history of the Mormons by longtime

Salt Lake City journalist T. B. H. Stenhouse. Stenhouse admires the efforts of the rescuers but calls the delays at the start of the trip "fatal and foolish." His book, *The Rocky Mountain Saints: A Full and Complete History of the Mormons, from the First Vision of Joseph Smith to the Last Courtship of Brigham Young*, includes an account of the trials of the Martin Company and the two ox trains by a man Stenhouse declines to name, who traveled with one of the trains. This "gentleman" notes that "great numbers" of people died at and just after the Platte crossing, that fifteen oxen died while the last companies were pulling up Prospect Hill, and that "several more people died and were buried at Devil's Gate." After that, he continues, "the track of the emigrants was marked by graves."[25]

Stenhouse attributes the delays at the start of the handcart journeys to church politics and greed. It was routine, he implies, for the Mormon agents in Liverpool to take kickbacks of half a guinea per passenger from the steamship bookers, and for agents in New York to take similar kickbacks from the railroads. Partly because of competition among Mormon agents for the graft, but also because of generic pride, arrogance, and rivalry, a lot of organizing wasn't done in the spring of 1856. Apostle John Taylor was in charge of Mormon logistics in New York; Richards was in charge in Liverpool. Taylor was nominally Richards's superior but Stenhouse implies that Richards, head of all European missions, publications, and transport, held a position of more glamor and prestige. So the two communicated badly and many details went unattended. Meanwhile, Taylor got back to Salt Lake City before Richards did, and had time to influence Brigham Young before Richards's return. When Richards arrived, Young "attacked him in the Tabernacle, held him up to ridicule and contempt, and cursed him in the name of Israel's God," Stenhouse notes. Richards maintained his position but lost his influence. And Brigham Young, decades later, suppressed a true story about the entire matter, Stenhouse says, that was due to run in the *Utah Magazine*.[26]

In 1878 and 1879, Martin Company survivor John Jaques told his story in letters to the *Salt Lake Herald*. Jaques mentions no deaths after the Platte crossing, nor anywhere else; his stories seem more didactic than historic. Wading the icy Sweetwater on the move to the new camp, one man lost his "fortitude and manhood" and burst into tears. His wife, "the stouter heart of the two," took charge and pulled the handcart across. The man's bare shins were wounded by ice chunks in the river, wounds which never healed until he arrived in Salt Lake City, and "the dark scars of which he bears to this day."[27] A day or two later, according to Jaques, Captain Martin and three other men left the cove to walk back to Devil's Gate, but lost their way in a sudden snowstorm. They gathered twigs and lighted many matches, trying unsuccessfully to start a fire. Finally, they tore off pieces of their body linen—the garments devout Mormons wear next to their skin and regard as holy—and were able to get a fire going. (Burton's journal mentions an iron cold but no fresh snow after the Martin Company's arrival at Devil's Gate.) Jaques refers to the new camp as "Martin's Ravine"—probably the first published reference to what has since become known as Martin's Cove.

In 1890, Daniel W. Jones, leader of the contingent that stayed at Devil's Gate to guard the wagon goods, published his life story as *Forty Years among the Indians.* Jones was one of the three scouts who first contacted the Martin Company and the two ox trains. He spent one night with the Martin Company after he'd gotten them moving again toward Devil's Gate and reported, "Several died that night." Once the emigrants arrived at the gate, he said, "many were dying daily from exposure and want of food. . . . The hand-cart company was moved over to a cove in the mountains for shelter and fuel; a distance of two miles from the fort." Jones traveled with the emigrants two more days after they left the gate, during which time he reported "much suffering, deaths recurring often."[28]

It seems likely the Martin Company emigrants continued to die all the way from the crossing of the Platte to South Pass and beyond. That even a majority of them died at the cove seems not to have been the case.

Harvey Cluff accompanied the rescuers at least in part because he had a financial interest in some cattle coming across the plains with the ox trains. At the cove one night, a fierce wind "levelled every tent to the ground," Cluff wrote in 1908. Marvelously, Cluff goes on, no one was badly hurt—and in fact he says nothing about human deaths at the cove or at Devil's Gate. He does, however, go out of his way to note that "cattle died daily," and "[t]he situation was, indeed, verry criticle. . . . No power could save the people from death but that of God." God, Cluff believed—and also Brigham Young: "The only glimmer of hope . . . was the utmost confidence in President Brigham Young's inspiration that he would keep the companies coming out to meet us."[29]

As more survivors' tales were recorded, many of the most poignant were located at the cove. Twenty-nine-year-old Patience Loader camped there in the snow with her mother, three sisters, and little brother, their father having died east of Fort Laramie. One morning the family was boiling a bone for breakfast when some of the young male rescuers invited "the girls," as Patience called herself and her sisters, to come sing at their campfire, where they had cut logs all around for seats. This the girls were happy to do, and sang for two or three hours. But the men had no food to spare, and when the girls returned, hungry, to their own tent, their mother confessed she had eaten the small bits of meat off the bone without them. The girls, Patience Loader Rosza Archer wrote in her old age, were happy to forgive her, and slept comfortably and warm despite the cold. In another story Patience tells, the mother dances in the snow to cheer up the girls, slipping and falling on purpose to bring on their laughter in that desperate time.[30]

The memoir contains not a word about the number of corpses at the cove, or burials; not a fragment that the future might call a fact in order to settle a question of which place, long later, had the more meaning based on which saw more suffering at the time. Only stories survived. Censuses of the dead were never taken.

# CHAPTER 7

# War

Nothing but a war of extermination will ever rid the country of their depradations, they pay no regard to treaties, and as their disease is severe, the remedy should be in proportion.
　　　　—*Private Hervey Johnson, Eleventh Ohio Cavalry, 1865*

Private Hervey Johnson of the Eleventh Ohio Cavalry came to the West an innocent, and learned along the North Platte and Sweetwater to hate and fear his enemies. Yet, finally, when it was time to go back to Ohio, he was willing to tolerate them, or at least allow them space on his mental map—an allowance that cost him little. His enemies, by contrast, remained in the West, and had to give up a great deal to do so. They surrendered an entire economy, the mobility that went with it, and land, land, land. The exchange was the result of a war, of course; one side won and the other lost, and so the exchange was uneven. But to a large degree, and often out of the invaders' view, Pvt. Johnson's foes kept dignity and wit—what might be called a way of life. They took their stories with them to the reservation, and left the plains behind them empty for the whites to concoct new ones.

The whites, as they arrived, told mostly victory stories. Or if their stories involved defeat—the story of the young Lieutenant Caspar Collins at Guinard's bridge, for example, or the story of Custer on the Little Bighorn eleven years later—the common versions mixed in valor with the killing as the stories were told and retold. Hervey Johnson's stories, however, remained in a trunk of family letters, unknown to the world until they were published in the 1970s. They show a war with unclear lines between victory and defeat, and unclear distinctions among friend, foe, and neutral.

The Platte was as dry as the road beside it when the Ohio soldiers reached Fort Kearny early in the fall of 1863. Three hundred miles upstream at Fort Laramie, a few puddles and trickles were left in the North Platte, and fishing was easy. Pvt. Johnson and his messmates used their cavalry sabers to spear fresh sturgeon, two feet long, out of the pools, and for the first time in weeks, his dysentery subsided and he felt something like an appetite.[1] His next post, six months later, was at Deer Creek, where he got to know the Bissonettes and learned enough Lakota words to say to the women, "marry me, I'll marry you; kiss me," he told his mother and sisters in a letter home.[2] Then he was stationed, briefly, at Guinard's, now called Platte Bridge, and finally, late in 1864, was moved out to the little post at the bridge on the Sweetwater.

The post lay exposed to wind and sun on a low bluff above the river, where the road dipped down to cross the bridge. The post had been expanded from Guinard's establishment but was still small, holding perhaps twenty troops and a telegraph operator, a little corral and a small parade ground within its half-stockade. On two of its four corners, sentinel boxes the size of telephone booths stuck up into the mountain air. A mile to the west, the big rock was clearly visible, and Devil's Gate five miles beyond. To the east, the Sweetwater wound off toward the North Platte. South, across the river, granite outcrops tumbled above each other to a height of twelve hundred feet above the river. Here and there, the plains nudged up into little canyons among the rocks. Cedars and pitch pines grew thickly in the canyons, and sparsely out on the noses of rock between the little drainages. To the north of the post, a low rise hid a shallow playa lake just beyond it. In spring this lake was large, and attracted water birds—terns, mallards, grebes, coots. By summer it often dried up, leaving a white layer of alkaline dust that was pure sodium bicarbonate—travelers called it saleratus and used it for baking powder. In winter after it snowed, the world was white in all directions. But even snow was welcome, because when the snow came, the wind died down and stopped.

Hervey Johnson liked it. Johnson was a Quaker farmer from Leesburgh, in southern Ohio, eldest of six siblings, with a brother and four sisters; his father had died when he was seventeen. He enlisted in 1863 at age twenty-four when it appeared the Civil War draft would soon catch up with him. This ensured he would serve among neighbors and friends in a regiment raised and commanded by a local man, Colonel William Collins, a lawyer and prominent citizen of nearby Hillsboro. Johnson also knew he would serve in the West, where Collins's unit had already put in more than a year—a far safer place than the killing fields of Virginia and Tennessee.

During his three years on the North Platte and Sweetwater, Johnson wrote a hundred letters home to his family on the farm. They are long on detail and short on sentiment; not only did he have a sharp eye and ear, he was wry and self-deprecating. He missed being home for the molasses-making, he wrote his sister Sybil, "but I don't think it would come very natural to me, it seems to me like it wouldent be home—that my natural place is out in the mountain wilds I have grown accustomed to this life."[3]

When Johnson and his comrades first arrived on the Sweetwater in November 1864, they found that the soldiers they were relieving had neglected to get in a winter's fuel supply. Just getting an extra wood-hauling wagon out to the post proved nearly impossible. Two soldiers, boys his sisters knew from home, started on the fifty-five-mile journey from Platte Bridge Station with a regulation six-mule army wagon. Two of the mules disappeared the first night—strayed or stolen, Johnson doesn't say—the wagon stuck in the snow, there was no wood for a fire, and so the boys came in the rest of the way with four of the mules but left the wagon. It was valuable, loaded as it was with arms and provisions for the post on the Sweetwater and three more from there to South Pass. When five men went after the wagon the next day, cold drove three of them back. The last two got near one of the missing mules but found armed Indians after it, and as the soldiers themselves were unarmed they thought better of a fight, and left. Johnson told his sisters that more men would be sent after the wagon the next day, hoping to find it unburnt and unlooted. Meanwhile, he added, "we have been burning the buildings for several days for fire wood, and if we don't get the wagon soon we must suffer."[4]

Supply was a constant problem. As 1864 turned into 1865, the soldiers were headed into the bloodiest year yet on the northern plains. But their minds, most of the time, were on the miles between them and the garrison at Platte Bridge Station, where their food and mail came from, and where the army had expanded Guinard's storehouses and corrals into a larger post. If all went well, it was a two-day journey, with a night in the open at Willow Springs. Wagons got stuck in wind-packed snowbanks, and it could take two or three days to dig them out. When it warmed, teamsters would strike out off the muddy road into the sagebrush, and get stuck as badly or worse in alkali bogs. Or the cold would come back, and cold itself could make an iron wall against travel. From time to time, men froze toes, ears, or fingers; if his mules or horses were stolen, a man could easily freeze to death.

Stories the men heard of Indian attacks always dripped with extra gore; still, the danger was real. But where corpses at Spotsylvania, Virginia, in 1864 were piled three and four deep in trenches after the battle,[5] men died singly on the North Platte and Sweetwater, or in twos. Most of their travel—to unstick a supply wagon, chase lost mules, or repair a telegraph line—was still, at this time, done in twos, threes, and fours. They were routinely vulnerable to ambush. It was a guerilla war, and so it was a war of nerves.

The larger war, in its way, had touched off this smaller one by igniting an already volatile state of affairs. During the 1850s, personal travel along the Platte-Sweetwater route gradually gave way to commercial travel as emigration dwindled and the freight business boomed. The first regular mail service between Independence, Missouri, and Salt Lake City began moving monthly in 1850. The mail was moving weekly by 1858, daily by 1859, and with it began systematic stagecoach service for passengers. Stations were needed for a change of horses every ten or twelve miles; stations offering meals were more rare.[6] In the spring of 1860 the Pony Express was established, and before it went bankrupt in the fall of 1861 with the completion of the transcontinental telegraph line, its riders electrified the territories with news of Lincoln's election, and five months later, the attack on Fort Sumter. In June 1861, the army withdrew its regular troops from the West to fight in the big war, and only gradually replaced them with volunteer regiments.

Meanwhile, steady traffic on the road worsened relations with the Lakotas, Cheyennes, and Arapahos. The pestering that Sarah Sutton found her party subject to in 1854 was part of a larger pattern. Begging slid into demands for payment, then butchering of strayed emigrant stock, and finally outright raids and theft. After gold was found near Pikes Peak, the Front Range of Colorado began filling quickly with miners and townspeople. The treaty of 1851 had earmarked that land for the Cheyennes and the Arapahos; the tribes when they signed had expected nothing like this. Now they were forced to choose: confront? or capitulate?

Raids increased after the army pulled out its regular troops in 1861. Their volunteer replacements were slow in coming; in the spring of 1862, Lincoln asked Brigham Young for help patrolling the roads. It was a plea that came both from necessity and shrewd politics: seeking a show of loyalty from the Mormons at so uncertain a time would remind them that they had in fact agreed to subject themselves to federal power four years before. Young sent militia captain Lot Smith and 106 mounted men east—the same Lot Smith and many of the same men who had burned army wagon trains in 1857. On the Sweetwater, they found the stage stations abandoned, the stock run off, and some of the stations burnt.[7] Col. William Collins and the first two companies of Ohio cavalry arrived in July, and with them was Collins's seventeen-year-old son, Caspar, along as an unpaid clerk and map draftsman. The younger Collins—the first boy in Hillsboro, Ohio, ever to own a diamond ring, his biographer noted—enjoyed himself most when out alone after grouse, ducks, or sage hens with his dog and shotgun.[8]

With the aging Jim Bridger as guide, the troops made a long march up the Sweetwater, met Lot Smith at South Pass, then looped around behind the Wind River Range, and headed back east over Union Pass to the headwaters of the Wind River before making their way back to the Sweetwater. Indians briefly attacked a supply train near South Pass, and some of the soldiers chased them, but otherwise there were no skirmishes and the two Collinses had the time of their lives. In the summer of 1863, Col. Collins returned to Ohio to recruit more troops—among them Hervey Johnson—and at the same time young Caspar Collins enlisted and was commissioned a second lieutenant.[9]

Raids and skirmishes became more frequent in 1863; by 1864 emigrants and freighters were demanding army escorts. Collins's resources were stretched thin by the stage company's decision to move its main east-west route farther south. Before, it had run up the North Platte, but beginning in 1862 the stages followed the South Platte up to its confluence with the Cache la Poudre, then up onto the Laramie Plains and west to Fort Bridger. The telegraph line, however, remained along the North Platte and Sweetwater, so now Collins had to protect two routes across what is now Wyoming.

At Deer Creek, in the summer of 1864, Pvt. Johnson began hearing more tales of killing. Three soldiers came to the site of an attack on the road, where

> arrows clothing beds flour bacon salt and other plunder, six dead men, one of them a Negro were seen by them scattered along the road, all of them had been killed by arrows, The indians were piling together plunder and burning it; The wagons were not destroyed, the harness was all cut to pieces by the indians to get the mules out. . . .

Two women, a little boy, and girl were reported captured in the same attack. The women and boy escaped, but soldiers found the body of the girl with arrows in it and a "large gray wolf eating the child," Johnson wrote home. The Indians reportedly had first begged bread and meat, then insisted on trading horses before they began killing the men with whom they had been trading moments before. Uncertainty was taking its toll, and blood thirst was overtaking Johnson's Quaker upbringing. "I could shoot an indian with as much coolness as I would a dog and I will do it if [I] can," he wrote. "I never want to see an indian come about where I am. . . . I would experience a thrill of pleasure in shooting such brutes, and I would not hesitate to take a scalp if opportunity offers."[10]

The enlisted men, hearing tales like these, were eager to chase the Indians responsible; Johnson went along on one or two such expeditions, which proved fruitless. The army never was able to catch Indian war parties on the northern plains; army victories came only when troops fell on entire villages. The best known of such attacks occurred November 29, 1864, on Sand Creek, a tributary of the Arkansas far to the south of where Johnson and his comrades were serving. There, a big village of about 100 Cheyenne and ten Arapaho lodges was awaiting final word on some recent peace negotiations. Before daybreak, about 650 Colorado Volunteers under Colonel John Chivington and 125 regulars from Fort Lyons attacked and began killing people indiscriminately, then scalping and mutilating the bodies. Perhaps a fifth of the village's population—135 children, men, and women—was killed outright, and many more were wounded. News of the atrocities rippled out quickly among the tribes. Within a few weeks nearly all the Lakota, Arapaho, and Cheyenne people who had been living between the South Platte and the Arkansas, deeply angry and feeling forced into a war they had not sought, began to move north. They stopped twice at Julesburg, on the South Platte just above the forks, and raided the important stage depot there, raided again at Mud Springs on the North Platte, and kept moving. They were headed for the Powder River country, north of the North Platte, where they had relatives, where there were no white people, and where buffalo still bunched and massed.[11]

Johnson and his comrades were new to the Sweetwater when they were telegraphed the events on Sand Creek. The version they heard quadrupled the Indian body count and omitted the soldiers' atrocities. By mid-February 1865, they also knew of the fight at Mud Springs and had heard lurid versions of the Julesburg raids—Johnson believed Indians had bored a hole in the skull of a still-living soldier, filled it with powder and blown it up—so it's no surprise he was convinced that "extermination" of the tribes was the best solution. "That is the style I would like," he wrote his sisters; "this way of following indians night and day like we did last summer has about played out with me. The kind of style is to find their village and let into it about daylight some morning when they dont look for anything in that line, then there is the prospect of some fun."[12] Similar remarks were making the rounds of barracks, posts, and road ranches throughout the West.

The colonel by this time had placed his son, Lieutenant Caspar Collins, in command of the four little garrisons above Platte Bridge. Even in the coldest weather, he had to make the five-day round trip from Sweetwater Station to South Pass twice a month. This was fine with Johnson, who found the lieutenant "a smart scholar but a perfect boy, and entirely incapable of holding the position of Lieutenant."[13] Neither Johnson nor young Collins understood yet how Sand Creek had affected the tribes, and how much bloodier and more constant the war was to become. Still, with news of the massacre and raids still fresh, the soldiers had mixed feelings when forty lodges of Arapaho camped a day's journey away, and those Indians began visiting often.

Young Collins made light of it. "Every day or two," he wrote home to his aunt, "the chief [of the village] would send in reports from the hostile tribes and then ask for 'grub,' old clothes, etc. and want to trade for my horse or steal him—either, I think."[14] In his attempt at a joke he may have been missing the chief's real message: Be careful; you're in trouble; these bands up on the Powder are serious. We, by the way, are hungry and poorly clothed, and you could help us out. The senior Collins was shrewd, and probably would have understood such a message. Johnson, too, seems to have been more in tune than his lieutenant to the politics of what was going on. The younger Collins, however, was often absent, and too brash to hear such things. He was only twenty.

Then, while the Arapahos continued to camp nearby, some Cheyennes or Lakotas, or both, raided the soldiers' horse herd.

**Sweetwater Station Idh. Ter.**

Sweetwater Station, 1865. Lieutenant Caspar Collins's drawing of the biggest of the four army posts under his command. Independence Rock is in the middle distance; Devil's Gate is the left-hand slit in the mountain range beyond. The road went through the low pass to the left of the Gate. Note the telegraph poles and sentry boxes. The artist has drawn himself in the lower left-hand corner, returning with his dog from a hunt. The area was part of Idaho Territory at the time. Courtesy of Denver Public Library Western History Collection.

"There goes an Indian with Old Bob!" a sentry called out from the sentry box. Bob was a lame mule the soldiers allowed to graze near the post. Four men armed themselves quickly, ran out and began shooting at the Indian, who left Bob and rode down toward the river. Another Indian appeared; the two of them splashed with their horses across the river to the south side, and quickly disappeared among the bluffs. There followed what must have been two hours or more of decoy, taunt, cautious chase, and confusion. The soldiers' herd of twenty animals was a mile and a half away, under the care of three herders. When Indians showed themselves on a low ridge between the post and the herd, the soldiers knew they were in trouble; they would have to risk a sortie if they were to save mules and horses. The standing agreement was for the herders to bring the herd to the post as soon as they heard firing, but they were too far off to hear the first shots and still unaware of the Indians' presence. Six soldiers went out on foot over the bridge, then divided—three to guard a potential route of Indian retreat, three others to help the herders bring in the horses. The Indians managed to separate the herders from half the herd, and could have left; but they wanted the rest. Only the soldiers' superior firepower—they had Spencer rifles, which could be fired seven times before reloading—prevented such an outcome. The Indians finally found their only escape route was to drive the horses right up over the top of the highest rocks—"in a place," Johnson wrote in haste, "where a man would hardly think of crossing on foot."

One soldier was shot in the hand by the Indians; one Indian was shot by the soldiers and fell forward against his horse's neck. Though they'd lost half their herd, the soldiers counted themselves lucky. The telegraph didn't work for most of the next two or three days. When it was working again for ten minutes or so, the sergeant didn't have time to wire out news of the horse thefts. News came in that St. Mary's Station, on the upper Sweetwater, had been burned two nights earlier. Lt. Collins had gotten close enough to see it burning, and had turned back to Three Crossings. The soldiers assumed—wrongly, as it turned out—that the five-man garrison at St. Mary's had been killed.[15]

The Arapahos from the village nearby kept up their visits after the horse-stealing skirmish. Collins was still absent, but Private Johnson picked up on an important detail: the Arapahos were looking for help. At the moment, they told the soldiers, they had four Cheyennes staying in the village. Could the soldiers come out and kill them?[16]

It was just a scrap of information, yet it contained peace, war, and all the uncertainties between. The Arapahos feared the Cheyennes, but didn't want trouble with them, the interpreter explained. Given the timing, these Cheyennes must have been bringing the war pipe to the village. If the headmen smoked it, it would mean they were willing to go to war. After Sand Creek, the Cheyennes had brought the war pipe to all the Lakotas, Cheyennes, and Arapahos of Kansas and eastern Colorado, and all who had smoked it had gone north with their villages to join their northern relatives. By this time, late February 1865, the tribes were in several large camps along the Powder—probably 15,000 people or more. Their horse herds were so large they had to move to new grass every few days. The northern and southern branches of the Cheyennes had been hunting and living separately more than forty years, and had much to celebrate as everyone decided what to do.[17]

For their part, however, these Northern Arapahos seem to have been reluctant; such a decision was not to be made quickly. Johnson calls their leader a "medicine man"; he was most likely Medicine Man, leader of the Long Legs who ranged the North Platte and Sweetwater, one of three main bands of Northern Arapaho at the time.[18] Seeing if the troops would solve their difficulty was just one available option; Medicine Man had also sent couriers to Little Shield and Black Bear, other Arapaho headmen, camped with their people near Platte Bridge. All these men led not by fiat or decree, but by persuasion, discussion, and, when possible, consensus. The consensus may have been against war. In any case the Arapahos near the Sweetwater told the soldiers a day or two later that the Cheyennes had left their village. Question averted, for a while.

Meanwhile, a telegraph operator at Platte Bridge eavesdropped on some Arapahos talking by sign with some mountain men, warning them that a small party of soldiers due to leave soon for the post on the Sweetwater would be killed by Cheyennes, and the mules stolen. Other than the operator himself, no one believed this warning. But the next day, Johnson reported, four *Arapaho*s professing friendship rode up to a wagon making its way from the North Platte to the Sweetwater, and after some conversation shot a young trooper dead. The driver managed to escape with two of the mules, and though the Indians kept him pinned down for hours, he held them off with his Spencer until dark and made his escape. That is, the driver said they were Arapahos, as perhaps they were. It does not seem to have occurred to Johnson that these could have been the same Cheyennes the Arapahos had warned the mountain men about—and perhaps the same four Cheyennes who had spent many days in the Arapaho village, counseling war.

In any case, Johnson's sympathy for his fellow trooper, Private Philip Rhodes of Petersburg, Ohio, led him to forswear any future sympathy for Indians. "I don't think Co. G. will be fooled again by 'good Arappaho' or 'good Sioux' or 'good Cheyenne.' We have learned a lesson, if there are any friendly they must keep off the road while we are on it, if they do not, they will be politely invited to keep their distance. The Arappahoes I believe are friendly, but it wont do to meet them, or for them to meet us with tokens of friend ship on the road. It has 'played out,'" Johnson wrote his sister Sybil.[19]

Indians attacked the stations more directly; soldiers continued chasing the Indians to little effect. Col. Collins's enlistment ended in March, and he went home to Ohio, where he wrote an insightful report on what he'd learned of the tribes on the upper Platte, and in which he showed that Sand Creek was already having bad consequences. In April, Lee surrendered to Grant at Appomattox and troops in the West began feeling it was time to go home. In May, Collins was replaced at Ft. Laramie by Colonel Thomas Moonlight of Kansas, who promptly hanged two Indian headmen without trial. In late July, the entire strength of the tribes gathering for months on the Powder—between fifteen hundred and three thousand warriors—swept down to the North Platte with hopes of wiping out the garrison at Platte Bridge. There, they attacked a few army wagons coming along on the road from the Sweetwater. Young Lt. Caspar Collins—who happened to have stopped at the bridge the night before on his way from Fort Laramie back to his command—found the Kansas troops at the post, their enlistments up, near mutiny and unwilling to fight. Collins led a detachment out to rescue the wagon train, but was killed in thick, close fighting when he turned back to help a wounded soldier, and had his borrowed horse bolt into the crowd of Indians. The detachment returned to the post with heavy casualties. All but three of the men with the wagons were killed as well—twenty-six soldiers altogether.[20] Raids and skirmishes continued along the North Platte and Sweetwater, but the army chose to take the main war north where it would remain, off and on, for twelve more years before Lakota and Cheyenne power was broken.

Hervey Johnson was transferred back to Fort Laramie in the summer of 1865, settling into a barracks routine. A corporal now, he had more to fear from soldier-prisoners he was ordered to guard than he did from Indian attack. As his discharge neared, he began to think again about civilian life. He thought he might take up land in Missouri, which he believed held a bright future now with slavery abolished.[21]

He also grew indifferent toward the foe he had once been so eager to destroy. When 500 Indians came to Fort Laramie for a treaty conference late in April 1866, Johnson feared the drunken Major Maynardier and the other officers would order the garrison to fall on the Indians and kill them all. A month later, with negotiations stalled, Maynardier muttered about goading the Indians into a suicidal attack, Johnson reported to his sisters. Perhaps once Johnson would have gone for the chance, but not now. And if Maynardier, or any of the other officers, should try such a thing, they wouldn't be safe from their own men, he hinted. Negotiations broke down altogether and the Indians left. Johnson started home in June, marching away from the Indian wars neither victor nor victim, and returned to Ohio to live the rest of his life unrecorded.

To the west, the Shoshones, too, found their economy disappearing and themselves left with the choice of whether to beg, starve, or steal. Early in the 1860s, some began raiding the overland road east and west of Salt Lake City. Colonel Patrick Connor and a regiment of California volunteers arrived in the city in 1862—about the same time the first Ohio troops arrived on the Sweetwater—to protect the roads and watch the Mormons. Connor took Indian hostages and, when that didn't stop the raids, he hanged the hostages. In January 1863, he led a column of cavalry and infantry to attack Bear Hunter's band of Shoshones on the Bear River in what is now southeast Idaho. The Indians were well informed, well armed, and fought steadily until their ammunition ran out. In the hand-to-hand fight that followed, the cavalrymen's revolvers made all the difference.

Once the warriors were killed, Connor ordered the troops to destroy the lodges and take the property—which they did, including wheat, flour, beef, and potatoes, most of it subsidies from the Mormons. They also took the 175 Indian horses. Then the soldiers killed the wounded, raped the Shoshone women, some of them as they were dying, and killed the children. Connor, usually a strict disciplinarian, made no attempt to restrain the men. At least 250 of the 450 Shoshones living in the village were killed. Though far less well known even now, it was a bloodier day even than the one at Sand Creek. And it had quicker results. That summer, the Shoshones were ready to make peace. The Mormons, despite their distrust of Connor and his soldiers, were not sorry to see Shoshone power broken. And Connor was promoted to brigadier general.[22]

Federal officials negotiated treaties with various Shoshone bands. Washakie, at Fort Bridger, signed first; the Eastern Shoshones agreed to reestablish friendly relations with the whites, to tribal boundaries, and to a $10,000 annuity for twenty years. Four more bands signed by mid-October 1863, and the Senate ratified all the treaties.[23]

In the wake of these successes, Connor was promoted again, to command of all the troops on the northern plains. Late in the summer of 1865, a month after Collins had been killed at Platte Bridge, Connor led a three-pronged expedition into the Powder River Basin. He had bad supply problems, however, and his only success was an attack on Black Bear's village of about five hundred Arapahos in September, on the Tongue River near present Sheridan, Wyoming. The Indians lost thirty warriors and drove the soldiers off, but suffered severe losses of horses and lodges and after that began draining the resources of other Arapaho bands.

The army's next step was to build three forts along the Bozeman Trail leading to Montana through the heart of the Powder River Basin. The Cheyennes and Lakotas, furious, managed to make life so difficult for the army during the next two years that a peace faction won the upper hand in a war-weary Congress, and the government again called in the tribes to negotiate. In the summer of 1868, the army agreed to abandon its forts in the Powder River country, and to stop travel on the trail.

Though the Cheyennes and Lakotas would remain defiant a few years longer, the Arapahos now began navigating a trickier route between confrontation and capitulation. The Fort Laramie Treaty of 1868 moved Washakie's band of Shoshones away from Fort Bridger and up to a large reservation on Wind River, north of South Pass, northwest of the Sweetwater and well away from all the main travel routes. The Lakotas and Cheyennes were left free to roam north of the North Platte and east of the Bighorns—the Powder River Basin was theirs again. But the Arapahos remained unlocated.

Medicine Man, Black Bear, Little Shield, and other headmen all signed for the Northern Arapahos, agreeing that within a year they would settle with other tribes—with the Lakotas at Fort Randall on the Missouri, or far to the south in Indian Territory (later Oklahoma) with the Southern Cheyennes and Southern Arapahos, or on the Yellowstone with the Crows. But the Northern Arapahos were uneasy about all three options. They felt condescended to by the Lakotas, the Crows had been their enemies for generations, and Indian Territory was too foreign, too far south, too hot. The Arapahos wintered on the Powder; the following year Medicine Man and the other headmen began negotiating with the Shoshones, via the army and the governor of the new Wyoming Territory, for Shoshone approval for the Arapahos to settle temporarily on Wind River.

The land, which once had seemed like one continuous thing with local variety—not so different that way from the sky, or the wind, or the weather—was breaking up now. Before, as Black Hawk the Oglala had told the whites on Horse Creek in 1851, you took what land you wanted and held it if you could. Now everything was fragments, angles, alliances, favors, permissions, and schemes. What had seemed to all like a useful solution crumpled quickly in front of a new gold rush. Miners poured in to new strikes at South Pass. When Black Bear's village of Northern Arapahos arrived on Wind River in March 1870, settlers blamed them for recent raids on miners. A mob of 250 vigilantes, with help from some Shoshones, attacked two peaceful groups of Arapahos moving from their camp on Wind River to trade in the new town of Lander. A dozen Arapahos were killed, including Black Bear. Soon the Arapahos left Wind River again and spent the next few years on the move, over a landscape losing its continuity to abstractions of ownership imposed from far away.

Close to home, the buffalo continued to dwindle. Medicine Man died in 1871. The Arapahos now drew their annuities at Red Cloud agency on the North Platte, near Fort Laramie, where the Lakotas were based, and hunted and wintered on the Powder when they could. When the Red Cloud agency was moved north to the White River in 1874, some Arapahos went south to Indian Territory, but nearly 1,000 stayed on the northern plains. A headman named Black Coal worked to keep up good relations with the army and that spring, for the first time, some Arapahos began working as scouts. In the summer, a band of Arapahos was camped on Nowood Creek in the foothills of the southern Bighorn Mountains when it was attacked by sixty soldiers and 160 Shoshone warriors from Wind River. As they had against Connor in 1865, the Arapahos resisted well but lost far more in horses, lodges, and possessions than they could afford.

Many Arapahos continued to draw rations at the Red Cloud agency—but they didn't want to end up there, fearful of being lost as a tribe altogether. In the spring of 1876, Arapaho scouts joined General Crook's column on that last major campaign into the northern plains—spearheaded by Crook, Custer and Terry—that ended with Crook stalled and Custer annihilated. Settlers after that were not convinced of the Arapahos' peaceful intentions, but the army was. More Arapaho scouts enlisted in the fall to help Crook hunt the fleeing Cheyennes and Lakotas. With Pawnee, Shoshone, and some Lakota scouts, they led the army to the headwaters of Powder River for the attack on Dull Knife's village of Northern Cheyennes. The uniforms, provisions, horses, guns, and ammunition the Arapaho scouts brought home to their families kept starvation at bay, and the respect they won from the soldiers eventually allowed them a final place to land.

Crook, according to the Arapahos, agreed to find them a reservation on the Tongue, and in the spring of 1877 the army backed the Arapahos in their desire to stay in Wyoming. Civilian authorities wanted the tribe to move south. In September 1877, three Arapaho headmen—Black Coal, Friday, and Sharp Nose—traveled with sixteen Lakotas to Washington, D.C., to meet President Rutherford B. Hayes and Interior Secretary Carl Schurz.

They could learn to live with the Shoshones, Black Coal told Hayes, Schurz, and the army officers. They had had trouble with the Shoshones along the Sweetwater and elsewhere, he said. But "now if you will let us join the Snakes we will get along first rate, and will have no further trouble. . . . You ought to take pity on us and give us good land, so that we can remain upon it and call it our home . . . where we can farm."[24]

It seems deeply ironic that Indians should be asking the president and the secretary of the interior for land. They returned to the Red Cloud agency by mid-October. Partly because the Kansas Legislature feared placement of "northern hostiles" in Indian Territory, the Arapahos were authorized to move to the Sweetwater instead. Soon they left the agency on White River and traveled west. Two weeks later they reached Fort Fetterman near the North Platte, by which time they'd already eaten all 155 cattle they'd been issued at the agency. Crook lent them arms and ammunition to hunt buffalo. By late November they reached Independence Rock, and they wintered there. In March, they divided into smaller groups and moved on. On March 18, Black Coal arrived with twenty-one lodges on the Shoshone reservation, and camped two days' ride from agency headquarters. He met with agent James Patten, who reluctantly issued rations for the Arapahos, protesting to his superiors that it was a bad idea. By May most of the rest of the Arapahos had arrived, and began the next stage of their history learning to subsist on short rations, resist Shoshone efforts to have them removed, and at the same time resist government efforts to undermine their culture and institutions altogether.

Again they mentioned the Sweetwater as a possible home when they met a year later with Territorial Governor John Hoyt to ask for a trader and agency separate from the Shoshones. Then in the mid-1880s, with the Sweetwater already heavily settled by white ranchers, they suggested the Tongue or the Powder.

These are minor facts, however, and make the Arapahos look like petitioners only. They leave out a sense of how dignity can enable survival. According to Arapaho tradition, Black Coal and his people arrived on the hills south of the hot springs near what's now Fort Washakie, and on the plains below they saw the Shoshones in celebration, racing horses in the dust.

Although their people had little use for each other, Black Coal and Washakie were friends. Black Coal got off his horse, cleaned himself carefully, put on his best clothes, braided his hair with a wrap on one side and a braid on the other to show he was a chief, and laid by all his weapons. He told his people that he would go down into the village, and if they saw him come out again into the open and wave a buffalo robe, it would be safe for them to come down. Then he walked, alone, down toward the big Shoshone pow-wow. He had prepared carefully so he would be clean if he was killed, and the Great Spirit would find him clean in death. No one noticed him at first; then the young Shoshone men noticed him and threatened to kill him. By signs he made it clear he wanted to see Washakie, his friend, and Washakie told the young men, "Who-ever touches this man will have to answer to me." Black Coal was safe then, and he and Washakie agreed to divide the reservation along the lines that still divide it today—with the Arapahos living out on the plains east of the hot springs, and the Shoshones living west of the hot springs, against the mountains.[25]

# CHAPTER 8

# Hayden's Gaze

Our camp near Red Buttes was . . . on a broad, grassy bottom of the Platte, in a sort of amphitheater, with the rocky beds rising to a great elevation all around us. . . . As we approached them from the east in the afternoon, the rays of the setting sun greatly heightened their color and brought them out in relief, so that we could readily see why they have been such prominent landmarks and have so long attracted the attention of the traveler.

*—F. V. Hayden, 1870.*

When the photographer William Henry Jackson posed fourteen men around a table in a field, propped a deer head on a keg for display, and allowed a dog to continue lying in the shade of a wagon, he was articulating complicated relationships among people, animals, and landscape—but he didn't think much about such things. He thought only of the pose. Once he had everything placed, he entered the photo himself, and stood as its fifteenth member at the right-hand end of the group. He turned his side to the camera, raised his left hand to his hip, looked slightly downward toward the center of the composition, and instructed an assistant to make the view. The assistant, the third cook or a teamster, reached around to the front of the tripodded camera, removed the lens cap for many long seconds, and then replaced it over the lens. "Red Buttes," Jackson wrote that night at the top of his diary page.

Then he added "Layover—Views of camp and of men in A.M."[1] Even today, it may be the great landscape photographer's best-known photograph. And it's full of people.

The camera was new that summer. From Omaha, where he kept his studio, Jackson had telegraphed for it to New York City, and it had arrived barely in time for him to join these men as their official photographer before they left on their expedition to the West. The camera recorded images on five-inch by eight-inch wet glass plates. Because they had to be wet to receive the images, the plates had to be exposed and then developed at once, before they dried out; prints could be made later.[2] Other field summers had taught Jackson the importance of traveling light; by 1870 he had reduced the outfit he needed to make his views to only about 300 pounds of stuff. Where before he'd needed a light wagon, now he could pack everything for a day's work onto a mule, and get to rougher country.

Because the negatives were so large, and because Jackson understood so well what focus, light, and various lenses could do, the pictures preserved an enormous amount of detail. But only in the weeks of August 1870 was Jackson becoming a great composer of images. In a single summer, he became a mature artist. Though he was innocent—unironic, Romantic, enthusiastic—his pictures, like this one, show he was beginning to engage the complexities of power.

Two cooks stand at the left-hand edge of the group, flanking a small camp stove with three black pots on it. From the stove rises a pipe with a right-angled elbow at the top, sending smoke behind the head of the right-hand cook. Next, six men stand along the rearmost plane of occupation, ending with Jackson on the right. But no two stand alike. Sanford Gifford, the painter, cocks a lanky shoulder upward and gazes toward us. Next, the geology draftsman Henry Elliott looks down toward the center of things; next to him, James Stevenson, second in command, leans forward slightly, hand outstretched toward his seated boss, of whom more shortly. Then a gap, through which we can see the grass stretch back to the base of the hills; then three more men—Schmidt, the naturalist, Carrington, zoologist, and Bartlett, listed as "general assistant." Then

Hayden Survey party, Red Buttes, August 1870. Sanford Robinson Gifford, the landscape painter, stands third from left. Hayden sits hatless at the rear of the table. William Henry Jackson, the photographer, stands at extreme right, left hand on hip. Photograph by W. H. Jackson, courtesy USGS photo archive.

another gap through which we can make out some horses grazing; then the dashing Jackson—wearing his long hair tied back, wearing a string tie perhaps, with the near side of his hat brim flipped up—then the hind end of a mule in the background; and finally, down the right-hand edge of the photo, a slice of wagon in whose shade in the lower right-hand corner luxuriates a dog, which has just stretched snout and forelegs into the sun.

In front of the standing men, five more men sit at a wooden table. They appear at ease; there are dishes, a pot and a pitcher on the table as though they had just finished breakfast, and one or two are holding cups. Left to right, they are Turnbull, secretary of the expedition, leaning forward with a forearm on his thigh; Beaman, meteorologist, who often assisted Jackson in the field; and at the back end of the table, Ferdinand V. Hayden, M.D., geologist and leader of the expedition. At the near corner, elbows on the table, looking off to the left, sits entomologist and agriculturalist Cyrus Thomas in a black frock coat. Behind him and to his right sits Raphael, an interpreter they had hired at Fort Fetterman. And further right, in front of Jackson, sits Ford, mineralogist, who may be stirring up batter in a dishpan. In front of Ford's shins, the deer head is propped with its nose on the top of a smaller keg, and the back of its skull against a taller one. The image is so sharp that it's evident the antlers are still in velvet.

Hayden, the leader, sits hatless at the back of the table. The men's postures are casual; most are wearing work clothes, yet the effect is formal. It's not just a group portrait of the 1870 members of the United States Geological and Geographical Survey of the Territories. It's a picture of power, of who's in charge. Hayden's face is at the center; the men's casual postures defer to his presence. Sun blazing off his forehead, left shoulder cocked just slightly back, he gazes out at us from well back in the group, dominating everything.

Hayden had an uncertain and difficult childhood, and seldom talked about it in his adult life. He was born in Connecticut in 1829 and was more or less an orphan until the age of thirteen, when he landed safely on an aunt and uncle's farm in Rochester,

Ohio. A few years later he entered Oberlin College, then a hotbed of abolitionism, but appears to have stayed out of politics and joined literary groups before finding his way to the natural sciences. In 1851 he entered medical school in Cleveland; there he met John Strong Newberry, a recent graduate of the same medical school and a rising geologist and paleontologist. Through Newberry, Hayden came into contact with the geologist James Hall, of Albany, New York. When Hall needed an extra assistant for a western collecting expedition he was organizing in 1853, he gave Hayden the job. Hayden's letters to Hall that spring—demanding, ingratiating, self-promoting, and idealistic—show the man who was to go so far in American science, and yet be remembered as a failure.

Thus it was that Hayden got his first look at western rocks at the age of twenty-four, from the deck of a steamboat belonging to the American Fur Company. The trip up the Missouri was slow for a brisk young man but it allowed for day after day of gazing at the riverbanks and bluffs, and a chance to talk over the meanings of the strata with Fielding Meek, whom Hall had deputized to lead the expedition. Meek was an invertebrate paleontologist of broad knowledge and curiosity, engaged then in using the fossils of ancient shellfish and other creatures to understand which rocks were older and which younger—part of the great worldwide ordering task of nineteenth- and early twentieth-century geology. They disembarked at Fort Pierre—the same fort where the tribes and the traders had waited two long winters without buffalo in 1832, '33, and '34—and headed southwest into the badlands along the White River. That bleached, gullied landscape is still one of the richest fossil localities in the world. But Indian disapproval and logistical difficulties forced Hayden and Meek to leave after just three weeks.

In that brief time Hayden learned valuable lessons, however. He learned chiefly that he loved the work, that no work would get done unless the details of finance, travel, and supply were attended to first, and that stable finance required stroking the patron.

In Hayden's time, geology was a visual science. A geologist needed a good eye to follow a rock layer, sometimes hundreds of miles, as it dipped and rose in and out of sight. He had to know fossils, too, and their order in time, as the fossils provided vital clues to when, relative to other layers, a layer in question had folded, faulted, or washed away.[3]

Hayden soon finished his medical degree and with its extra cachet and his own ambition advanced quickly in the natural sciences. Within a year or two he was collecting on the upper Missouri and Yellowstone rivers for men at the highest reaches of American science, including Spencer Baird of the new Smithsonian Institution and Joseph Leidy of the Academy of Natural Sciences in Philadelphia. Hayden generally worked alone in the field, but continued to work with Meek to understand the meaning of his finds. Together, they published sixteen scientific papers, the most important of which was a stratigraphic column—a chart that named the layers and showed their relative order and thicknesses—of the rocks on the upper Missouri. It remained a standard reference point for decades. With Meek's help, Hayden was becoming an important scientist. In 1856 and 1857, he accompanied Corps of Topographical Engineers explorations to the Black Hills of Dakota, the Missouri, and the lower Yellowstone. In 1858 he spent two months collecting with Meek in Kansas, and in 1859 he joined another Corps expedition, this time with Captain W. F. Raynolds on a fifteen-month trip that failed to locate the sources of the Yellowstone.[4]

The army moved too slowly for Hayden, however. He made frequent side trips solo, and thus was at odds with the officers in charge. Then the Civil War came, and he too became an officer, an army surgeon who amputated wounded limbs. Soon he was running hospitals, and with that experience emerged from the war a shrewd manipulator of bureaucracies.

And he seems already to have become famous for his haste. Whites repeated what supposedly was a Lakota story: that the Indians called him the-man-who-picks-up-stones-running; that having once emptied a sack he was carrying and found it full of rocks they thought him crazy, and afterward left him alone.[5] After the war he accepted a professorship in geology and mineralogy at the University of Pennsylvania. But it paid little and he kept collecting, to supplement his income and satisfy his curiosity. In the spring of 1867, his friend Spencer Baird in Washington learned that Congress had approved a survey of the southeastern counties of the brand-new state of Nebraska. Hayden got the job, and a similar one the following year leading a survey, with side trips, along the new Union Pacific line to its temporary terminus at Fort Bridger in the brand-new Wyoming Territory. Though these surveys were under the auspices of the General Land Office, which was in charge of the westward march of the sale of federal land, they were not square-mile-by-square-mile land surveys. They were on-the-ground inquiries into just what was out there; they were systematic, yet designed to cover lots of country, primarily to find where minerals might lie and where crops might grow best.

For settlement had been outstripping legal niceties for a long time. The grid of federal land surveys had been stepping westward from Ohio since shortly after the Revolutionary War, but for generations, squatters, prospectors, and cattlemen had kept ahead of it, claiming squatters' rights—"preemption rights" they were called as custom moved into law—to the choicest lands. To keep ahead of the disorder advancing ahead of the land grid, Congress decided to finance organized teams of explorers, allow them to draw supplies from army posts, and send them off to locate and publicize the resources of the West.[6]

By 1870, four surveys had emerged: Clarence King's Survey of the Fortieth Parallel, an army-financed civilian operation that worked eastward from California; Lieutenant George Wheeler's Geographical Surveys West of the One Hundredth Meridian, an all-army operation that confined itself to the dry Southwest; John Wesley Powell's all-civilian Geographical and Geological Survey of the Rocky Mountain Region, best known for its explorations of the Colorado River; and Hayden's all-civilian Geological and Geographical Survey of the Territories. Competition for funds and support among the four would grow steadily through the 1870s, until consolidation was in order. In the final maneuvering, Hayden would lose out. Partly because of his own weaknesses, partly because his

competitors outlived him and controlled the accounts that were
written, he has come down in history as a failure. In 1879, King was
named the first director of the United States Geological Survey. He
was soon succeeded by Powell, the one true reformer of the group,
who would end up losing important fights of his own.

These postwar surveys were in a direct line from the explorations of Frémont, and of Raynolds and others of the 1850s. Like the
earlier efforts, the new surveys were motivated as much by politics
as by science; they were as much about exploitation as they were
about understanding. The land would continue to be fragmented
and objectified, though it had more stages to go through before it
could be fully, privately owned.

In 1869, Hayden's survey was moved out from the General Land
Office to a position directly under the secretary of the interior,
and its appropriation doubled to $10,000. He led a party south
along the Front Range of Colorado and over Raton Pass to Santa
Fe. Hayden collected tons of fossils, his artist Henry Elliott sketched
the landscapes, and in the final report, Cyrus Thomas of the frock
coat wrote, with Hayden's tacit assent, that rain follows the plow—
the theory that breaking prairie releases locked-up moisture into
the atmosphere and increases rain. The idea would catch on fast
because farmers wanted to believe it so badly, and railroads were
happy to help them dream their dreams. Eight thousand copies of
the report sold out in three weeks. In future reports Hayden continued to mix science with hopes of bonanza, well aware that if the
public liked what he produced, Congress would hear about it, and
his surveys would continue to grow. It seemed as if there was always
a great day coming in the West.[7]

Similar enthusiasms had first swept Jackson, the photographer,
west in 1866. He had grown up in upstate New York and Vermont,
but his family moved often; he later remembered Spanish moss and
palmettos overhanging a moonlit river, when the family followed
the father to the Georgia frontier. The restlessness Jackson inher-
ited from that time stayed with him through his life. As a child
he showed skill with a pencil and his mother bought him drawing

books, but at fifteen he went to work in a photographer's studio in
Rutland, Vermont, coloring and retouching photographs—pains-
taking and repetitive work. In the Civil War he spent a year as a
soldier, sketching landscapes and encampments, before returning
to Rutland in 1863, then to Burlington, where a bigger studio paid
him more. Now twenty, he joined a literary club and they read Shakespeare, Dickens, Emerson, Holmes, and Thoreau, and the American nature poets, Whittier, Longfellow, Bryant. Nature in America
was an Eden that needed only human presence—solitary people
who understood it for what it was—to bring out its true meaning. In
1866 a sweetheart jilted him and he lit out for the Territories.

Jackson and two friends landed jobs in St. Louis with an ox train
of freight wagons, which took them to Salt Lake City. There, broke,
his clothes in rags and his boots worn through, he hit bottom, wrote
home for money, and lived for a month with a charitable Mormon
family while waiting for the funds to arrive. He bought passage on
a wagon train bound for Los Angeles. His diaries show him learning from his fellow travelers—on that route past the meadow where
Mormons had murdered the Arkansans nine years before—a contempt for Mormons and Paiutes that was apparently routine on the
trail. In the spring of 1867 he signed on with a crew herding hundreds of wild horses back over the same route. It was frantic work;
the herders were expected to keep extra watches on behalf of their
boss. All the while he was busy sleeping with the wife of the man
whose train they had merged their outfit with, early in the journey.

In Omaha, Jackson landed a job in a photography studio, at
wages as good as he'd ever made in Burlington. Working steadily,
with a room of his own to live in, must have seemed pure luxury
after his year on the trail.

While learning how to make a living in the West, Jackson had
been giving himself a visual education at the same time. Sketches
like the one he made of Chimney Rock left no little human figures
in its foreground—no houses, no soldiers' huts, villages, streams,
or farmsteads—no sign at all of human habitation or movement.
Everything seemed blasted by a new, blank enormity. The world
was too big to be beautiful. Whether it was picturesque or sublime

would have to remain unanswered while he grappled, for a while, with rocks, distance, and sky.

Omaha, meanwhile, was booming; Jackson worked in the photography studio for most of a year before his brothers joined him in 1868, and with help from their father they bought out the business. The town was the eastern terminus of the westward-building Union Pacific, and was thronged with workers. They wanted pictures of themselves to send home, singly and in groups. Tourists, too, wanted pictures—not of themselves but of the exotic world they'd come to see. Mountain views they wanted, scenery, splendor, and if in stereopticon slides, even better.

The tourists wanted also pictures of Indians. Jackson began making regular visits to the Otoes, Omahas, and Pawnees who lived on reservations near Omaha. To the growing selection of negatives he added views of the large Pawnee villages of mud houses, and of individuals posed alone in slanting sunlight. The Indians appear to be offering themselves to the viewer's gaze, but in fact they are being offered. They are passive props to the viewer's preemoeptions.

Jackson and an assistant, Hull, left his brothers to run the business and spent the summer of 1869 along the Union Pacific, the year the railroad was completed. The landscapes are great, innocent pictures, in which human and natural elements compete for power as Jackson learns his craft. They carefully kept the glass negatives of the scenics, as they could make prints from them over and over again.

In the squalid, vicious, bustling railroad towns they photographed businesses, homes, work groups, and families, developing and printing as many images as they could sell, then washing the plates to use again at the next town on the line. In Cheyenne they cleared $60 in three days, not bad in light of the $25 per month Jackson lived on during his best-paid days as a retoucher. Oddly, when Jackson and Hull stopped to deliver a batch of prints at Madame Cleveland's, a Cheyenne brothel, who should walk in but Hayden and "some military friends," Jackson wrote in his diary. The scientist "acted like a cat in a strange garret"; if they spoke, Jackson did not record the conversation.[8]

Leaving Cheyenne, they were asked by a young vendor of snacks and newspapers for 1,000 scenic views that he would resell to tourists. Late in the summer, still traveling, Jackson got word from his brother Ed in Omaha that a New York photographic publisher wanted 10,000 prints of pictures from the UP line. The railroad had split the West like a ripe fruit, and already it was offering up its lucre.

When Hayden walked into Jackson's studio in Omaha in July 1870, the young photographer already had a national reputation for his pictures. It was their first meeting of consequence. Hayden liked what he saw.

More even than the odd vigor of the landscapes, Hayden was drawn to Jackson's specific respect for rocks. There they were, in picture after picture, massively layered, detailed, and *identifiable*, sometimes accompanied by but never subordinate to people, trees, or railroad tracks. Hayden offered to cover Jackson's expenses for the summer as official photographer for the Survey. Jackson would be expected to make prints for the Survey for free, but he would be allowed keep the negatives. He knew his new wife, Mollie Greer Jackson, could run the business expertly while he was gone—she was much better at it than his brothers. He accepted. On the first of August, he caught up with the expedition at Camp Carlin, an army supply depot outside Cheyenne.[9]

One way to bring the past closer is to hunt up its locations. A visitor today to the floodplain where the Survey camped near Red Buttes finds more pines and junipers on the hills behind it, more cottonwoods along the river, wire fences following various property lines, more sagebrush, less grass. The vegetation is so different it's difficult to locate the area; the real clues lie in the ridgelines and rock strata of the hills in the background, and in the frank logic of the spot as a good place for men to camp and mules to graze. Of course, the rocks remain unchanged.

Hayden writes in his report for the summer of 1870 that it was the rocks that drew him north from Cheyenne.[10] But he almost certainly wanted to make historical connections as well. He too wanted to hunt up the locations of the past—places with nostalgic names that congressmen would recognize. The Survey traveled north from Cheyenne past the foothills of the Laramie Range—the same neighborhood another tourist, Francis Parkman, had wandered twenty-four years before—then linked up with the old emigrant road and turned west up the North Platte valley. They traveled with four heavy wagons and two light ambulances; the teamsters and cooks generally kept these to the roads, while the artists and scientists ranged and roamed alone or in small parties, generally on horseback. Hayden assigned tasks and kept track of what everyone was doing; still, it was a fairly loose arrangement. Of the 501-page report he hustled into print the following winter—ten times as long as any previous report he'd written—Hayden wrote the first two-fifths. The rest was contributed by various scientists, some of whom were on the expedition and others who wrote afterward from observation of its collected samples. The final report rambled in describing the route in a diary form, rather than concentrating on specific scientific questions—as it would have if Meek had had a hand in it.

Jackson kept his bulkier gear in one of the ambulances, and had a lighter outfit that he could pack for a day's work on Hypo, his fat, cropped-eared mule, named for one of his darkroom chemicals, hyposulfite of soda. They passed La Bonté Creek and Deer Creek, whose onetime trading posts were abandoned, probably gone. Jackson notes in his diary that they crossed the Platte at "Caspar," but if his use of that name indicates any ruins remained of the burned army post or Guinard's bridge, he doesn't say so. Hayden uses the word "landmark" at Red Buttes, and the same word at Independence Rock; soon afterward he calls Devil's Gate "another well-known locality."[11] Clearly, he intended the names of these famous spots on the emigrant road to echo in his report and in Jackson's photo captions.

He may have been seeking similar effects when, in July, he had encountered the Hudson River School landscape painter, Sanford Robinson Gifford, in Denver. Gifford, in his late forties, had come west with two friends on a sketching trip, looking to satisfy the same new demand for western subjects that Jackson had found so lucrative.[12] By this time, Gifford was a mature artist who had done well painting New England, the Hudson Valley, and the Catskills, like many of his contemporaries. Unlike them, he had a taste for more exotic locales. He painted in Europe for more than two years in the mid-1850s, and in 1868 and 1869 had extended a second European tour to spots farther east: Cairo, Beirut, Athens, and Constantinople. He is regarded as a luminist, which means he often painted looking directly into the light, like Turner but without the turmoil. He was good at deserts and seashores. In them, light fills the sky and casts a hazy stillness that is still dynamic—an emptiness from which it is difficult to look away. When Hayden described Wyoming's rock formations to Gifford, and invited him to come along as a guest of the Survey, the painter left his friends and came.

Gifford traveled with the expedition for six weeks. Though twenty years apart, he and Jackson quickly became friends. Gifford spent nearly all his time with the photographer, lugging the equipment, setting up the views and, now and again, taking over photography altogether. He also took the trouble to make himself useful around camp and on the trail, and at the same time managed a large number of oil sketches for himself. Often he painted the views Jackson photographed. All the while, Jackson was getting a crash course in landscape composition.

Meanwhile, the country along the road was recovering from the devastation of emigrant travel. Jackson reported plenty of antelope in his diary; then, the morning after they had left Red Buttes, Jackson, Gifford, and Beaman, the meteorologist, started out across country from their camp at Willow Springs. "Distant sight of lone Buffalo," Jackson recorded that night. "Cautious approach—commencement of hostilities—the Chase—Excitement!—Much firing but not effective."[13] They quit, for a time. Later they spotted a herd of nine—in a later autobiography Jackson numbers it at "thirty or forty"—but these buffalo, too, got wind of them and galloped off through the thick sagebrush. Still later, Jackson, Gifford, and probably Beaman made a long detour downwind of three more buffalo and finally, with help from others in the party, managed to kill all three. Though Hayden and Jackson both had passed this way before, neither remarked any improvement in the look of the country. Still, thirteen buffalo between Willow Springs and Horse Creek amounted to a great many more than people were seeing five and ten years earlier. With the nation's east-west artery now moved elsewhere, and the tribes pushed north of the North Platte, the country was empty of humans other than themselves, and seemed almost as rich in game as it had been in Frémont's time.

They camped two nights at Independence Rock. Hayden was stirred by the geology, and understood its main parameters perfectly well—that Tertiary sediments there lap up against granite outcrops, which are far older—"jut close up against their base" was how he put it. He understood correctly that Independence Rock is made of the same stuff as the surrounding granite ridges, and that its dome shows erosion by exfoliation, peeling off the outside as it continues to expand from within. In his excitement, he climbed the granite ridges just south of the Rock, and from there he could look and look to his heart's content:

> From the summit as far as the eye could reach in every direction granite ranges could be seen, of varying lengths, from one hundred to fifteen hundred feet above the surrounding plains. . . . In some of the broad intervals are the most beautiful terraces or benches, sloping gently down from the base of the mountains to the valley. Not a sign of water could be seen in any of these mountains at the present time. A few cottonwoods and groups of quaking asps, in some of the ravines on the sides, gave evidence that water issues from them at certain seasons of the year. A few stunted pines struggled for existence among the crevices, and some rare shrubs and ferns were all the vegetable life observed.

All true. Then he continued, "It seems as though the Sweetwater flowed through this valley for fifty miles or more with scarcely a tributary to add to its volume." That observation is not true, though it appears that way from the top of those rocks. Hayden's affection and enthusiasm for the country are palpable. But whether he would love to exploit it, or love to leave it alone, was a question Hayden

View down Sweetwater, from the top of Independence Rock, 1870, with the Hayden Survey's tents and wagons in the middle distance. Photograph by W. H. Jackson, courtesy USGS photo archive.

and the nineteenth century, with one or two exceptions, were not quite yet ready to ask.[14]

For Cyrus Thomas, the frock-coated "agriculturalist," there was no question; the valley was obviously exploitable. It looked to him as if the whole Sweetwater could be productive farmland if irrigated out of the river—three miles on either side for a ninety-mile length. His quick math made it 540 square miles, or 350,000 acres—pure dream, it has turned out.[15] Even now, ranchers irrigate only occasional hay meadows in the valley, not more than a hundredth of the acreage Thomas predicted.

The first day at the Rock, Jackson made some pictures, but it was cold and windy. The following day was clear and still. Jackson, Elliott, and perhaps Gifford led Hypo up the Rock to try again. He faced his camera downriver, east toward the Platte and a pair of peaks beyond it. Elliott lounges with his sketchbook in the right foreground, but the rocks are quickly sloping away, and in the right middle ground, just beyond the river, the viewer's eye quickly finds four tents and as many wagons. Two horses graze to the left of the tents, near the river; and the broad channel of the river itself flows briefly up the middle of the picture before bending off to the left. The big rocks that Hayden climbed for a better view of everything slope into the picture from the right; these are the same rocks into which the Sweetwater garrison's horses disappeared when the Indians drove them right over the top.

But despite foreground, middle ground, background, and sky, this is no conventional composition. A full third of the picture is nearby granite that Jackson allows in from the left on a long diagonal. It shows in such close detail one knows without thinking that the rock is rough to the touch and warm from the sun, with a breeze cutting around its edges. Still the viewer's eye rests finally not on the granite but, again, on the receding river at the middle of the picture—out there in space and emptiness, flowing away and leaving behind a stillness, from which it is very difficult to look away.

That same day they left the rock, packed up and headed up the road toward Devil's Gate. They did not camp, but Jackson, Gif-

View up Sweetwater, from the top of Devil's Gate, 1870. Jackson's photos asked as many questions as they answered. Photograph by W. H. Jackson, courtesy USGS photo archive.

ford, and Elliott climbed to the top with the camera and looked out again over a receding sweep of country—upstream now, to the west. Again in the foreground, diagonals of granite, though now the immediate rocks make a shallow vee. In the middle distance on a flat by the river, just a single wagon, one of the ambulances, and a tiny man is standing halfway between wagon and riverbank. Gifford and Elliott crouch on the right-hand side of the vee, looking away and outward. Again, the eye follows up the middle of the image, over top of the wagon, to the river as it snakes and loops and finally disappears toward the low, hazy mountains and the sky.

In a single image, Jackson hands us depth, space, hints of future human occupation, and an appearance of documentary verisimilitude that in fact is packed with emotion by the way the forms sweep the eye down and then with a big *whoosh* out—to infinity. At the center he also hands us the same qualities that centered the photo at Red Buttes: Hayden's power, and Hayden's ambiguity.

There are no corrals yet, where later the Sun Ranch will headquarter its empire. There is no sign of the Lajeunesse and Archambault cabins where the French-Shoshone families lived, nor any abandoned handcarts, though what will be called Martin's Cove is just a couple of miles along the rocks to the right. There is very little brush by the river compared to now, and the space between the two nearest meanders looks sandy, still, perhaps, unrecovered from decades of damage from emigrant cattle. Mostly, it looks appealingly empty. But it's not.

Already there are stories attached to the land, stories the camera doesn't record—stories of competence and incompetence, of suffering, survival, commerce, war, and loss. In the coming decades, as modern land ownership becomes possible, a few people will arrive with plans to stay. They, and their stories, will come into conflict. What the camera fails to capture is whose stories will stick to the land, and why.

# CHAPTER 9

# Grazing in Paradise

Seminole and the eastern end of Sweetwater Hills were formerly favorite hunting-grounds, but of late years the Indians,
Cheyennes, Arapahoes, and Sioux have not been regular in
their annual expeditions to these localities.
    —*Frederic Endlich, Hayden Survey geologist, 1877*

Sun family stories—the smoothest, most well-worn, cared-for
kind—hold that the French Canadian Thomas Beausoleil ran
away from home to the West at age twelve. In St. Louis he fell under
the wing of Dakota, a French trapper who looked out for him and
taught him the ways of the frontier. These are the stories Tom Sun
himself must have told. They turned up in articles about him during his lifetime and in notices of his death in 1909, they have been
retold many times since by his heirs and descendants, and they've
been repeated again in newspapers and books. By the time he died,
"he was loth to talk for publication and would shut up tight if he
thought we were trying to put down anything he said," the *Carbon
County Journal* reported. When he was alive he was admired and
feared, and between-the-lines evidence over time seems to show he
wanted it that way. Early on, he understood the value of a reputation. When it was in his interest, he was never loathe to publicize
his skills and his name. As the stories circulated and his reputation
solidified, so did his hold on the land.

    A few surviving documents show a rougher, more angular version
of Sun's early years. A Thomas Sun served for six months as a private

in a regiment of Maine infantry in 1861, early in the Civil War, before he was discharged for sickness, aged eighteen. Tom Sun bought a mining claim in Carbon County, Wyoming Territory, in March 1873, from an Andrew S. Burt, who was represented in the transaction by Boney Earnest, Sun's longtime friend and partner. In 1880, the same year Sun filed his first land claim at Devil's Gate, he told a census taker he was born in Canada. In 1882, with the cattle business booming, a Cheyenne newspaper devoted two long and admiring articles to the man and his ranch. In 1883, when he married Mary Hellihan, a Rawlins newspaper called him "the well known frontiersman, who has battled with nature and the red man in the Rocky mountains, for the past twenty-five years," which if true would put him in the West since the late 1850s—unlikely if he was still east in the army in 1861.[1]

In 1889, as we shall see, his name became permanently linked with the hanging of a man and a woman in a rocky gulch near Independence Rock, just a few miles from Sun's ranch headquarters on the southwest side of Devil's Gate. In 1899, Sun had a long conversation about Frémont with a University of Wyoming geology professor who was hunting dinosaurs. Sun told the professor, who wrote it up for *National Geographic*, that the Pathfinder's version of events the day the boat capsized in the canyon was wrong, that the party had dumped upstream in water that was not so wild. He had learned this, Sun said, from his longtime friend, mentor, and foster father, Dakota, the same Descoteaux who had accompanied the Pathfinder to the top of the peak in the Wind Rivers and saved the double-barreled rifle when the boat capsized in the canyon. The story is interesting not only for its content but for how it links Sun—through personal acquaintance, if not actual presence—to the country along the Sweetwater going back nearly sixty years. Finally, in 1900, a census taker reported that Sun couldn't read or write, and that he was born in Vermont. Although he was illiterate, the rancher would have understood by then that a foreign birth, if it became known, could jeopardize his title to his land.

More than land, however, it was a hunger for gold that first drew white men north from the line of the Union Pacific Railroad. Discoveries near South Pass filled the gulches there with miners. Frantic little boom towns sprang up—South Pass City, Atlantic City, Miner's Delight—and an army post at Camp Stambaugh. A new fort was built about halfway across the southern tier of the Territory at Fort Fred Steele, where the oncoming Union Pacific was due to cross the North Platte; the UP linked up with the Central Pacific to become transcontinental in 1869. At the same time, Lakota, Cheyenne and Arapaho people stayed generally north of the North Platte after the treaties of 1868; the Shoshone stayed generally west, along the base of the Wind River Mountains. White people swelled the new railroad towns strung across southern Wyoming Territory, but other than soldiers and prospectors, few ventured north.

Tom Sun's friend Boney Earnest—Bonaparte Napoleon Earnest—arrived ahead of the railroad at the new town of Rawlings Springs in May of 1868, when it was just surveyors' stakes and graders' shacks. He threw in with a band of Denver miners bound for South Pass, and on his way got his first long look at the Sweetwater. They traveled northwest past sand dunes and playa lakes, through Whiskey Gap to Devil's Gate, where they picked up the old emigrant road and followed it to the gold camps. For four more years, mining and prospecting took him elsewhere—Nevada, Idaho, California, and Utah—Boney would recall in the 1920s. In 1872 he returned to Rawlins, by now a prosperous railroad town and shipping hub with a shorter name.

At that time he met Tom Sun, a tall, dark-haired, dark-complected French Canadian in his late twenties. They formed "a joint stock company of two," for "trapping, hunting, and prospecting for gold and silver and other precious metals, besides scouting for [the] Government and," Boney wrote, as though it were just another commercial proposition, "fighting Indians."

He added, "This kind of life was not very remunerative, but always pleasant and exciting."[2]

The army had built Fort Fred Steele where the railroad crossed the North Platte. Soldiers from there found gold and silver prospects in the mountains north of Rawlins, and newspapers boomed the discoveries. Claims clustered where Whiskey Gap cut between the Ferris and Seminole mountains—yet another corruption of Seminoe, Charles Lajeunesse's old nickname—twelve miles southwest of Devil's Gate. In the spring of 1872, the *Laramie Sentinel* mentioned Boney as superintendent of the prospering Seminole Company at Seminole City, near Whiskey Gap. The city already had eight log houses, two saloons and a store, and any day there would be stage service from Rawlins and a thrice-weekly mail. Boney's ore was yielding between $13 and $26 per ton, and soon lead and silver mines in the Ferris Mountains were going strong as well. New discoveries were reported daily. One partnership expected to have a quartz mill running in just two months more.[3]

For several years, the papers reported only the good news, always a promising show from the mines, always a potential investor debarking at Rawlins and heading north for a look. Often gold, sometimes silver, copper, lead, and iron were in the prospects. In September 1875, Boney escorted Ferdinand V. Hayden himself to the Ferris Mountains to inspect the Matilda Jane. Hayden "believes it is a valuable mine and will pay big," another paper reported.[4]

There were no really big strikes, nothing like South Pass a few years earlier. Reports filtered out, too, of interest in the chemical possibilities of those dried lakebeds near the Sweetwater that emigrants a generation earlier had mined for saleratus. Soda lakes, they began to be called. Extracting it would require not much more than a shovel and a wagon.

From the newspapers' point of view, however, the soda lakes appeared to be deep in Indian country. At the same time, the papers began to mention buffalo around Whiskey Gap, or in the Rattlesnake Hills west of Red Buttes, and report that bands of Indians had been seen there, hunting; grass and game apparently were returning.

In the summer of 1874, Boney Earnest and a comrade were attacked downstream from Fort Steele by a band of Indians they estimated as two hundred strong. Boney may have exaggerated the size of the war party by five or ten times, but he may be right in thinking these were the same Indians who attacked the Seminole mining camps shortly afterward and killed a miner named Russian Ed. Colonel Anson Mills of Ft. Steele led about two hundred troops north from Rawlins.

Newspapers dubbed it variously the Sweetwater or the Big Horn expedition.[5] Mills established a big base camp in the meadows near Independence Rock, then led his troops north on a nineteen-day scout to the foothills of the southern Bighorns. They headed down the Powder River, briefly, then back south to Red Buttes and Independence Rock. Their worst luck was the loss of twenty-four horses in a snowstorm. They saw no Indians, though they assumed from the scarcity of game that Indians had been there ahead of them, before scattering north and east at the army's approach. "[C]onsequently the trip was fruitless," a Salt Lake City correspondent reported. By "fruitless" he meant no combat, no fight. "The Indians ought to be exterminated for living in such a country," he went on. "Plenty of grass for our animals, and good water, is the only thing I can say in favor of such a country," he concluded.[6]

The Indians they were chasing were probably Lakotas and perhaps Cheyennes; Arapahos already were unlikely by 1874 to be mounting long-distance raids. The papers mention Buffalo Bill Cody as a scout on Mills's expedition. Decades later, Boney Earnest recalled that he and Tom Sun also scouted for Mills as well that season.[7]

That may have been the last time the two partners drew government pay as scouts. But soon they were known as Indian fighters in the press in a way they hadn't been before. Sun was spotted in Rawlins in March 1875 with reports of having prospected the year before near the mouth of the Sweetwater and north into the Bighorns. "Mr. Sun is an old mountaineer," the *Laramie Sentinel* reported, as though introducing him to its readers, "and is, perhaps, better acquainted with this country than any other person in this vicinity, and is an authority in geography hereabouts." In April, a mail carrier reported that seventeen Indians had run off six horses at the Ferris mines. In May, Indians ran off four oxen belonging to William Hunt, who was trying to make a living on nearby Sand Creek. Hunt vowed vengeance, and, since the army wouldn't help, told the paper he would "get up a company of the best Indian fighters in the country" to get his stock back. Meanwhile, Sun and a man named Frank Harrington, prospecting near the mouth of the Sweetwater, were feared dead.

By the end of the month, however, Sun was quite alive and back in town for groceries. He reported that while he, Earnest, and Harrington were hunting Hunt's cattle, Indians pulled a switch and stole all their food and extra clothes while the white men were away from their camp. "Sun did not report what was done in return," the paper reported, "but it is surmised that all accounts between the party and 'Mr. Lo' have been amicably adjusted." ("Mr. Lo," an allusion to Alexander Pope's "Lo, the poor Indian!" was common code for Indian in the western press, often used to ridicule eastern sympathies for the tribes.) And the paper assumed as well that a company of cavalry, headed off toward the Seminole mines, wouldn't come up with much. "If they only go far enough they will find a few just as peaceable Indians as the sun ever shown upon," the paper punned.[8] Tom Sun was a force in the country, a man who knew how to build a reputation.

Meanwhile, capital was needed to develop the mineral prospects. After the railroad was built, a Baltimore physician named George B. Graff must have decided there was more money to be made in the newly accessible parts of the West. He looked first for gold and silver, but he knew geology and chemistry better than most of his competitors, and realized there might be money in sulfur, saltpeter, and the salts of soda—carbonate of soda, sulfate of soda, nitrate of soda. By 1875, Graff was well known around Rawlins. He kept his connections in the East too, and that same year a friend in New Haven, Connecticut, introduced him to Lammot du Pont, of the gunpowder du Ponts of Delaware.

Du Pont hired a mining engineer, Irving Stearns, to go inspect Graff's prospects. Graff took Stearns to the soda lakes near Independence Rock. Graff had been reporting that three inches of new salts crusted onto those lake bottoms each year, and thought millions of tons could be dug out at little expense; Stearns took samples, and when examined in du Pont's labs back east the results looked promising. By the spring of 1876, du Pont was eager to come out for a look himself.

Coincidentally, the day after Custer's disaster on the Little Bighorn, du Pont wrote the officer commanding Fort Steele for advice on the country north of Rawlins. There were no Indians around the soda lakes just now, the commander replied, but they could always show up on short notice, and the Sweetwater country "was one of their favorite haunts." In October, Graff advised du Pont that the Territory was safe.

In Rawlins they rented wagons and horses, bought tools, groceries, and 3,300 rounds of ammunition. There were ten in the party, including Graff, Stearns, du Pont, various cooks and wranglers, and the two guides: Tom Sun and Boney Earnest. They saw no Indians; all that ammunition was primarily for hunting. And du Pont got the time of his life. North of the mountains en route to the soda lakes, he and Sun, on horseback, chased a herd of elk for seventeen miles, the tycoon wrote home later. By the end of the chase, the elk had gained about two miles.[9]

Prospects of a soda-salts boom likewise stayed just out of reach. Graff led a party including Wyoming Territorial Governor John Hoyt on an elaborate two-day trip to the lakes two years later, but not much seems to have come of it. A lawsuit over ownership of the claims was settled in du Pont's favor in 1879, and the powder man's heirs owned the properties all the way up to 1977, when they were sold for $67,000.[10]

But by the late 1870s, mineral prospects closer to Rawlins clearly were not paying out. A party of the Hayden Survey returned to the valley in 1877. Government geologist Frederic Endlich reported only one store left at South Pass City, no one working the Ferris and Seminole mines, and a stamp mill there abandoned. "Indians and the railroad have produced isolation of this region," he reported, "which once bid fair to have a prosperous future." At Devil's Gate they found a few old cabins in ruins, piles of abandoned telegraph poles and tangles of abandoned wire, but no one, late in August, living there. At Independence Rock they found the remains of the army post where Pvt. Hervey Johnson had been stationed, and the remains, too, of what probably had been Col. Mills's base camp on the Indian chase three years before.

But now, eight years after the completion of the transcontinental railroad, eight years after the Sweetwater Valley ceased to be on the nation's main trunk road from coast to coast, Endlich found the hills and valley filled with game. It was early fall. Fog was thick in the hills south of the Sweetwater, fog and a cold, drizzling rain. "We heard elk 'squealing,'" he reported. There were deer and antelope, too. "The entire hill appeared to be alive with game." In the timber the men found themselves surrounded by elk; first a smaller band, then a band of four hundred. They shot two, a cow and an old bull, but both got away, wounded.

Sun and Earnest, meanwhile, were bringing clients steadily to the country. Earnest guided a party of English hunters from Rawlins all the way to the new Yellowstone Park. Sun stayed in the Sweetwater hills and valley with a party that included two Englishmen and the widow of the late president of the Bank of California, her children and a governess. One or both of these parties almost certainly contained the English sportsmen Endlich met near Whiskey Gap. One day he joined them, chasing buffalo. It got late: the English had to get back to their camp. Endlich and his companions kept on, and finally found two bulls "which were captured after an exciting chase," he reported. "It is surprising for how many bullets a buffalo can form the receptacle without dropping."[11]

And it is surprising how many animals a few men were willing to kill. The following year, Sun guided Edwin C. Johnson, a Connecticut mahogany importer and capitalist, on a six-week hunt. On the headwaters of Sage Creek, well east of the North Platte, they found elk in herds of a thousand or more, and abundant antelope and black-tailed (mule) deer. Primarily, they were after trophies. "See big bands of elk by the hundreds but big bulls scarce," Johnson wrote in his diary September 2. "I finally kill a nice one after Story has missed him twice. Put his horns into a tree [to retrieve later] and take tenderloins and tongue and leave the rest to rot." And

September 6: "Reach camp with two horses loaded with heads[,] tired and hungry."

A week later, out to collect elk heads they'd left the night before, Sun and Johnson surprised a grizzly feeding on one of the carcasses. As the men approached, the bear ran off and they followed it. Snow began to fall. The bear retreated into a canyon thick with pines, spruce, and fallen timber, the brush and tree limbs thickening with snow. They killed the bear in the thick brush. It took two hours to skin him. When Sun, six feet tall himself, stood and threw the skin over his shoulder, both ends dragged on the ground.

In nine days they killed ten bull elk and numerous deer and antelope. After almost two weeks they broke camp, headed back across the North Platte, and stopped for mail and a day's rest at the little settlement on Sand Creek. Then on to Sun's ranch at Devil's Gate, where Tom appears to have been well established.

That night at Sun's, Boney Earnest and two young Englishmen showed up with reports of plentiful buffalo to the north, up Horse Creek. Johnson, Sun, and Johnson's friend Story found the same herd the next day: "Story and I kill one big fellow and wound another. Tom cleans head, but I don't want it," Johnson wrote in his diary on September 17. By the 22nd, Story appears to have had his fill of killing. "He's too lazy to hunt," Johnson reported. "Tom and I go out for a look at the country. See three old buffalo bulls and I kill all in their tracks, for which I feel dreadfully ashamed, did not think I had hit all. Saw some black tail [deer] but killed none."

They returned to Sun's ranch, and Story rode off alone for Rawlins. But Johnson still hadn't gotten a bighorn sheep, so he and Sun rode east to the big canyon of the North Platte, where Frémont had dumped the rubber boat thirty-six years before. They scouted the rocky canyon walls for days, without luck. Back to the ranch again, then up into the granite hills behind it to the north and west. Still no sheep. At last they started for Rawlins and the railroad. On the way, they spent the night in an abandoned cabin, full of what Johnson called "mountain rats." They were down to eleven cartridges. The next day in the hills nearby, Johnson got his ram.

In Rawlins a political convention was in full swing, and every room in town was taken. Sun and Johnson slept in a hallway. "I feel a bad attack of rheumatism coming on in my left shoulder," he wrote next morning in his diary. "So ends the best hunt and trip of my life."[12] Sun had made an important friend, who would have money to invest when the time came.

Sparse as they were, these episodes of prospecting and commercial hunting would not have happened had the Arapahos, Cheyennes, Lakotas, and Shoshones still been hunting north of the Ferris and Seminoe mountains and along the Sweetwater. But the tribes' economies had been broken elsewhere. And when the Arapahos spent a few months at Independence Rock in the winter of 1877–78 on their way to the Shoshone Reservation, whites, if any were there, seem scarcely to have noticed. Perhaps Tom Sun's reputation kept them away from his ranch at Devil's Gate. Or perhaps he wintered in town.

Endlich, the government geologist, left a clear picture of what all that grass would mean for the future of the valley, though he didn't understand what he was seeing. On the same drizzly day he and his men wounded a cow and a bull elk, they found a cabin in one of the valleys east of Whiskey Gap, and men there putting up hay. At the Sand Creek settlement, yellow and back currants abounded along the creek banks and haymaking was already a business: men were cutting wild hay in the meadows and shipping it by wagon sixty miles to Rawlins, a grassless place with plenty of animals to feed. Then one evening late in August 1877, he and some other members of the party climbed Independence Rock and watched the long, slow show as fourteen riders bedded down a herd of 2,800 cattle bound east for Fort Laramie.

The men were "fully armed," Endlich reported. "Mounted on good 'cow-horses' the herders proceeded to 'round up' the stock, preparatory to camping for the night. . . . it was astonishing to see upon how small an area so many animals could be crowded together."[13] His use of quotation marks indicates the novelty of the terms, and the word "cowboy" seems still to have been outside his

Tom Sun, in a studio photo from the early 1880s, around the time he trailed his first herd of Oregon cattle to the Sweetwater Valley, married, and started a family at Devil's Gate. Courtesy of Wyoming State Archives.

vocabulary. Turning the herd onto good grass along the river, allowing it to graze, getting it calmed and compacted, would have taken
hours. Endlich must have watched for a long time, as afternoon
sloped into evening. An economy was changing before his eyes.

The cattle were almost certainly shorthorned Durhams trailing
in from eastern Oregon. Texas cattle, with their long horns and
wild ways, had proven too lean, disease-prone, and hard to handle.
The Durhams, by contrast, were placid, stolid, trail-hardy, and just
built, it seemed, to put on meat. By the following year, 1878, the
valley was beginning to fill up with stock. Governor Hoyt, on his
visit to the soda lakes, saw 25,000 cattle along the Sweetwater, the
newspapers reported, probably an exaggeration. Sun himself had
a hay meadow and at least a few cattle by then, Johnson noted.
And when the two men came out of the granite hills still sheepless,
they found five thousand cattle, recently arrived from points west,
grazing along the river upstream from Sun's new ranch.[14] These,
Johnson noted, belonged to a man named Stewart, who owned the
Quarter Circle 71 Ranch, already a bigger operation than Sun's,
and long to remain that way.

Early in 1880, Sun would take up a Desert Land entry on a section at Devil's Gate. By doing so, he began the three-year process
that would allow him legal title to a still unsurveyed square mile of
government land at the heart of a huge range he had every expec-
tation his cattle could graze till doomsday. With mining in decline,
and game only a transient, unreliable kind of plenty, it was time
now to fix title on some land. To run cattle, a person didn't need to
own much land outright; most of the land could remain in government hands and the grass was free. But Sun, Stewart, and a few others in the valley realized sooner than most that if a person owned
some land, with water on it, he could control a great deal more.
Legal title was one route to control. There were other routes, too.
A smart man would realize that certain stories, once circulated,
could further strengthen his hold.

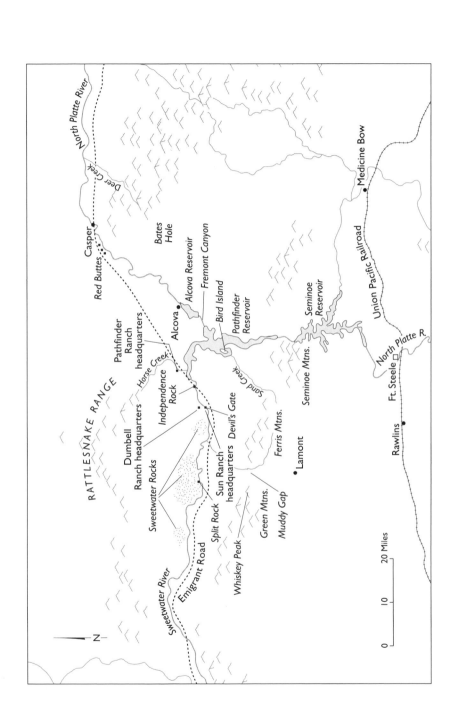

North Platte River

Deer Creek

Casper

Red Buttes

Bates Hole

RATTLESNAKE RANGE

Pathfinder Ranch headquarters

Horse Creek

Alcova

Alcova Reservoir

Fremont Canyon

Bird Island

Pathfinder Reservoir

Medicine Bow

Union Pacific Railroad

Seminoe Mtns.

Seminoe Reservoir

North Platte R.

Ft. Steele

Dumbell Ranch headquarters

Independence Rock

Devil's Gate

Sand Creek

Sweetwater Rocks

Sun Ranch headquarters

Ferris Mtns.

Lamont

Rawlins

Split Rock

Green Mtns.

Muddy Gap

Whiskey Peak

Sweetwater River

Emigrant Road

N

0    10    20 Miles

# CHAPTER 10

# Township and Range

> But one day in 1875 Mr. Grant told me they had just closed a
> contract for extensive government surveys along and in the
> vicinity of the Union Pacific Railway, and the execution of
> which would take us to the west boundary of Wyoming Ter-
> ritory and keep us in the field till winter. I cannot adequately
> express the happiness that was mine when I heard this glori-
> ous news.
>
> —*Billy Owen, about 1930*

Formal land law first entered the Sweetwater Valley in the person of an ambitious, short-legged little surveyor named Billy
Owen, not yet twenty-one years old when his employers sent him
from Laramie to Rawlins to meet Tom Sun. Billy found Sun "a tall,
rawboned man of very dark complexion." They met in the office
of a Rawlins lawyer. "Tom looked me over very much as he would
have done with a steer he contemplated buying," Billy remembered
fifty years later, "but his countenance gave no inkling of his mental
estimate of me."[1]

All his life, Billy seems to have worried about others' estimates
of him; everything to him was a race. He had to show himself the
fastest walker, runner, and climber on the survey crew, the best shot,
the hardest worker, and the quickest study of his craft. For besides
competition, he loved the work; he loved the mental exercise of it
as much as the physical. He loved trigonometry and he loved dead

reckoning; he loved the mules, he loved camp life, and he loved the equipment. In particular, he loved the Burt's solar compass, which, with its tripod, weighed twenty-three pounds.

Government contracts required use of solar compasses, as they showed true north and south by means of the sun, not by an unreliable magnetic needle. All his life Billy remembered the day when he noticed a survey crew near Laramie—"just east of Laramie," was how it lingered in the memory of an old man always aware of the compass points. He was eleven or twelve; this would have been about 1870, the railroad still a novelty and the creator of a permanent demand for knowing whose property was whose. Curious, the boy approached the men. His future employer showed Billy how the compass worked. "[W]hen he showed me the sun's image on a little silver plate and explained how it gave the meridian . . . I was completely enthralled for I always delighted in anything pertaining to astronomy."[2] He may at that age have delighted in the sun and stars for themselves, but it's safe to assume he soon came to love them for their utility. They allowed a trained person to lay an abstract, orderly pattern—a grid from heaven, it must have seemed like—on the uneven, disorderly land. Reference to the pattern would allow even untrained people to distinguish whose land was whose, and then the land could be used peacefully, and without conflict. At least, that was the idea.

The idea didn't really come from heaven, of course; it came from Thomas Jefferson. After the Revolution, while the loose-knit United States were still governed by the Articles of Confederation, Jefferson led the committee that wrote the law dividing the public domain into square townships, six miles on a side. The new grid would be laid on land that suddenly now belonged to the new national government, provided one ignored all tribal claims, as most whites did. Among the compromises necessary to form a nation were the states' agreements to relinquish their longstanding, pre-Revolutionary claims to western land, in particular the land north of the Ohio River and west of the present western border of Pennsylvania and Maryland. The Land Ordinance of 1785 provided that townships were to be further surveyed into thirty-six sections of a square mile each. The first government surveys began in what is now southeast Ohio in 1785. A second ordinance, in 1787, set up a mechanism by which territories could be established, and later admitted as states on an equal footing with the original thirteen. More important for this discussion, the Northwest Ordinance, as it came to be called, allowed for sale of the lands at one dollar per acre, or $640 per square-mile section. Conflict immediately arose between speculators, who wanted to be able to buy the land wholesale and hold it until later demand would inflate prices, and small farmers, who wanted to buy land in small lots on easy terms, for immediate use. The speculators won the first round. The ordinance allowed for the sale of nothing smaller than a full section. Within a few weeks, Congress approved the sale of more than six million acres in the Ohio country, most of it to just two associations of speculators.[3]

Conflicts between land speculators and small farmers would continue, however, to pull Congress first one way, then another. Under the new Constitution, the new federal government needed the land-sale revenues to pay off the war debts it had assumed from the states. Land speculators continued to find friendly ears in Congress, while small landowners continued to clamor for the right to buy smaller and smaller plots on easier and easier terms. Congress, as it always has, dealt with a difficult problem piecemeal, and by the time Billy Owen and Tom Sun headed north from Rawlins in a wagon in July 1880, there were at least six different ways a person could legally take up federal land in Wyoming Territory. Many settlers cheerfully ignored all six for decades. Sun, though he could not read and could only write his name, had a good lawyer, and he seems to have been eager to protect his interests by taking advantage of everything the law would allow him.

For his part, Billy seems not to have had any particular desire to own land for himself, only to bring all the land he could walk over in a lifetime under a system of orderly survey. He was fourteen when he started working summers for William Downey and Mortimer Grant, the surveyors who'd first shown him how the solar compass worked a few years before. In 1875, when he turned sixteen, Billy's employers landed the contract to survey the alternating sections of railroad and government lands along the route of the Union Pacific. The Union Pacific and the Central Pacific were given enormous land grants to undertake the otherwise losing proposition of building a railroad across a continent where few inhabitants might want to ship anything in or out. The land was given the railroads in alternating, square-mile sections, stretching like a checkerboard twenty miles north and twenty miles south of the right of way. In 1875, Downey and Grant started surveying about in the middle of the Territory and worked westward toward the Utah border.

They worked fast. Billy remembered years later that Downey ran one crew, Grant the second, and with just those two they were able to finish the work in a single season. Being near the railroad helped; the UP provided a boxcar for horses, wagon, and equipment, and a second car for the men's bedding, food, and tents. Each party, in open country, could finish the interior and exterior lines in a thirty-six-square-mile township, eighty-four miles altogether, in about a week. The compassman would send his flagman out ahead along the appropriate direction. While both were still

Billy Owen, probably in the late 1870s, when as a teenager he went to work for Downey & Grant in Laramie, surveying the checkerboard lands along the Union Pacific Railroad across Wyoming Territory. Courtesy of American Heritage Center, University of Wyoming.

in sight of each other, the flagman would stop, realign himself by the compassman's arm gestures, and plant a flag precisely on the proper line. Then the two chainmen would start from the section corner where the compassman had set up his instrument, to measure the distance to the next corner. Probably they used a sixty-six-foot, hundred-link Gunter's chain, standard already for 250 years by Billy's time. This odd device simplified the surveyors' arithmetic, as it allowed all distances to be conveniently divided into twos, fours or tens, as needed; ten square chains made an acre, and eighty chains made a mile. Monuments were set at every section corner and at the half-mile spots between them. Usually the monuments were rocks, with a depression dug around them. Once or twice Billy used big dinosaur femurs.

And speed, more than accuracy, was on everyone's mind. The sooner the land was surveyed, the sooner the railroad could sell it. The land-grant railroads became, by default, land companies as much as they were railroad companies: especially in the early years of their existence the bulk of their profits came from selling off the land they'd been granted free. The checkerboard system had originally been worked out to prevent monolithic blocks of land from ending up in the hands of speculators, and to help raise the value of the alternating sections that remained in government hands. Once the Homestead Act of 1862 made government land available for free, however, it had an opposite effect, deflating the value of the surrounding railroad lands. White people were slow to move into the area in any case, and in southwest Wyoming, where the land is so dry it has minimal use even for grazing, the great majority of the checkerboard sections are still either government or railroad property.[4]

In Billy's time, everyone had high hopes for riches. Downey and Grant were paid by the mile; all incentives were to get as many miles covered as fast as possible. Just as, among cowboys, the horseback arts became prized, among surveyors the most admiration went to long-legged stamina and a keen sense of direction. Billy didn't let his short stature slow him down, however. "I wasn't particularly fast," he wrote, "on a square heel-and-toe walk—my legs were too short—and when my companions got a little ambitious and speeded up I was compelled to go into a dog trot to keep up with them. Now, that was my favorite pace."[5]

In 1878, his smarts and eagerness got him promoted to assistant compassman. His boss, William Downey, cared enough about science and history to arrange it that Billy's crew topped the Snowy Range the day of the total solar eclipse, July 29. On Medicine Bow Peak, 12,013 feet above sea level, they used the telescope on their Burt's compass "and turned it till the sun's image fell on the little plate." As they watched, the little bite out of the sun's disc grew bigger and bigger until, just before totality, they looked west. "Over that vast forest the moon's shadow was advancing with a speed and a rush that almost took one's breath." Totality lasted two and a half minutes, during which it was too dark, Billy remembered later, to read his watch, and the corona was more colorful than a rainbow or the northern lights.[6]

That year and the following, they worked south of the checkerboard, up the valleys of the Laramie and North Platte rivers toward Colorado. Working from a baseline of latitude, the so-called Third Standard Parallel, which runs east and west about three miles north of the Colorado-Wyoming border, they would first establish the exterior borders of the townships, then return later to run the interior lines, dividing the townships into sections. Each Wyoming township was given a township number, moving sequentially north, and a range number, moving west from the Sixth Principal Meridian, which runs north-south through southeast Nebraska. Independence Rock, for example, is located in Township 29 North, Range 87 West. And the townships that Billy and his colleagues were surveying in those summers included Township 24 North, Range 85 West, in the upper valley of the North Platte. The settlers there, at least according to Billy, were eager to have the government grid laid on the ground so they could take up legal claims.

In 1880, Downey and Grant were hired to run 105 miles of the line between Albany and Carbon counties. That same year, Billy's bosses thought enough of him to send him to Rawlins alone on a smaller job—to locate some ranches on Sand Creek, north of the

Seminole mining district, and to locate a couple of mineral claims for Tom Sun.

Unless they had reason to hurry, it would have been a two-day wagon ride from Rawlins to the little settlement on Sand Creek, where Sun and Johnson had stopped to pick up their mail on their hunting trip two years earlier. Billy found the ranchers there, too, eager for a survey to firm up their squatters' rights. He reported that he and Sun stayed at the house of one of the five ranch families that had hired him. As there had been no public-land grid run in the district yet, Billy surveyed the ranches the old-fashioned way, by metes and bounds. He tied his surveys to hilltops, stream confluences and the like, noting the distances and compass bearings between them, and counting on his clients to help him plant the flags and run the chains.

More people and cattle were coming into the country at that time. Even though they must have known that the government survey would arrive in their valley before too much longer, the fact that these families took the trouble to hire Billy shows some unease on their part—or at least a need to legalize what they had. Either on the spot or later, Billy gave them plats showing their property lines, and field notes describing the steps he'd taken to mark out the pieces they wanted.[7] From these, they could have worked up more conventional descriptions after the township-and-range grid was laid over the land a year or two later. And they could have done those descriptions themselves; the system was so simple.

Across the Midwest and West, the same system is still in effect. You can describe any piece of land by describing its niche in the grid. Take a 640-acre section. The so-called northeast fourth would be the 160-acre square in the northeasternmost quarter of the section. The northeast fourth of the northeast fourth would be the forty-acre square in the northeasternmost quarter of the quarter section, and so on. In a thirty-six-section township, the sections are numbered from right to left from the upper right—northeast—corner, then from left to right across the second, six-section tier, and so on. For example, the south half of the southwest fourth of the northeast fourth of section 31, Township 25 North, Range 86 West, describes a twenty-acre, east-west running oblong—half a quarter quarter section—with its southwesternmost corner in the center of the southeasternmost section—number 31—of that particular township's thirty-six sections.

The grid worked well as a mechanism for describing and identifying a particular piece of ground, and therefore it made land simple to claim, buy, and sell, because everyone could easily understand which piece was under discussion and exactly how big it was. But this pattern of equal-sized squares also carried with it, as time went on, assumptions about other kinds of homogeneity. Congress passed laws that assumed, at their heart, that one section would be worth about the same as the next. Across much of the Midwest, with its relatively even terrain and even rainfall, this was true. But after the Civil War, as the grid continued out into the semiarid high plains and beyond, that equality of quality, section to section, evaporated.

In 1841, Congress passed the Preemption Act, which gave legal status to the old custom of squatters' rights. Settlement on the parcel of public land was required before a family could file a claim on it, but survey was not. A single man, a family, or a widow—not a single woman, note—could "enter," that is, take up, 160-acre, quarter-section parcels for $1.25 per acre, cash. The government would not issue the patent until a formal survey had been made and approved at some later date. Because of its terms, this system was often called a cash entry.

In 1862, with the Civil War on and the South unrepresented in Congress, Congress passed the Homestead Act, which allowed a family head or a single adult man *or woman* to enter a claim on 160 acres. The so-called "entryman" (or woman) could get a patent for free after five years if he or she could prove on the testimony of two credible witnesses that he or she had lived on and worked the land the entire time. This was called "proving up." Because the land it offered was free, and because free land for the small, white landholder was the strongest single ideal that swept the Republicans to power in 1860, the Homestead Act has been remembered when many more commonly used methods of taking up federal land have long been forgotten. Few people proved up, especially in the drier regions. As the grid began to tic-tac-toe the plains of central Nebraska and western Kansas, 160 acres were simply too few to support a family. People began to discover that not all sections were the same. Most had cactus, some had canyons, some had mountains, some had creeks and hay meadows, some had alkali flats. Few had much water, and only the ones with mountains had forests. All, from time to time, suffered prolonged drought. But almost as damaging was the false hope that came with equally long wet cycles. Enthusiasts like Cyrus Thomas, Hayden's frock-coated "agriculturalist," became convinced the world was getting better permanently, because, from time to time, it got wetter for a while.

Because Thomas and others like him had convinced the nation that rain not only would follow the plow but that more trees, too, could cause more rain to fall, Congress in 1873 approved the Timber Culture Act. A person could enter on 160 acres and, after seven years, prove up on them for free—if the person also planted and cared for 40 acres of trees on the 160-acre claim. Such a feat was nearly impossible in Wyoming, but that didn't prevent a number of entrymen in the Sweetwater country and elsewhere from filing Timber Culture entries. It was a convenient way to control a piece of land for nothing for a long time—seven years. Finally the law caused so much fraud it was repealed in 1891.

More successful was the Desert Land Act of 1877, which offered a full square mile—640 acres—of arid land for $1.25 per acre to any claimant who brought water to it and grew a crop within three years of filing. The law did not specify how much water need be brought, nor how many of the 640 acres need be watered, and so in Wyoming at least it became the quickest way for a person to acquire title to the most government land.

And finally, soldiers leaving the army were given land bounties—coupons—redeemable for 100 to 1,000 acres of government land, depending on their rank. This practice began in the Revolutionary War and continued up to the Civil War. Speculators often bought up the scrip at deep discounts, and sold it later at face value to people with cash to buy land. Long after new bounties ceased to be issued, land scrip continued to circulate.[8]

Theoretically at least, once the township-and-range grid arrived, each settler family on Sand Creek would have been able to assemble a ranch of 1,120 acres. The family could combine a 160-acre cash entry, a 160-acre Homestead claim, a 160-acre Timber Culture entry, and a 640-acre Desert Land entry. Only cash entries and homestead claims required actual residence on the land; the other two types were often popular with people trying to hold the land from a distance.[9]

Next stop for Sun and Owen was the mining district in the hills nearby where Tom needed Billy to locate a couple of mining claims. Such claims on public land came, and still come, in two categories: placer claims and lode claims. Placer claims are for mineral resources that lie on the surface—gold in a gravel bed, for example. Lode claims allow a prospector to claim a mineral vein, or lode, where it comes to the surface, and at the same time to follow it underground as far as it leads. Lode claims are nearly the same size as the twenty-acre placer claims, but only one shape—600 feet by 1,500 feet. Under the mining law Congress passed in 1872, a claimant can hold either kind of claim indefinitely by doing $100 worth of work on it per year. If the claimant ever decides the claim is valuable enough to own, he can buy a patent for just $2.50 per acre, after he's done at least $500 worth of improvements on the claim. In the mountains, they located two of Sun's gold claims, the Emeletta and the Deserted Treasure, and headed back for Rawlins.

There, Sun's lawyer Homer Merrell informed him that the two claims had been disputed, and the matter would have to go to court. That meant they needed an *official* survey of the two claims; something Billy could be licensed to do in a few weeks, when he turned twenty-one, but not until then. So Sun went back to his ranch, and Billy waited in Rawlins until his birthday, August 22. Merrell had it all worked out. Approval arrived by wire from Cheyenne, the closest outpost of the federal General Land Office, and Billy became a deputy U.S. mineral surveyor for the Territory of Wyoming. Sun came back to Rawlins, Sun and Owen headed back out again for the claims, made the official survey, and Sun won his case. And according to Billy, at least, the rancher was always grateful.[10]

The survey business boomed as the township-and-range grid extended north from the checkerboard. In 1881, Downey and Grant won enough contracts to keep twelve full crews going. Billy started out in charge of a crew of five men, but soon seems to have been in charge of several crews more. They worked north from the railroad at Medicine Bow, angling northeast across Sheep Creek to Bates Hole, then across the North Platte and past Red Buttes to Poison Spider Creek and the Rattlesnake Mountains, then south to the Sweetwater at Independence Rock, and up the familiar emigrant route to South Pass.

By the time they got to Bates Hole, there were thirty men in the party, and the cook was feeling overwhelmed. Billy took an empty wagon and headed south to Fort Steele. The government contract allowed Billy to draw any supplies he needed at army posts, which he proceeded to do. He also counted himself lucky to find an experienced hand willing to sign on as cook. This was Jim Averell, thirty years old, just discharged as a sergeant a few days earlier after two five-year hitches in the army. Billy may not have known that Averell had shot a man to death the year before in a bar in Buffalo, far to the north on the edge of the Powder River Basin. He also may not have known that Averell had spent several months since then in jail in Rawlins, awaiting what turned out to be a favorable disposition of his case—charges were dropped. Or Billy may have picked up the talk about Averell's past, and hired the man anyway. A decent cook was a lucky find.

So it was that Billy and his crews brought township and range to central Wyoming. Fifty years later, Billy would recall the high points—including a wild, disorganized bear hunt when thirty men armed with six rifles and two pistols but a thousand rounds of ammunition chased three bears through thickets along Bates Creek—more than he did the routine survey work. And in his memory he collapsed two years of effort, 1881 and 1882, into just 1881. But he also kept survey notes, as he was required to do, which preserved such detail as the particular monument set at each section corner and quarter corner, but also included a more general description of the terrain of each township. For T29N, R86W Billy wrote:

> The ~~land in~~ surface of this Township is generally rolling with some hilly and mountainous land in the SE portion ~~and~~ and considerable amount of level River bottom along Sweetwater River. It is covered with vegetation of Sage brush and Bunchgrass. Timber of Pine and Cedar.
>
> The soil is 2$^{nd}$ & 3$^{rd}$ rate. The Township is well watered by the Sweetwater River which runs near the centre from S.W. to N.E. There are ~~three~~ four Soda Lakes in the N.E. ~~W.~~ portion, containing carbonate of soda. Some portions of the Tp. Are excellent for agriculture and it is 1$^{st}$ class for grazing purposes.
>
> A very prominent land mark is in this Township viz : Independence Rock on the Old California Trail and its crossing with the Sweetwater River. upon the slope of which, is situated the corner to Secs. 9-10-15-16.[11]

In the next township to the west, T29N, R87W, Billy made no note of Devil's Gate, though he did say there were "many settlers and improvements" in the area. One of the improvements would have been Tom Sun's ranch.

Methodically protecting his interests, as always, Sun had entered a Desert Land claim in February 1880 on 640 acres in sections 34 and 35 along the Sweetwater near Devil's Gate. Billy may have done that survey too in 1880, when he did the locations for the Sand Creek ranchers and the mineral claims for Sun. On the initial Desert Land entry, the claim would have been described by metes and bounds. Billy came to the Sweetwater valley a second time in 1882, bringing with him the township and range grid that served Sun's purposes perfectly.

Sun filed his affidavit of final proof on the claim late the same year. In it he swore, and two witnesses swore likewise, that he had done everything necessary to take title to a square mile of public land under the Desert Land Act. He swore that he was thirty-seven years old, a stock raiser in Carbon County. He swore that he was a native-born citizen—not true, according to what he told the 1880 census taker. But had he admitted in the affidavit that he was not native born, he would have had to declare his intention to take up citizenship and then follow through.[12] He swore that he had made the initial entry nearly three years earlier, February 28, 1880, and that the land in question occupied a series of forty-acre squares running east and west through sections 34 and 35 along both sides of the river. He swore that he had irrigated the land, as the law required—not the first two years, but successfully enough the third year to raise "hay, oats, alfalfa, potatoes, and other vegetables" on the east end of the claim, the end closest to Devil's Gate. He swore he raised ten acres of vegetables altogether, and cut about fifty tons of hay off the rest of the land. He dug three main ditches, one a sixth of a mile long, a second 600 yards long, and a third between 500 and 600 yards long to bring water to the land from Rush and Pete creeks, Sweetwater tributaries flowing up from the south. Many smaller ditches took the water from the main ditches out onto the land. The main ditches, he swore, were three feet wide and two feet deep, and water flowed in them, in 1882, from May through July.

Sun's claims are supported by affidavits from two witnesses. George Graff—the same George Graff who had brought Lammot du Pont to the Sweetwater six years earlier to check out the soda prospects—swore that he had known Sun for twelve years and known the land at Devil's Gate for ten. Graff swore he'd visited the property five or six times in 1882. He put the vegetable plot at three acres, not ten, but otherwise backed up Sun completely. Edwin Johnson, Sun's hunting client from 1878, swore he'd known Sun for five years. And he was familiar with the claim, he said, from living near the land, and on it, and from helping dig the ditches.

Both men also swore, as the affidavit required witnesses to do, that they did not have "any interest, direct or indirect, in this entry," its land, or its water. Graff almost certainly held various mineral properties jointly with Sun over the years, but probably no real estate. Johnson, by contrast, had by this time invested heavily in the ranch at Devil's Gate. He wasn't just a visiting friend and ditch digger that summer; he was a full-fledged partner and would remain so for several more years. Sun almost certainly used Johnson's cash to buy cattle; Sun's name alone went onto the land patents and property deeds.

Finally, on the Desert Land affidavit Sun swore that he held legal title to the water he had brought onto the land and planned to continue irrigating perpetually. But that ownership, he added, "is not a matter of record." Sun didn't really need a water right on the river; the meadows there were naturally fertile enough to grow any hay he needed to cut. And he was running a ranch in any case, not a vegetable farm.

The following summer, 1883, Tom Sun paid the remaining $640 he owed on the claim; the patent was finally issued to him in 1889. On December 18, 1883, he married Mary Agnes Hellihan, a twenty-seven-year-old Irishwoman with family in Omaha, who had worked five years at the railroad hotel in Rawlins. Their first child was born in 1884. The scout, prospector, hunting guide, and now stock raiser had become a family man. His family would hold the land for a long time.

Where filing the documents and paying the fees would give him permanent, legal title to a small piece of the public domain, cattle and custom would give him control of a great deal more. In 1882, Sun began stocking his range in earnest. From Rawlins he took a handful of drovers with him by train to Utah, and then northwest by stage through Idaho Territory to eastern Oregon. There, in Baker City, he hired more men, bought horses and wagons, and bought 2,800 Durham cattle, descendants of the animals that settlers had been trailing west for four decades. The Durhams, as we have seen, were far superior to the Texas cattle then arriving in other parts of Wyoming. Sun and his drovers took them east on the old emigrant route—across the sagebrush plains and lava rocks of Idaho, into Wyoming, over South Pass, down the Sweetwater, and home, probably a four-month trip.[13]

When he got to Devil's Gate, Sun turned the cattle loose. Already, the country was starting to fill up. Just downstream, on the other side of Devil's Gate, a man named Schoonmaker had started the Dumbell Ranch. Farther downstream, six miles below Independence Rock where Horse Creek flows into the Sweetwater from the north, a man named Foley had started the 76 Ranch and was running cows on the good grass along the river and by the creek. Upstream from Sun, two brothers named Jackson were running cattle on the Sweetwater near Split Rock. Farther west lay the Durbin brothers' headquarters and beyond the Durbins, up by Three Crossings, was the Quarter Circle 71 Ranch, soon called simply the 71.

The first cattle herds to be brought into the country were small and their owners watched them closely, keeping the animals close to the ranchers' dugouts or cabins, and protecting them from weather and predation. By the early 1880s a more efficient custom was spreading over the ranges—more efficient, at least, in terms of human labor. Ranchers turned the cows loose and hoped for the best. For a time, it worked splendidly.

Twice a year they had to gather the cattle, in spring to brand the new calves, and in the fall to wean the calves from their mothers and choose which ones to trail to the nearest railroad and ship. The rest of the time, summer and winter, cattle were left to their own devices. The grass seemed endless, labor costs were low, and beef prices, early in the decade at least, stayed high. Profits soared. Word got out. A new kind of boom was on, a cattle boom. Money flowed in from eastern and British investors who bought herds sight unseen on book counts—cattle tallies based solely on a theoretical rate of increase, one year to the next. Besides Edwin Johnson of Connecticut, Sun took on a second partner, St. John Rae Reid, an Englishman and like Johnson a former hunting client. Unlike many ranches, however, Sun's continued to be run by its original owner. In 1880, there were about three million head of cattle in Wyoming. By 1886 that figure had tripled.[14]

Grass was free, and the range unfenced. Like Sun's, most cattle were run from a small patch of claimed or patented land over vast stretches of land that was still public. As long as the grass was free and the country uncrowded, there was little incentive for a rancher to take up much land at all. His cows ran loose and mingled with his neighbors'. For the system to work, there had to be a neighborly way to separate them from time to time, so that some cattle could be sold and profits taken. Informal at first, more organized as the years went by, the custom of the roundup arose.

Solitary representatives—reps, they were called—from different ranches in a district would work together on a single crew to gather, sort, and brand the cattle if it was spring, or gather, sort, and wean them if it was fall. Each crew would work for a single foreman, supported by a cook with his chuck wagon, and a horse wrangler to handle the herd of replacement mounts. The roundup would follow the shape of the particular country—up one drainage, over a divide and down the next, gathering and working the cattle as it went. The spring work could extend well into July. The fall's work might begin as soon as August. Cowboys stayed busy the whole time from the last snowfall to the first. County-based and, later, Territory-wide associations of stock growers were formed to plan out the logistics of these roundups—which ranches would commit which resources and how many reps to cover which territory.

The system worked well at first, but things got dicier as more herds were brought in. Added competition for grass meant the herds didn't increase as fast as the book counts showed they should. With so much beef coming to market, prices flattened. Investors got nervous. Some cowboys began building herds of their own, using methods their employers had encouraged for years. They branded so-called mavericks, the cattle that slipped through the roundup unbranded and were therefore, for all practical purposes, unowned. Distrust grew between owners and employees with small, private herds until the suspected thieves were banned from the roundups altogether. Eventually, the blackballed men started roundups of their own.

Then a drouthy summer further weakened a range already weak from overgrazing, and a terrible winter followed. Cattle died by the millions on the northern plains. Owners of the big outfits that remained began blaming all their woes on cattle thieves. Finally, in 1892, two dozen members of the Wyoming Stock Growers Association would hatch a plan to hire two dozen professional regulators from Texas, and would ride with them north into Johnson County and kill small owners and thieves.

When Sun began stocking his range with Oregon cattle, the so-called Johnson County War was still ten years away. The fault lines were real enough between owner and worker, big landholder and small, first comer and newcomer, but the earthquake hadn't come yet; the faults had yet to slip. Such forces are easy to see in hindsight, but nearly invisible close up.

One person did see what was going on, however, at least in a general way. John Wesley Powell saw that people trying to make a sustainable living on arid land were headed for trouble. He understood that it wasn't just a matter of people and land, but that it was a three-way difficulty. It was about people, land, *and water.* The township-and-range system was only about people and land. It took no account of the great gap in value between watered land and dry in arid country, and therefore it would not keep trouble at bay. He proposed a new model that would encourage cooperation, instead of speculation and monopoly.

In 1878, Powell, Hayden's competitor in Washington, wrote out his ideas and proposed solutions in a report for the commissioner of the General Land Office, the arm of the Department of Interior charged with transferring public land into private hands. Best known then and now as the explorer of the Colorado River, Powell, like Hayden, was chief of one of the four government surveys in the West, and as such was often in conflict with Hayden for government funds for science. Congress soon would consolidate the four surveys into the U.S. Geological Survey. Powell would emerge as its director, and with his new power would try to put his ideas in action.

With the Homestead Act only sixteen years old, the Timber Culture Act five years old, and the Desert Land Act only a year old, it was already clear to Powell that the public-land system was a tool of monopoly and thick with fraud. Railroads had turned the quirks

of the land system into monopoly power, and now mining and cattle companies were doing it too, Powell believed. Soon, he feared,
the most power of all would flow to whoever could monopolize the
water. It was not too late, he was sure, to change things.

To begin with, the General Land Office itself was outrageously
corrupt, both in Washington and in its branch offices in the western territories. Congress kept the clerks' pay low, morale stayed
low with it, turnover was high and the officials were susceptible
to persuasion by outside interests. Cronyism was rampant at the
higher levels, and yet protests from the region most affected—the
West—were nonexistent. People wanted land; they didn't want government officials paying much attention to how closely they followed the rules for taking it up.[15]

From his years directing his survey in Utah, Powell had an alternative model in his head: a Mormon model, not based on the township-and-range grid, but based on the qualities of arid landscapes.
Mormon traditions of land use were not particularly democratic—
high-status Mormons got a lot more and better land than low-sta-
tus Mormons—but they were decidedly cooperative. The Mormon
theocracy in territorial Utah made land available to settlers only in
ten to eighty-acre blocks, and made sure there was enough water to
irrigate all the blocks available. Grazing land was a separate cate-
gory. With these models in mind, Powell recommended in his 1878
report that the government needed to come up with two new categories for agricultural land in the West. Under the first, concerning irrigable lands, a farmer or a family would own no more than
eighty acres, but any nine or more landholders could organize an
irrigation district, using only land that government surveyors had
certified as irrigable. Powell was silent on how the irrigation projects should be organized, designed, and financed. But he was clear
that the irrigators should own the water jointly, and trusted that
they would be able to design and build projects that would benefit
all who held a stake in them.

Grazers, too—men like Foley, Schoonmaker, Sun, the Jacksons,
and the Durbins on the Sweetwater in 1882—would have to cooperate if they wanted to take up public land. Powell recommended the

public land be available in pasturage homesteads. Each homestead would be large—at least four sections, 2,560 acres, with a water right attached to each homestead sufficient for growing twenty acres of hay to feed the cattle or sheep through the winter. These ranches would be organized into grazing districts of, again, nine or more landholders each. Once organized, the district members could graze their stock in large, common, unfenced pastures, much as the Mormons had already been doing for decades. Congress drew up two bills, but they never got out of committee. Powell's ideas were met by a vast silence.[16]

Late in the 1880s, Powell persuaded Congress to put all public land sales on hold while his agency surveyed and sorted irrigable lands from non-irrigable, grazable from not. All the new data, he was sure, would then make for good new law, establishing orderly, cooperative use of the public domain. The moratorium soon collapsed under pressure from the very interests it was meant to keep at bay, and Powell's career collapsed with it. Still, on quiet days along the Sweetwater, it's hard not to hear the winds of missed opportunity, and to wonder how things might have turned out in the West had Powell's ideas succeeded.

All that was a decade in the future when Billy Owen, with a cook named Jim Averell on his survey crew, first brought the township and range grid to the Sweetwater Valley. Fifty years later, Billy remembered Averell as "diligent and industrious . . . punctual and courteous . . . never out of humor," the last, especially, a quality rare among cooks. Yet Averell carried a deck of marked cards, and said he had made a good deal of money over the years in the army, playing poker. "And yet," Billy continues in his recollections, "I would have trusted Jim Averell with a mission even where a goodly sum of money was involved."

In early fall, the survey crew camped on the meadows on Horse Creek, a mile or two upstream from its confluence with the Sweetwater. Some small irrigation ditches branch through those meadows now, and big cottonwood trees shade the houses, barns, and corrals of the headquarters of the Pathfinder Ranch. Away from the corrals you can imagine the place without its improvements, trees, or ditches and tell that, even then, it would have been a lovely spot. Averell, Billy recalled, asked for "the numbers"—the township and range descriptions—of the land where they were camped. He wanted to file on the land and settle there as soon as he could, Billy remembered.[17] It didn't happen quite that way, or quite that soon.

When Billy Owen brought the township-and-range grid to the land along the Sweetwater, a story came with it. It was an abstract pattern, a new story that nevertheless contained centuries of understanding of how an elemental thing like land could become a fragmented thing to be owned. It was a system and so it was a silent story, invisible, little spoken of, but no less real for that. Averell and Sun stand as well as any two figures for what happened: the new story tangled with the old custom, the system that Sun and the other firstcomers felt obliged to preserve.

Personalities had a good deal to do with what happened as well, especially because a third personality, the wild card in a deck already marked for trouble, was a woman. She was very stubborn. After her death, the Cheyenne newspapers would name her Cattle Kate.

# CHAPTER 11

# Neighbors

Next morning I took a pony that formerly belonged to my daughter and visited the place where she was hanged. It is on the south side of the Sweetwater where a small canon runs up into the rocks and at a point where some small pine are growing at the head of the canon. After going around a little I came upon the very identical tree she was hanged on. It was a pine tree where some large rocks raised out of the ground about four feet high near a large limb that extended out from the tree over the rock, and from what I could learn it was from off this very rock they were swung into eternity.

—*Thomas Watson, 1889*

A person who steps out from under the deep shade of the cottonwoods around the Pathfinder Ranch can see ten miles in any direction, and in some directions thirty or more to the crests of distant ridges. No neighbors are visible anywhere and, except for pines and junipers in the gulches among the granite hills, no trees. South of the ranch a 500-foot outcrop known sometimes as Averell Mountain rises up from the west side of Horse Creek. It blocks the view down toward the Sweetwater and to the Sentinel Rocks beyond, but a person can still see to the southwest toward Independence Rock and Devil's Gate. About a mile north of the Pathfinder headquarters, one notices a passing car or semi from time to time, its windshield glinting in the sun. This is Wyoming 220, the main road from Casper to Rawlins.

When I visited the ranch one day in late June, Ruth Stevenson was sitting at a table by her picture window, steadily pushing the redial button on her telephone. An entry deadline was looming for a Fourth of July rodeo down in Nebraska; Ruth was obligingly taking care of entries for her grown sons and ranch hands. But it seemed every other rodeo family in the West had the same idea at the same time, and the number was constantly busy, so Ruth kept pushing the button. Finally she got through, and took care of her business. Except for one small girl sitting quietly on the couch, everyone else—family, employees and their families—was over at the Dumbell Ranch at Devil's Gate, branding. The week before, Norman and Gaynell Park of the Dumbell and a similar contingent of relatives and employees had been here at the Pathfinder for the Pathfinder branding. But now Ruth's house was quiet. The corrals outside her window were empty, and just two or three horses frisked in a small pasture beyond, driven up from Horse Creek, she said, by the bugs. It was a bright, hot day.

The Stevensons' house lies under big cottonwoods about four miles north of Horse Creek's confluence with the Sweeetwater. Ranch headquarters also includes sheds and metal barns, a utilitarian jumble of corrals, and two smaller houses for the two employees and their families. About a quarter of a mile south, the owner's house, newer and larger than the Stevensons', lies at the end of a lane lined with cottonwoods, and in a field to the right of the lane a chapel points a steeple at the sky. The owner, John Berra, a construction contractor, lives in St. Louis, and owns other ranches too. He bought this one from the Stevensons in 1989, when its name was changed to Pathfinder, and after that the chapel was built. Before then, the ranch was most often still called the Sanford Ranch, for the family that had owned it before Stevensons, since the 19-teens. Ruth and her husband, Haney, still run the ranch, and are expected, she said, to show a profit.

The ranch extends just a few miles north from headquarters, but many miles east toward the North Platte and south beyond the Sweetwater toward Sand Creek. It and the Dumbell are both large ranches, even by Wyoming standards, though neither is as big as the Sun Ranch was at its biggest in the 1980s and early 1990s. The Stevensons have always "neighbored" with the Parks, Ruth said, by which she meant sharing the work at branding time, and perhaps other times when a crowd is handy: haying, weaning, and shipping. They and the Parks do not neighbor with the Suns on the far side of Devil's Gate, she said, nor with the employees of the Farm Management Co., the Mormon Church subsidiary that bought half the Sun Ranch and runs it now as the Handcart Ranch.

The Stevensons and Parks still brand the old way; they "rope the calves and drag them to the fire," Ruth said. Sometimes she reminds her grandchildren they should pay attention, as the system may not last much longer. More and more ranches use mechanical squeeze chutes that hold the calf still while a single person brands, castrates if it's a bull calf, and vaccinates. The new way is easier on the calves and allows them to return more quickly to their job in life, gaining weight. The old way is more picturesque, and, for humans, more sociable. Brandings are remnants of the old roundups.

Except for the highway traffic on Route 220, the country is much emptier now than it was in the summer of 1889. That year, there would have been several cabins visible down Horse Creek toward the Sweetwater, and perhaps one or two to the north, as well. Billy Owen's former cook, Jim Averell, and a woman named Ella Watson, who may have been his wife, had back-to-back, L-shaped, 160-acre Homestead claims, with the long limb of the L running east-west across Horse Creek about where the Pathfinder headquarters is now. The big cottonwoods were still unplanted; Horse Creek was treeless, though the grass would have been good for one or two hundred yards on either side. Watson had a cabin on her claim, and a fenced pasture of around sixty acres. The main road crossed Horse Creek south of where the highway does now, and swerved closer along the west side of the big rock outcrop to cross the Sweetwater on a bridge. Averell maintained a road ranch near the bridge—a store, saloon, and post office—and Watson helped him run it.

In the fall of 1887, a cowboy named W. H. Harvey and a partner hired on as night herders with a crew moving 1,000 steers from northwestern Wyoming diagonally across the state to the shipping yards at Rock Creek, east of Medicine Bow. They kept watch over the bedded herd at night. Then they would breakfast with the rest of the crew, sleep through the morning and early afternoon, ride to catch up with the rest of the herd, and go to work again at nightfall. In October, they were awakened near the Sweetwater one morning by a cold rain, after the herd had gone on ahead. Thinking to get out of the wet, they knocked on the door of Averell's store and asked the woman who answered if they might sleep in the big shed. "Mrs. Averill," as Harvey remembered her decades later—her man being nowhere about—insisted they take her spare bed, with warm blankets in a clean room, and wouldn't hear their protests that they were too dirt-caked to sleep indoors. They slept well. She woke them in time to catch up with their job, gave them a hot meal, and refused any payment. "No cowboy is going to make a bed in a cowshed while we have a house," she told Harvey and his friend. "This couple was afterwards murdered," Harvey remembered years later, but he was vague about how, or why: "some said by hired killers from the large cattle interests."[1]

Watson and Averell were a couple; he was right about that. They shared Canadian origins, turbulent pasts, and, by the time they met, a desire for the stability that comes with owning land and property.

Averell was born in Ontario in 1851, and came to Wisconsin in the early 1860s. As a youth he worked in a sawmill before enlisting in the Thirteenth U.S. Infantry at Oshkosh in 1871. The record shows him five feet, seven inches tall, with black hair, gray eyes, and a light complexion. Five years later he was discharged at Port Gibson, Mississippi, and listed as a "good, honest, reliable soldier." Soon he reenlisted for a second five-year hitch at Chicago, this time in the Ninth Infantry, and was eventually posted to Fort McKinney, near the brand-new town of Buffalo, Wyoming Territory, on the east side of the Bighorn Mountains. And oddly, for a soldier, he bought a house in the town.

Any plans he had for the future, however, unraveled in May 1880, when he shot Charley Johnson in a Buffalo saloon. Johnson had threatened Averell's life repeatedly in the previous six weeks, and was rushing Averell when Averell shot him. But Johnson was unarmed. He died a few days later. Two deputy Carbon County sheriffs escorted Jim 225 miles south to Rawlins to face charges. The road led along the front of the mountains to Red Buttes, where it joined the old California route to the Sweetwater. Even then, on his first trip through the country, it may have occurred to Averell that somewhere near Independence Rock—where one road split off for Rawlins and the older headed west for South Pass—was a logical place for a business. In Rawlins, various bail settings, court schedules, and perhaps occasional overcrowding meant Jim was in and out of jail all winter. He was in jail March 22, 1881, when George "Big Nose" Parrott, sentenced to hang for the murder of two popular deputy sheriffs, tried to escape and failed, and was lynched by a mob the same night. In April, Averell again was released on bail. His lawyer kept filing for continuances on the grounds that witnesses were not available, and finally the case was more or less abandoned. Averell then reported to nearby Fort Steele to serve out the rest of his enlistment. He was discharged June 19, after which Billy Owen hired him to cook for the survey crew. Meanwhile, he had managed to sell his house in Buffalo from a distance, for $700. He was building a stake.

In February 1882, Averell married Sophia Jaeger in Wisconsin on her twenty-second birthday. They settled on Sand Creek, the little community north of the Ferris Mountains. They were well liked there, by all reports, but the marriage was short. She died in September of childbed fever, a few days after delivering a premature, stillborn baby. Her body was shipped home to Wisconsin.

Around this time, Averell came into contact with the Durbin brothers, Tom and John, who had built a sizable ranching operation north of Cheyenne and now were buying herds and moving cattle onto the Sweetwater and Sand Creek ranges. Jim may have worked for them, and they may have backed him on a land deal they hoped to benefit from later. The spring after Sophia died he filed for a cash entry on 120 acres about a mile west of Cherry Creek, a Sweetwater tributary that flows north off the Ferris Mountains. A

Jim Averell. First a soldier at Fort McKinney near Buffalo, Averell left the army in 1881 and signed on to cook for Billy Owen's survey crew. Later he opened a store near the mouth of Horse Creek on the Sweetwater, on the Rawlins-to-Fort McKinney road. Courtesy of Wyoming State Archives.

year and a half later he filed a Timber Culture claim nearby, 160 acres on Cherry Creek itself.

The practice of using so-called false entrymen—to claim land, hold it until proving up, and then deed it over to the person who really wanted it all along—was illegal, yet common; the collusion it involved was almost impossible to prove. Many large ranches were assembled this way, with the cowboys filing the initial claims and proving up with cash provided them by their employers, then turning the land over to the boss.

Durbin headquarters were on the Sweetwater, a few miles west of Tom Sun; Averell's Cherry Creek claims lay about seven miles south of that. An 1885 map also shows a Durbin cabin on Cherry Creek, about where Averell's claims were; they may well have been one and the same.[2] Furthermore, the Durbins' ledger book shows a debt of $360, owed them by Averell, incurred sometime before

1884 and settled in 1887. The loan would precisely cover his outlay, at $1.25 per acre, on the two claims—$150 up front on the cash entry, $200 due eventually on the Timber Culture claim, plus, $10 in, say, fees or incidentals. Of course, final payment on the Timber Culture claim wouldn't have been due until seven years after Jim first filed on it late in 1884. Still, the amount of the loan and its timing are suggestive.

These are just scraps of information, but combined with other scraps, a pattern of possible motives starts taking shape. Averell, according to one account, relinquished the Cherry Creek claims to Robert Butler, a Philadelphia publisher. Supporting that account, a bill of sale survives in Carbon County records, showing that Averell sold a ranch—in the same section as his first claim near Cherry Creek—on February 28, 1884, to Butler and a partner named Horton. Averell got a very good price, too—$2,500. The property included houses, stables, corrals, two horses, ranch supplies, and haying equipment—but no land claim. Butler filed a claim where Jim's had been the same day as the sale, and another Durbin, Richard, filed a claim on the same piece on March 4, five days later.[3]

Beyond that, the record is silent. But the scraps suggest a sequence: that Averell added his army discharge pay to the $700 from his Buffalo house; that he saved his wages from the survey crew, married a Wisconsin friend from earlier days, moved to Sand Creek, and started building a domestic life; and that on the survey crew or while riding herd for the Durbins, or both, he had spied out the country. Sometime before or after Sophia died, he began investing money and labor in the spot near Cherry Creek, and improved it in a remarkably short time. It worked. His timing was superb; he sold out to eastern buyers just as the cattle boom was nearing its peak. Only ten months passed between filing and sale. The man seemed able to choose well and move fast when it came to land deals. His time on the survey crew would have made him familiar with the range and the invisible-grid system that now defined it; clearly, he was using his knowledge of both to his own advantage.

But the Durbins, if they had thought Jim was cooperating with them to help them get title to the land, may have felt outflanked, if not double-crossed. The 1885 map shows signs that Durbin cattle ranged all the way from a spot west of Sun to the North Platte—300 square miles or more. Not that they would have expected to "own" this range in any exclusive sense; still, the ranch near Cherry Creek lay about in the middle of this range. If the Durbin brothers did in fact lose it, in their minds, to Averell's willingness to take a profit where he could, it's not a loss they would have forgotten. They would have held a grudge.

Averell's next move was the store, near the crossroads and the river. Early in April 1884, just five weeks after the Cherry Creek ranch sale, the Rawlins paper noted that Averell "went out home to the Sweetwater" with a load of lumber and other building supplies.[4] There he built his road ranch, half a mile north of the crossing, out of the way of spring floods. Almost certainly, he was investing his profits from the ranch.

It was a promising time; the country was filling up. Sun, on the far side of Devil's Gate, was now married and soon would start a family. Edgar Schoonmaker was well established at a ranch on the near side of the Gate. The Durbins had trailed in 2,000 head from the railroad at Medicine Bow the previous year. In 1884, the year Averell arrived on the Sweetwater to stay, they began serious expansion. Already they owned ranches and meat-packing plants; now they reorganized as the Durbin Land and Cattle Company, taking on three Chicago investors who owned a livestock commission firm, which became the Durbins' marketing arm. They were integrating their operations vertically, just like any good nineteenth-century industrialist. And with the new capital, they brought in still more cows—15,000 head, to be exact, of Texas cattle—to their Sweetwater and Sand Creek ranges.

By this time, too, a man named Robert Conner was running a big ranch from a headquarters seven miles up Horse Creek from its mouth. He had been born in the Lehigh Valley of eastern Pennsylvania in 1849 to humble origins, but family fortunes improved after his father died and his mother married a local coal and railroad capitalist. Bob Conner and his brother Sam were both appearing in the Rawlins papers by 1879; Sam managed mines in Utah and

Bob, by the mid-1880s, was running the ranch. Lew Smith, Conner's foreman, filed a claim at the mouth of Horse Creek, and two other men filed claims the same day farther up the creek. They may have been neighbors, but most likely were Conner employees, too.[5]

More ranches and cattle meant more people, still mostly men, who would have been happy to pick up a few necessities at Averell's store and cut the dust with a drink. An even bigger cattle boom was underway up in the Powder River Basin and, for the time being, the road from Rawlins to Buffalo was the shortest way to get there from a railroad. Averell probably did more business with travelers than with locals.

But it wasn't just cattle that brought people in. People expected a railroad, too, to ship out all kinds of newly discovered minerals. By the summer and fall of 1883, the Cheyenne and Rawlins papers were reporting possible rail routes north from Rawlins to the soda lakes at Independence Rock, with a branch to run via the Sweetwater Valley to Yellowstone Park, and another to head northeast toward Red Buttes. Right-of-way surveys were in full swing by the summer of 1884.

Officers of the Wyoming, Yellowstone Park and Pacific Railroad Company included Wyoming Territorial Governor William Hale, Lammot du Pont, and a certain John Bothwell. Bothwell had been kicked out of the army in 1870 for financial chicaneries, worked five years for newspapers, and by now was a New York broker involved from time to time in shady stock deals involving Utah mines. In March, just as Jim Averell was contemplating his move to the Sweetwater, some of these same capitalists, along with former Wyoming Territorial Governor John Hoyt, Schoonmaker, and John Bothwell's brother Albert, were planning a move to the Sweetwater in a much bigger way. They incorporated as the Central Association of Wyoming, with an eye toward developing minerals, agricultural land, irrigation works—and towns. In July, the Bothwells led a two-week field trip. Hoyt and Schoonmaker were in the party, also the territorial geologist, Samuel Aughey, the Cheyenne banker and cattleman A. R. Converse, capitalists from England, Pennsylvania, New Jersey, and New York, and a representative of Standard Oil.

Probably, they stopped at Averell's store. Perhaps they liked the look of the country. More likely, the Bothwells persuaded some that land claims were a cheap way to gain a toehold. In any case, Aughey, both Bothwells, Edgar and Jeanette Schoonmaker, and two others filed land claims along Horse Creek inside of five weeks that summer, from mid-August to mid-September.

Finally, on December 27, 1884, the *Carbon County Journal* reported that survey parties of "the Bothwell Railroad" had returned to Rawlins and gone into winter quarters. And that was it. But the town-development idea survived, particularly in the mind of Albert Bothwell. If a railroad wouldn't produce a town, then perhaps a town could be produced that would attract a railroad. Either way, the person who owned the town lots stood to make good money.[6]

Meanwhile, a few more women began to appear in the Sweetwater Valley. Sun married Mary Agnes Hellihan in 1883; she had been working at the railroad hotel in Rawlins. The names of Schoonmaker's daughter, Harriet, and his wife (apparently), Jeanette, turn up on land claims around the same time. And one of the claims on Horse Creek was held for a while by an Anna Partington. But women were still scarce. Ranching was a male occupation. Like sailors, most cowboys who worked the big ranches lived celibate lives, interrupted by a debauch once or twice a year, when they got to town.[7]

Averell, however, seems always to have had a more settled, respectable life in mind. Fifteen months after he'd hauled his first load of lumber out to the Sweetwater, he got around to filing a Desert Land entry on 160 acres around his road ranch, and ten months after that, he married, or came very close to doing so.[8] Ella Watson was ten years younger than Averell, and like him had been born in Ontario and had come to the states as a teenager. With her parents and siblings she moved to a farm near Lebanon, Kansas, when she was about fifteen. In 1879, at eighteen, she married William Pickell, Jr., and moved in with him and his father on a nearby claim. Billy Pickell soon proved alcoholic, abusive, and unfaithful. In 1883 she left him, and moved to nearby Red Cloud, Nebraska, then to Denver, Cheyenne, and Rawlins—where, like Mary Agnes Hellihan before her, she worked at the railroad hotel.[9] She would have met Averell there. She

Ellen Watson and her first husband, William Pickell, in Kansas around 1882. She joined Jim Averell on the Sweetwater in 1886. After her death, the Cheyenne newspapers dubbed her "Cattle Kate." Courtesy of Lola Van Wey, George W. Hufsmith Collection, Casper College Library.

was a big-shouldered woman, tall, 165 pounds or more, slightly cross-eyed, with dark hair and eyebrows, good cheekbones, and a strong chin. She joined Averell on the Sweetwater in May of 1886.

Too many scraps of information can sometimes obscure a bigger picture. Here were two people, no longer quite young, he a widower and she divorced, making a life and livelihood in the middle of nowhere not by ranching but by selling socks, cartridges, tobacco, bacon, flour, and whiskey to any who asked. They were an island of domestic enterprise and middle-class hopes plopped down at the intersection of feudal estates. They were running a business. The cowboy W. H. Harvey's story seems to show they were trying to do so honorably. It's hard to see how they could have been a threat to anyone in the district. But threat they were nonetheless, say their deaths.

The big ranches of the 1880s—ranches like Sun's, Conner's, the Durbin brothers', and the one Bothwell dreamed of and would assemble soon—depended for large profits on free grass, hard work, a limitless range, and cheap labor. Cowboys were paid $30 per month, spring through fall; experienced hands were paid $40. It was low wages even then. Nearly all were laid off at the end of the fall, and a tolerant custom arose that the single men could ride the grub line during the winter months—move discreetly for longish stays from one ranch to another, bringing news and gossip, and relying on free food as they did so. If such a system seems benignly feudal, in fact there were too many loose ends for it to last.

For one thing, the roundups were porous. Calves—mavericks, the cowboys called them, or slicks for their smooth sides—slipped unbranded through the system every year. Many of the big ranches paid their cowboys a bonus for each slick they branded, as an incentive to increase the boss's herds. As long as the book counts kept increasing, no one minded much. It didn't take long for the cowboys to realize there was still plenty of unclaimed land, and that slapping a new brand on a few slicks was a quick way to start a new herd. Soon the Territorial legislature outlawed the practice and declared unbranded calves the property of the state to be sold at auction after roundup, with the proceeds going to the Wyoming Stock Growers Association. Members were allowed to buy the mavericks at deflated prices. Nonmembers—including many of the members' cowboys and foremen—were kept out of the sale.

As a result, the new law only deepened class divisions and heightened rancor. Soft prices, drought, and the terrible winter of 1886–87, the worst anyone could remember, all followed in swift succession. Stock losses were highest in Montana, Dakota, and the Powder River Basin of Wyoming, less severe on the Sweetwater. Still, ranch after ranch went under and cowboys were thrown out of work. More began to take up land, and start small herds. A moral hierarchy of cattle theft emerged: mavericking wasn't so bad; changing an existing brand was worse; killing a cow to quiet her protests while stealing her calf was worst of all. Remembering, many of them, how they had first built their own herds, the big ranchers suspected any man with a herd that was small but growing.

Some of their employees and former employees, meanwhile, grew more open about their intentions. Ed Lineberger, foreman of the Rand and Steedman ranch on Sand Creek before he was fired in 1883, branded his cattle *OE*. His employers branded *OX*; people assumed Lineberger started his herd by branding mavericks, or by adding horizontal bars to the brand on Rand and Steedman's calves, changing the *X* to an *E*. Similarly, the Searight brothers, headquartered on the North Platte near Red Buttes, branded an *H* and a goose egg. The Durbins' foreman, Tom Collins, started branding cows with a spectacle image—two circles connected by a nosepiece—and Jack Cooper, foreman of another ranch, started a herd of his own with the Spear *H* brand. The goose egg was easy to change into one lens of the spectacles; the *H* could be changed to a Spear *H* just by extending the crossbar to the left and adding a spear point on the end.[10]

Tensions continued to rise. Now and then a man was shot in a quarrel, or a horse killed, or a rancher burned the haystacks of a neighbor suspected of stealing his cows. Watson and Averell, meanwhile, continued to take legal and logical steps to acquire land and make a life.

Though Averell made his living on the Sweetwater as a storekeeper-saloonkeeper-postmaster after 1884, and occasional surveyor, he apparently wanted to ranch, too. Four times between April 1885 and December 1888, he approached the Carbon County brand committee to register a brand, and was turned down every time. The brand he proposed had two vertical lines connected by a bulbous curve on the bottom—a jug. The committee's job was make sure no new brands were the same as or too similar to any existing ones. It's unlikely, therefore, that Averell would have continued proposing the same design unless he suspected they were turning him down for some other reason, and that changes of people on the committee would improve his chances. He approached the committee a final time in February 1889 with a new brand—J Bird, it was called, a *J* with the profile of a bird's head next to it—and again was rejected. Perhaps he just wanted to brand a few horses. Perhaps he really did want to go into the stock business, like nearly all his neighbors.[11]

Finally, it was Watson, not Averell, who ended up with a herd, though Jim's knowledge of land law almost certainly helped her get one. Newspaper reports after his death noted that he had once protested the legality of a land claim of Conner's; this may well have been Conner's Desert Land entry on Horse Creek about three miles upstream from its mouth, which was canceled in April 1886 but reinstated a year later. Averell had filed a Homestead claim on the L-shaped 160 acres a short way south of Conner's just two months earlier. Between Averell's and Conner's claim lay an eighty-acre Timber Culture claim, also on Horse Creek, belonging to Schoonmaker, whose main ranch was still over by Devil's Gate.

In November 1886, Watson filed a complaint against Schoon-maker's Timber Culture claim, saying he hadn't kept up the plow-ing and cultivating required to hold the land. Anyone who wanted a say in the matter was summoned to appear February 14 in Rawl-ins. Schoonmaker did not show, however, to contest Watson's com-plaint, and so his Timber Culture entry was eventually cancelled, and the General Land Office ruled that Ella could exercise a pref-erence right to file a homestead entry on the same ground. She did so, on 160 acres instead of 80. Her papers show she had already settled there in August 1886; she may not have known of Schoon-maker's prior entry until she tried to file in the fall. Her improve-ments on the claim, she noted, included a two-room log house, irrigating ditches, and some plowing, worth $425.[12] By the spring of 1888, then, she and Averell held legal claims to the two L-shaped 160-acre Homestead claims crossing Horse Creek, just south of Conner's Timber Culture claim.

Next steps were a herd, and a brand, and a water right. Ella's friends maintained after her death that she bought a small herd of footsore cattle, perhaps twenty or thirty animals, in October of 1888, from an emigrant bound for Washington State. No bill of sale survives, but on December 3, she applied for a brand. The brand committee rejected her request. On December 10 she filed a statement of a proposed ditch at the county recorder's offices in Rawlins. She planned to bring water from a headgate on Horse Creek north of Conner's claim, down along the west side of the creek, and across his claim to her claim, most likely to water a vegetable garden and a hay crop for her new cattle. The proposal was ambitious; the ditch would have been two miles long, with at least a mile of it on Conner's claim. In April 1889, she solved her brand problem simply by buying one from John Crowder, a stockman from down on Sand Creek. For ten dollars, she got the right to brand *LU* on her own herd.[13]

If matters had rested there, she and Averell—despite their unorthodox and uncustomarily *legal* approaches to making a living on Horse Creek and the Sweetwater—might have lived longer lives. They hadn't figured on another neighbor's capitalist ambitions. Albert Bothwell still clung to his scheme of starting a town and selling lots. He'd planned his town—Bothwell, he called it—for the west side of Horse Creek, right there on the sagebrush, in the middle of nowhere.

Albert Bothwell had not been idle since he and his brother John led the investors to the Sweetwater in 1884. Albert spent the following year overseeing the new Central Association's oil interests at Oil City, a now-vanished hamlet west of Red Buttes near the headwaters of Poison Spider Creek, and had taken over Tim Foley's former 76 Ranch headquarters at the mouth of Horse Creek sometime that year. Bothwell controlled land along the Sweetwater, too. He began ranching in earnest in August 1888, when he bought out E. A. Page's R Lazy S brand and brought 1,500 head to the Sand Creek range. By that time Watson had been on Horse Creek two years and Averell four.

A more elaborate scheme was on Bothwell's mind, however. On August 22 and 23, 1888, seven different men filed four Homestead claims, two Desert Land entries, and a Timber Culture entry on parts of seven sections of land just west of the Conner, Watson, and Averell claims on Horse Creek. Within two weeks, they made the land a town. The east half of one of the sections was surveyed as the Town of Bothwell, the plat was filed with the Carbon County recorder, the streets and alleys were dedicated to public use, and the land claims were turned over to the new Wyoming Town and Investment Company of Atchison, Kansas.

Towns, in fact, were turning up all over the place. In June 1888, the Fremont, Elkhorn and Missouri Valley Railroad reached a spot on the North Platte two miles east of the old Fort Caspar site. The town of Casper popped up at the end of the rail line. Quickly, it became a shipping point for cattle and a jump-off point for freight, and eclipsed much of Rawlins's business in the process. At the same time, the town of Bessemer was incorporated on the bench above the post office and crossroads at the Searight brothers' ranch near Red Buttes.

The new towns felt they needed their own county; soon a proposal surfaced to lop Natrona County off the northern end of Carbon County. The county line would run just south of the Sweetwater; Averell's store would be in Natrona County. He and Watson approved the proposal at first, though later she signed a petition withdrawing her earlier approval. Casper's new paper, the *Weekly Mail*, lobbied heavily for the new county; large landowners like the Durbins opposed it on the grounds they had nothing to gain but a boost in their property taxes to support the new government. In February 1889, Averell wrote a long, articulate letter to the *Mail* declining to take a position on the immediate issue. But he made it clear where his real sympathies lay:

> . . . we find two distinct views taken in the matter: namely, by the settlers who have come here to live and make Wyoming their homes and the land grabber who is only camped here as a speculator in land under the desert land act. The former are in favor of dividing Carbon county, believing it to be for the welfare and proper development of the country, and the latter are opposed to the organization of Natrona county or anything else that would settle and improve the country or make it anything but a cow pasture for eastern speculators.

The Wyoming Town and Investment Company had by this time begun to circulate pamphlets praising the town of Bothwell's attractions. The *Mail* railed against them, and Averell, too, warned the paper's readers not to be swindled:

> Do not be misled in the matter of the town of Bothwell. There is not one house in that town, and you can with safety say that the town of Bothwell is only a geographical expression, and its influence can not go far against the new county organization. If something can be done to help settle the country up and use the beautiful water of its many streams which are now going to waste, have Natrona county organize; if not, leave the country as it is. You may ask, "What can be done to better the situation?" Change the irrigation laws so that every bona fide settler can have his share of the water; and as soon as possible, cancel the desert land act, and then you will see orchards and farms in Wyoming as there are in Colorado.[14]

There is a real intellect behind Averell's sentences, one that understands the politics of the moment and the relative powers of its opposing forces: land baron vs. stockraising settler; speculator vs. populist. John Wesley Powell himself in all his fights to fix western land law could not have asked for a clearer expression of support. Averell had a reputation among his neighbors as an educated man; one story even made him a Harvard graduate. He wasn't. Nor was he the saint some writers have portrayed. By this time he was heavily in debt to a relative and some Rawlins merchants, and he had, after all, killed a man in a bar nine years before. But he was smart, he could see what was going on, and he wasn't afraid to go public about what he saw.

The investors had their town; all they needed to make the investment pay off was people. People wouldn't come buy town lots if they didn't hear of the place. Circulars weren't enough; like Casper and Bessemer, the town of Bothwell needed a newspaper to boom the town. Early in April 1889, the investors arranged for lumber and a printing press to be shipped from Rawlins out to the Sweetwater. The town's first—and, as it would turn out, only—residents were Isaac Speer, one of the investors and an agent for the town company, and H. B. Fetz, editor of the *Sweetwater Chief.* They built one building, a "shack," the *Carbon County Journal* would call it later. It was just tall enough that a person, standing on its roof with binoculars, could watch a buggy and a group of men on horseback travel two full miles before a fold in the land obscured them.[15]

Stories of the Watson-Averell lynching pull apart and converge, merge and pull apart again like strings of twine in a piece of abandoned burlap—some parts strong, some weak, and until you start tugging it's hard to tell one from the other. The least reliable versions are still the best known. They appeared in the Cheyenne papers within days of the event: Jim's saloon was a "hog ranch"—a kind of rural brothel; Ella was a brawny, foul-mouthed, bronc-riding prostitute who took calves in payment for her favors; both were cold-hearted cattle thieves; and they were playing cards and drinking whiskey at midnight when twenty stockmen-regulators burst sternly through the door crying "Hands up!"

The Rawlins and Casper papers published much better accounts in the following weeks, based on interviews with eyewitnesses. But these, too, showed confusions of timing and geography. Fairly reliable versions were given a few days after the crime in two coroner's inquests, only one of which was recorded. And a handful of stories, never written down, survive among Sweetwater ranching families. These still have their narrative pedigrees attached: who, exactly, told what to whom, and who then told it to the teller, which gives them a credibility lacking in the Cheyenne newspaper accounts. One hundred seventeen years is not so long a time, really—a lifetime and a half. Just as people can get stories terribly wrong in a day, they can keep them unchanged for a century.

By the end of the third week in July, roundup number 26 of the Wyoming Stock Growers Association's 1889 statewide system was branding calves and slicks at Beulah Belle Lake, on Schoonmaker's Dumbell Ranch, eight miles north of Devil's Gate and an equal distance west, roughly, of Averell's store. The roundup's commissioners—its three most important men—were Sun, John Durbin, and Albert Bothwell. The roundup would have had a foreman, too, who bossed and tracked all the work. These three men, as owners of the bulk of the cattle that were being worked, would also have been riding and living with the cowboys much of the time since the roundup began in mid-May.

They started in the desert south of Muddy Gap, at Lost Soldier near present-day Lamont, worked south to the railroad, then east along the UP line past Rawlins to the North Platte. There they turned north, downstream all the way to the Sweetwater, then up the Sweetwater past Bothwell's ranch, Averell's store, Sun's and Durbin's home ranches to Split Rock and Three Crossings. From there they turned north again, up Sage Hen Creek through the Granite Mountains to the headwaters of Dry Creek. Then, while some of the wagons worked north across the Rattlesnake Range toward the southernmost headwaters of the Powder River, others headed back down Dry Creek toward the Sweetwater again.

At Beulah Belle Lake, they would have been finishing up two months of the hardest work of the year. The commissioners may already have felt they had time to attend to another problem that had been on their minds for a while. But their purpose focused further when some of the roundup cowboys late in the week found twenty dead cows. The animals had been recently shot, and their calves were nowhere about.[16]

Early on Saturday, the 20th of July, the roundup hands knew they were not to ask where Sun, Bothwell, Durbin, one of Durbin's cowboys named Ernie McLean, and a fifth man were headed when they rode out east into the morning. The fifth man, Robert Galbraith, was a well-known Rawlins railroad mechanic who had come to the Sweetwater country to buy a herd from Bothwell. All but one of the men were on horseback; Tom Sun drove his buggy, with room in it for a couple of extra passengers. They headed first for

Bothwell, that is, for the office of the *Sweetwater Chief.* Out there a mile or more from Horse Creek, lumber still yellowish raw or newly painted, the shack stuck up out of the sagebrush with nothing else around, equipped with a printing press to tell the world what Bothwell was about to become.

The men sent McLean on toward Horse Creek and Ella Watson's cabin and pasture to see what was up. At the *Chief,* the rest stopped in for a chat with Fetz and Speer, and found that Bob Conner had already arrived from his ranch farther up Horse Creek. At this point, local tradition maintains, someone broke out the whiskey.

A mile to the east, Ella and John DeCorey, a young cowboy from Lander who worked for her, had walked down Horse Creek toward the Sweetwater, where a band of Shoshones was camped. As they were walking, McLean rode past them and then back again, as though assuring himself of their whereabouts. At the camp, Ella bought a pair of moccasins and put them on. When she and DeCorey got back to her cabin, they found six men; Conner now had joined the others. Sun was driving his buggy and the rest were mounted. Everything started happening at once. Durbin began to pull down her wire fence and drive her cattle out into the open range. The other men told Ella to get in the buggy; they were taking her to Rawlins. When she wanted to go into the cabin to change her clothes, McLean and Conner barred the way to her and DeCorey. Bothwell threatened to rope her and drag her to death if she did not cooperate. Still protesting, she got in the buggy. Sun is not mentioned in the contemporary accounts of this moment; we may imagine him quiet at the reins, dark eyes on the horses and at the same time watching everything else.

Also on hand was Gene Crowder, fourteen, another friend, in Ella's pasture trying to catch a pony when the men drove up. The whole party started heading south now, driving the cattle before them down toward the river and Averell's store. When Crowder tried to ride around the little bunch and get ahead of it—forty-one animals by later reports—presumably to warn Averell, Durbin grabbed his horse's bridle and stopped him. So Crowder simply helped McLean move the cows, and the whole procession continued, slowly moving down the creek, the jumble of rocks high on their right, the midday sun high and hot above them.

They met Jim heading out through his second gate, driving an empty wagon, bound for Casper for supplies. Durbin and Bothwell told him to throw up his hands, he was under arrest. On what warrant? Averell asked. Durbin pointed a revolver in his face and said the gun was warrant enough. They made him unhitch his team and climb into the buggy beside Ella. Then, instead of continuing down toward the river, they left the cattle and headed back up around the north end of the rocks. This would have kept them out of sight of Jim's store, and of any friends or travelers lingering there out of the heat on a Saturday midday in July.

Crowder and DeCorey tried to follow, but Bothwell threatened them further. Instead, they hurried away in the opposite direction, down to Averell's store, where they found Frank Buchanan, a friend of Averell's, and Ralph Cole, Averell's teenage nephew from Wisconsin, who had been working for him since spring. Buchanan understood immediately what was going on, armed himself with a revolver, saddled a horse, and headed west to intercept the larger party.

They had come south along the west side of the rocks, and were nearing the river when Buchanan came to where he could see them, he later told the *Casper Weekly Mail*. Buggy and riders dipped down into the riverbed, and then, instead of continuing on across, turned right and traveled upstream for two miles, toward Independence Rock. At one point all stopped for a long, loud argument. Buchanan could not hear what they were saying. At last they turned left, and headed up into a gulch in the rocks south of the river, thick with cedar and pitch pines among the granite jumble.

Buchanan followed, probably up a separate gulch, keeping himself hidden from the others, and tying his horse when the rocks became too steep. He crept forward, still armed only with his revolver, until again he was close enough to see what was going on. Averell was standing on a rock, under the limb of a small pitch pine, lariat around his neck and over the limb. Be game, Bothwell was saying to him; jump off the rock. Watson stood next to him, on the same rock under the same limb. McLean was trying to get a noose around her head as well, but she kept weaving and dodging, making trouble, making it difficult. Buchanan began to fire, twice emptying his six-shooter, but was too distant for the gun to have much effect. The men fired back with their Winchesters, and drove him off.

Though dead, the tree is still there. The gulch is now called Spring Canyon; the rocks are called Sentinel Rocks. The tree is not large, twenty-five or thirty feet high, and even its largest limbs, blackened now from fire or lightning decades ago, would be too brittle to hold the weight of a pair of kicking, desperate people. There are two rocks at the base of the tree. Only one is big enough for two people to stand on before being pushed into space. Living, the biggest branch could have been limber enough to hold them without breaking, yet stiff enough to hold them off the ground. It was a short drop. Their toes, once the branch took their weight, would have been inches from the dead pine needles and the dirt.

Watson's little herd of cattle was driven to Rawlins by Durbin's and Bothwell's cowboys and sold, and the two landowners apparently kept the proceeds. Durbin bought Ernie McLean a train ticket out of Rawlins the next day. Frank Buchanan told his story to the newspapers, but was gone from the area by mid-September and never heard from afterwards. Gene Crowder also left and never told his story. The *Carbon County Journal* implied it was common knowledge Buchanan had been paid off. DeCorey sent his version in to the papers from Steamboat Springs, Colorado. Ralph Cole, Averell's nephew, who had come to Wyoming in the first place for his health, got sick in September and died. The coroner came from Casper and cut the stomach from the boy's body and took it back to Casper in a jar, but a chemical analysis showed no sign of poisoning.

The remaining five lynchers were charged with murder in Rawlins. They made no attempt to deny their part in the deed, yet they were allowed to pledge securities for each others' bail. In October, a grand jury convened, but as it was clear the prosecution was not going to be able to produce any witnesses, the grand jury did not return an indictment, and the lynchers were free.[17]

Being dead, Averell and Watson were of course unable to prove up on their claims on Horse Creek; their little pieces of land eventually were absorbed into Bothwell's ranch. Conner sold out a few years later to a man named Taylor, who brought in sheep. Durbin eventually retired to Denver, and the Suns absorbed his and other claims on up the Sweetwater. The "town" of Bothwell was gone by the end of the lynching summer; Fetz moved to Rawlins and started the *Rawlins Republican*, a competitor to the *Carbon County Journal*. Bothwell himself stayed on Horse Creek until 1916, when he sold out to Stewart Sanford. By the mid-1890s the country was already being used much as it is now. There was one ranch on lower Horse Creek, one on upper Horse Creek, Schoonmaker on the Sweetwater just downstream from Devil's Gate and ranching a long way up Dry Creek and its tributaries, Tom Sun ranching on the Sweetwater upstream from Devil's Gate and expanding west, southeast and south.

It's interesting in the accounts of the lynching to note the mention of fences. Watson apparently had fenced a pasture to hold her forty-one head. Jim's meeting the lynchers at his so-called second gate implies he, too, had fenced the perimeter of his claim and also built an inner fence, perhaps to keep animals away from his garden and dooryard. Durbin, who controlled more land and cattle than the rest of the lynchers put together, showed his annoyance by his immediate move to tear it down. Bothering to fence such a small piece of land must have seemed petty and mindless to him, evidence of Watson's wish just to be difficult, abrasive, defiant to the roundup and the way business was done. Averell's letter to the *Mail* about land grabbers and speculators must have stirred a similar annoyance. These people had it all wrong, the cattlemen decided ahead of time, and needed to be removed. They were defying tradition by fencing such little pieces of land and expecting to make a living off the pieces. It was too much. Then whiskey and the midday sun overheated their judgment, and the cattlemen decided to make an example of their two problems. Hanging is a public kind of murder.

The bodies hung about thirty-six hours before a deputy sheriff, a small posse, and a coroner's jury cut them down the following Monday morning. But even though they were out of sight of the river and the road, even though the posse had to scramble and climb to find them, they hung long enough to make their point. And they hang there still, in the memory of the valley and the state, as a reminder of who was in charge, who owned what, and the lengths that power will go to, to get its story told the way it chooses.

# CHAPTER 12

# The Magic Touch of Water

A fitting monument to the sturdy explorer, John Charles Fremont, a mighty figure of the romantic pioneer days, this giant
structure of modern masonry rears its lofty crest on the site
where the explorer was wrecked in his attempt to reach the
Missouri River by water, and a wondrous valley made fertile by
the magic touch of water now greets the eye where once the
Indian and buffalo reigned supreme.

*—George Wharton James, 1917, on Pathfinder Dam*

One raw May morning in 1897, a man got off the train in Rawlins
and boarded a stage for the Sweetwater country. Hiram Chittenden was a captain in the Army Corps of Engineers, on detached
duty from his posting in St. Louis. The ride north was cold and,
when the coach topped ridges, fiercely windy. He found the midday meal at the Stern Ranch disgusting and expensive; then the
way got worse through the sand hills south of the Ferris Mountains
and on through the Sand Creek gap. They reached the Ferris post
office by 5 p.m. From there the driver detoured west to drop Chittenden nearer Devil's Gate. It was a two-mile, moonlight walk to the
Suns' ranch. Tom and Mary Sun gave him supper. He was in bed by
ten, exhausted and elated. His two passions, water control and the
western past, had been joined.

Chittenden was born in upstate New York in 1858, graduated
from West Point in 1884 and won a commission in the elite Corps

of Engineers. Early in his career, he was posted to Yellowstone Park, where he directed construction of the park's first roads and bridges. By 1896 he was in St. Louis, at the head of a commission charged with surveying the Missouri River from its mouth to Sioux City. In August of that year, orders came through channels for him to survey some reservoir sites. In fact, the real orders came from higher up. They issued from U.S. Senator Francis E. Warren of Wyoming, who controlled more or less all connections between his state and the federal government.

The senator had slipped an appropriation for a survey of likely Colorado and Wyoming reservoir sites into Congress' main vehicle for porkbarrel spending, the annual Rivers and Harbors Bill. He had done so in consultation with Elwood Mead, Wyoming state engineer and thus the state's chief water officer. Mead understood the interplay of federal, state, and private irrigation interests as well as anyone in the West; he was nearly finished with a long effort to bring order to Wyoming's water laws, water records, and water-rights disputes. Warren and Mead had already picked the reservoir sites, and when Chittenden passed through Cheyenne on his way to Rawlins, Mead had given him topographical maps and other information from his files.[1] And Chittenden knew, as he went out next morning for a daylight look at Devil's Gate, that as long as he was in Wyoming he was expected to be Warren's man.

Sun took Chittenden up a rise behind the ranch. They had a good view of Devil's Gate to their right, and to their left, looking across the valley toward the mountains, Chittenden photographed a rich-looking hayfield Sun had irrigated out of a loop of the stream. But it was the deep, narrow notch of the Gate that first caught Chittenden's attention—"a perfect site for a reservoir dam," he would write in his journal. He and Sun next climbed to the top and there, the engineer let himself feel swept by a larger sense of time at the place. He was convinced he was seeing a spot where the returning Astorians, probably the first white men to cross South Pass, had stopped in 1812. But the place plucked his own memory, too. It reminded him of the view of the Hudson from West Point, and when Sun pointed out Independence Rock, Chittenden saw it

Hiram Martin Chittenden. Amateur fur-trade historian and professional army engineer, Chittenden proposed a dam at Devil's Gate in 1897, after visiting the Sun and Bothwell ranches. Courtesy of American Heritage Center, University of Wyoming.

"rising like an island from the sea." Water, water; land, land. Here was a man who planned to take the convergence beyond simile, and make it fact.

Wyoming is white in winter, gray-tan as the snow melts, green in May and early June, and often tan again by the Fourth of July. After that, even when seen from the air, the tan plains dominate the world. The gullies are tan, the washes, draws, arroyos, gulches—tan, tan, tan, tan. Then the plane flies over a watercourse—the Sweetwater, for example, or the North Platte. And there, along the edges of the stream, runs a strip of vivid green.

Chittenden was point man for a movement to widen that green with human engineering. Irrigation was an industrial, populist dream of making barren places fertile and productive for the benefit of as many people as possible. It would eventually turn into a socialist operation because it would take rivers of state-controlled capital to set it in motion.

The dream rose out of stories people told themselves. They could make the desert bloom, the story went; they could make a dry world wet. If the prophecies of Cyrus Thomas and others that rain would follow the plow had failed to come true, there remained an alternative. Take the little water that flowed already, store it, spread it, and *use* it on the land.

To the extent the water would make the land produce more, irrigation would add cash value to the properties. Most saw the effort as a benefit to all. The new value could be spread evenly among the people, like steady water from a once unreliable stream. But a few saw irrigation not as an article of hope or progress but as something more mundane, something they could use to their own advantage. They saw prospects; they saw ways to make themselves rich. They told themselves a slightly different story, and patiently waited for the main chance.

Albert Bothwell, still ranching at the confluence of Horse Creek and the Sweetwater, proved a more expansive host than Sun. Chittenden the engineer was impressed by Bothwell's ranch; the place seemed prosperous, with a substantial network of irrigation ditches. Chittenden the traveler warmed to the household, finding the family delightful and urbane: Bothwell's wife Margaretta, her two children by a previous marriage, and a Miss Wadsworth, also on hand. Chittenden took quickly to Bothwell's conversation—geology and evolution were the rancher's passions—and to his library, packed with books by his idols, Darwin and Darwin's disciples, Spencer, Huxley, and Tyndall. And Chittenden the historian delighted most of all in Bothwell's story of how Independence Rock got its name.

When General Frémont, the story went, first came up the valley, word preceded him that he and his party would arrive at the Rock on July 4, and he would give a speech. Couriers galloped up and down the trail with the news, so that travelers at the Rock would stay there, and travelers behind would catch up. Soon a big crowd gathered. They placed the general in the best carriage they had, and hauled it to the top with him in it, then hauled it back and

forth along the top of the rock for a while, in triumph. Then the
general spoke powerfully on the greatness of the day. Afterward,
six young couples, already properly engaged of course, joined
him at the summit, "and there, on this sublime natural altar, surrendered their independence pair by pair in voluntary bondage
to each other." That is, Frémont married them on the spot. And
from the lovers' formal *surrender* of independence, the rock took
its name.[2]

The fact that the Frémont story came from a man willing to
lynch his neighbors takes nothing from its appeal. By this time
Bothwell's ranch stretched five miles along the river; he more or
less owned the lower Sweetwater valley. We can imagine him understanding the power and the money Chittenden represented, and
choosing the most charming stories he knew to describe the country he controlled.

In fact, Bothwell's relations with neighbors may still have been
rocky. "He farms out portions of his ranch to small farmers," Chittenden noted in his diary, "but finds great difficulty in securing
competent men." What "farms out" means, exactly, is hard to say; it
implies something different from simply renting to a tenant. It was
still common practice for large ranchers to use dummy entrymen
to expand their holdings—common, illegal, and as we have seen,
nearly impossible to prosecute successfully. Natrona County land
records for the 1890s show Bothwell buying up smaller pieces in
the area from time to time at modest prices; he could easily have
financed neighbors' initial filings with the intention of buying the
patents once proved up. At the same time, like any rancher today,
he used bigger blocks of land as collateral for large, regular loans,
presumably to keep his operations running.

Beginning about 1888, Albert Bothwell's older brother John, the
Wall Street broker, got involved with a company that had acquired
rights to 45,000 acres of railroad land in northeast Utah along the
Bear River, and to a damsite on the river. The Bear River Canal,
greatly increasing the value of those lands, was finished in 1893.
Albert Bothwell appears to have been financially involved with the
Bear River plan too, at least for a short time.[3]

In the spring of the lynching year, 1889, Albert began studying how the steppe stretching from Devil's Gate, past Independence Rock and over to Horse Creek might be irrigated. Like the Bear River project, this would greatly increase the value of the irrigated land, and most likely was linked in Bothwell's mind with the rosy prospects for lot sales on the Bothwell townsite.

That August, the month after the lynching, Albert Bothwell, Edgar Schoonmaker, and Rawlins businessman John C. Davis incorporated as the Sweetwater Land and Irrigation Company, with John Bothwell and a John C. Baird as trustees. The plan was to take water out of the Sweetwater by means of a flume at Devil's Gate and empty it into a ditch on Schoonmaker's ranch on the downstream side. The ditch would run along the foot of the hills ten miles northeast to where Fish Creek trickled into Horse Creek. Then more ditches would run from that confluence all the way to the Platte. The canal would run twenty-five miles, would fall 2.64 feet per mile, could take all the water from the Sweetwater, and would cost $100,000, the *Sweetwater Chief* reported. The paper went on to note John Bothwell's involvement in both the Bear and Sweetwater River projects as a sign of the local project's soundness.

It wouldn't have worked. The Fish Creek–Horse Creek confluence is twenty feet higher in elevation than Devil's Gate; a gravity ditch from the Sweetwater couldn't even have reached Horse Creek, let alone have irrigated the entire valley. Bothwell can not have done any kind of rigorous survey. The whole scheme makes sense only as an attempt to inflate the price of what he already had for sale—land.[4]

Prior to the Mead-Warren collaboration and Chittenden's visit to the Sweetwater, there had been little or no government involvement in irrigating the West. Now, popular, national forces were gathering. After bad droughts in the late 1880s, it began to appear that if the arid West was ever to reach its dreamed-for potential, it needed more water on more land than natural stream courses would allow. Irrigation was the answer; ditches and canals could carry water from rivers to cropland.

Soon, irrigation congresses, led by boosters hoping farmers
and capitalists would catch on to the idea, were cropping up at
state, then national levels to promote the irrigation story. Pressure
from these groups led by 1895 to the passage of the Carey Act,
named for Joseph Carey, Wyoming's other U.S. senator. The act
made one million acres of the public domain available to each of
sixteen states and territories in the arid West. States would oversee
private companies' design and construction of water projects on
this land, and the land itself and the water rights to make each
piece productive would end up in the hands of settlers.

It never worked much better than Bothwell's plan to run water
uphill. There was never enough capital, there were never enough
settlers, and, with just ditches and canals to move water around,
there was never enough water. Ditches could expand a rancher's
creek-bottom hayfields enough that he could grow hay to feed his
cows all winter. To grow a real crop, though, a crop like corn or
beans or sugar beets, a farmer needed water far into the late summer—all of August and half of September. With sufficient water,
such crops could support a family on forty or eighty acres. Without
extra water, western rivers were unreliable by the end of the growing season, if not—as Pvt. Hervey Johnson had discovered coming
up the Platte in September 1863—completely dry.

Within a year of the 1895 legislation, it was clear to Mead, Warren, and a few other engineers and politicians that it wouldn't work.
If agriculture was ever to get a foothold on the western plains, there
needed to be a way to store the water of those rivers when spring
and early summer flows were high, and then release it to the farmers' crops in August and September.

The answer, apparently, was dams, with big reservoirs behind
them to store the water until needed. Only then would there be
enough water to grow the crops. The farms would bring in families
by the tens, scores, hundreds of thousands to the West, completing
the conquest of the region, making it at last the stable, well-used
place it was always meant to be.[5]

A similar dream of conquest had driven Frémont five times
across the continent, and the dream can be traced via Frémont and

his mentor, the French geographer Nicollet, back to the Enlightenment and the *philosophes*. The dream was mixed, too, with the more
immediate motives of exploiting natural riches that had drawn
Hayden and Jackson up the Sweetwater Valley, mixed again with the
small-farmer ideal that had stirred thinkers from Jefferson to Powell.
Now the dream had come to the valley again with Chittenden, the
engineer. And yet Chittenden had been sent by a man who would
have said his job was a practical one; he had little time for dreams.

Western newspapers called Francis E. Warren "the great Getter,"
which they meant as praise.[6] Better than anyone, Warren understood that his Senate career depended on a long, steady and steadily
increasing flow of federal dollars back to his home state. Warren and
Mead by this time had come to understand that only the federal government had pockets deep enough to finance big-dam construction.
Mead liked the idea because he knew it assured a reliable flow of
water for farmers. Warren liked the idea because it assured a reliable
flow of money for constituents, and thus votes and power for him.

The senator had persuaded his colleagues to add a reservoir-
site survey into the 1896 Rivers and Harbors bill by arguing that,
without it, the bill contained nothing for the interior West, which
has no harbors and almost no navigable rivers. Like thousands of
legislators since, he understood how to use a study—a little survey
like this—to wedge open the budget door for later. And finally,
he threatened that he'd never vote for the bill again if the other
senators didn't go along with him. They shrugged, and went along.
Colorado was added to the study to keep it from appearing completely parochial. Chittenden was at least somewhat familiar with
Wyoming from his years in Yellowstone, and seemed like the logical
man for the job.

Chittenden stayed an extra day at Bothwell's. The next morning,
the two men galloped east through twelve miles of thick sagebrush
to the rim of the North Platte Canyon. They peered over. The engineer found the sight as splendid as any in Yellowstone Park—there
was the water, five hundred feet below, running between nearly vertical walls. The angle was too odd for decent photographs, however,
so they turned right along the rim until they found a place where

Chittenden could clamber down closer. He came to a spot inside a right-angle bend with good views up- and downstream, probably just one bend down from where Frémont and the boaters had stopped for their brandy-and-sausage breakfast. But Chittenden recognized it only as the "fiery narrows" of the Astorians. Climbing back out, he had to stop and rest several times. Meanwhile, we may imagine Bothwell at the top, holding the horses, his mind on water volumes, land values, the past, and the future.

Chittenden delivered his report to Congress in December 1897, with maps, photographs, and drawings of proposed irrigation works. Of the three sites in Wyoming and two in Colorado, Devil's Gate, wrote Chittenden, "stands almost without exception as the most favorable site for a great masonry dam in the world."[7] Plugging the narrow notch with a stone-paved dam would store maximum water at minimum cost. Though the notch is 330 feet deep, the reservoir could be dammed to a depth of only 100 feet above the river level. Water depth would be limited by a dip in the ridge to the east—the same low pass where the old emigrant trail came through. Still, a dam 100 feet high would back water twelve or thirteen miles up the Sweetwater valley. It would hold about 327,000 acre-feet—an acre-foot is enough water to cover an acre of land to a depth of a foot. And it would cost, according to Chittenden's estimate, $276,484, or about 85 cents per acre-foot stored.

Chittenden's estimate included $75,000 to buy out the property to be flooded. There was talk that year, as there was in the past and would be in the future, of construction of a railroad up the Sweetwater valley and over to Lander. Chittenden felt the railroad would soon get built right along the river, and that therefore the government would do well to take over the site and build the dam—or it would end up having to pay to move a railroad.

Devil's Gate, however, wasn't the wisest place for the government to put its money, he argued—at least, not yet. There was much more demand at a site in northern Wyoming along Piney Creek, where farmers were already irrigating and wanted more water. It was not a large project, and would cost considerably more per acre-foot stored. But it made the most sense to provide water first where people already wanted it.

Finally, Chittenden made the argument Warren wanted to hear, that western reservoirs in general were indispensable to development, and that only the national government had the resources to build them. In effect, he was turning the populist story socialist. Chittenden argued that the national government should also own the land the water would flood as it backed up behind the dams, and own as well the rights to the water necessary to fill the reservoirs. States and private interests should be left to operate the dams and ditches. And the water itself should be free.[8]

Warren wanted Congress to hear these arguments from an apparently nonpolitical outsider. This was the real purpose—that is, Warren's purpose—for the survey. Yet Congress, distracted by the war with Spain and then the assassination of a president, didn't do much with it for a while. Finally, with an extra push from the new president, Theodore Roosevelt, Congress passed a complicated law authorizing federal involvement in western water projects while attempting to pacify a conglomeration of conflicting interests. Still, the Reclamation Act of 1902 did make a few things clear: the federal government would build dams and projects, and run them once they were built. It would allow new ways for farmers to take up unclaimed plots of the public domain. These farmers would pay for the water and land they received, on increasingly favorable terms stretched over long periods of time. The payments would go into a revolving fund to finance future projects, thus allowing the Reclamation Service and its eventual successor, the Bureau of Reclamation, an insulation from Congress' annual budget processes that later some would claim allowed the agency too much autonomy. Finally, under the 1902 act, the government would own the rights to the stored water, buying them if necessary, and it would own the reservoir sites, buying them if necessary, too.

Underneath the socialist story of greater state control, the populist dream remained—that the scheme could benefit everyone. At the same time, Bothwell was keeping his eye the part where the government would buy the land.

Wyoming's largest rivers, as we saw earlier, follow similar patterns as they make their way. They rush out of mountains, wind slowly across basins, dive through narrow canyons, and then slow down again to wind across other basins. The pattern challenges water engineers, and in 1902, at the birth of the U.S. Reclamation Service, the engineers were only just beginning to sort the challenges into obstacles and opportunities. Canals and ditches, for example, are more difficult and expensive to build if the land they cross is relatively flat; the ditches have to wind farther along the landscape's contours to get the water where it needs to go. With more slope, the ditch cost falls; the ditches can get there more directly. Dams are easiest, cheapest, and strongest to build in high, narrow canyons, but the canyons themselves, if plugged, don't provide much storage volume for water. So ideal damsites are near the upstream end of a narrow canyon, where a wide, high-sided valley spreads out just above.

Within weeks of the passage of the new act, the service's top engineer, F. H. Newell, came to Devil's Gate to check on Chittenden's earlier conclusions. Four holes were drilled before winter, and the early results looked promising: nothing but solid granite under the sand. In February, the *Natrona County Tribune* thrilled at the prospect of $600,000 in government dam and irrigation spending for local merchants, of "water to burn" once a Devil's Gate reservoir was built, and of homes for 4,000 people on the newly watered land.[9]

A service hydrographer, A. J. Parshall, already believed however that the head of the canyon below the Sweetwater/North Platte confluence was the best damsite. The valley above was broad, the river there sloped gently. In the canyon the rock was solid and seamless, and the opening was only 80 feet wide at the bottom. Water would back all the way up to the base of the Seminole Range, twenty miles south. Only a few small ranches, Parshall reported to Newell, would have to be condemned and purchased, and they would add only slightly to the cost. Newell was pleased.[10]

The newspaper, meanwhile, continued to thrill itself over the enormous profits to be made on land that could be irrigated by a dam at Devil's Gate. Pieces available for $5 per acre now would be worth fifteen times that much in three years, the paper was certain; the optimistic tone continued all spring and most of the summer. The Chamber of Commerce caught the fever and voted to help the county pay to improve the road from Casper to Devil's Gate. until Four more holes were drilled at the Gate in July, bolstering the paper's hopes. Finally in August, George Field, surveyor for the Reclamation Service, admitted to the paper that a dam might not be built at Devil's Gate, his preferred site. If, however, the results of drilling and survey work showed that a dam in the big canyon below the confluence was a better idea, then one would be built there, he said.

The Reclamation Service had in fact been coming around to Parshall's point of view for months. Field's crews had been surveying the Sweetwater and the North Platte since April, 120 miles from Devil's Gate to Orin Junction. In early May, Parshall and Field visited Devil's Gate, and then apparently returned to Casper by way of the other damsite, in the big canyon.[11] Such a trip would have taken them right past Bothwell's ranch. It's easy to imagine the gregarious old lyncher buttonholing the two technocrats from the Reclamation Service on their way by. In any case, Bothwell made a very interesting purchase inside of a week.

A year earlier, a Florence Kelly had made a 320-acre Desert Land entry on the lower Sweetwater, about four miles down from Bothwell's ranch headquarters and four miles up from the confluence. On May 8, 1903, within a day of Parshall's and Field's visit to the Sweetwater, Kelly made the final proof on her place, which would have required a cash payment of $400 two years earlier than the law required. On May 13, she sold the plot to Bothwell for $500.[12] And all this while, the newspaper and, apparently, all its readers except Bothwell and some Reclamation Service employees, still expected the dam to be built at Devil's Gate.

In July the service began boring test holes in the big canyon. The crews had a difficult time of it, running their diamond-tipped drills from boats tied and anchored in the moving river on the canyon floor. At the same time, the government engineers were finally beginning to get good information on the water supply.

The Sweetwater was turning out to be a trickle compared to what Chittenden had thought. Extrapolating from the best data he had, Chittenden had deduced a mean flow in the river of 319 cubic feet per second. In 1903, however, the Reclamation Service measured a *maximum* Sweetwater flow of only a little over 400 cfs and flows on August 1 of nearly nothing at all, with an average through the year of around 75 cfs—a quarter of the volume Chittenden had been thinking about.[13] Damming the Sweetwater would provide enough to fill local ditches, but nothing more. And the engineers, by the end of 1903, had a lot more in mind.

By late October, the drilling crews had managed to sink eight holes at the North Platte damsite, showing that here, too, there was only solid granite under the riverbed.[14] They found the canyon downstream from the Platte-Sweetwater confluence deep enough and solid enough to hold a dam 200 feet high, high enough to back more than a million acre feet of water into the North Platte and Sweetwater valleys. To put that water to its most efficient use, the engineers had only to find the places where the land would allow the water to spread the farthest—where the green strip could be widened to its maximum extent. That such a place was 200 miles away, along the North Platte where its valley flattened as it left Wyoming and flowed into Nebraska, was not, from the point of view of the federal government, a real problem. At Whalen, five or six miles above Fort Laramie and 200 miles downstream from the big dam, they planned a little diversion dam to guide water into canals on both sides of the river. Then they could use both dams to regulate the water flow as needed at different seasons of the year.

The engineers investigated ways to irrigate all along the North Platte, starting with a ditch that would take out at Alcova, a townlet nine miles downstream from the damsite, and water fields at the mouth of Poison Spider Creek near Red Buttes: too expensive. Another ditch would have gone from Red Buttes to Douglas on the south side of the river, another from just downstream from Glenrock but on the north side of the river all the way past Douglas to Orin Junction. These were abandoned, though the Alcova-to-Red

Buttes idea would resurface successfully in the 1930s, in conjunction with another reservoir and dam.

Toward the end of 1903, the engineers began calling the big dam Pathfinder, and its proposed impoundment Pathfinder Reservoir, in honor of a fabled Frémont known vaguely to have lost his surveying instruments when his boat capsized.[15] Engineers now were more practical men, and would never allow such a thing to happen. If they were also fulfilling dreams of control familiar to any child who ever played in a stream, sending water where they wanted it to go, when they wanted it to go there, that was their business and their privilege.

Central Wyoming was "bubbling with ecstasy," the *Tribune* reported, at the prospect of the government spending even more—a million dollars to dam the Platte. "[H]igh and clear," editor A. J. Mokler wrote, "comes the song of prosperity." Lots in Alcova were selling briskly, and Boney Earnest was building a saloon. There would be money to be made on freight to the damsite and, who could say? There might even be an electric railroad built all the way to Alcova.[16]

Final approval of the site came late in 1904. Construction began early the following year with the drilling of a large diversion tunnel, 480 feet long, to take the water around the site while the dam was built. The first stone was laid in August 1906. The dam itself rose 218 feet above its rock foundation—nearly twenty-two stories high. It was 80 feet wide and 90 feet thick at the base, 432 feet wide along the top—a football field and a half—and just 10 feet thick. The entire structure, faced with large granite blocks, filled with a "cyclopean rubble" of concrete, and arching elegantly upstream, was completed in June 1909. A spillway 600 feet long was cut into the granite on the north side of the dam—the river at the damsite flows briefly east—to allow overflow at times of highest water. About a quarter mile south of the dam, however, a long earthen dike was needed to raise the ground there to a height even with the top of the dam. The dike was finished in May 1911, after more than a year of work, allowing the reservoir to reach its maximum capacity and marking the formal end of construction.[17]

Mattie and Boney Earnest, about 1925. By this time their ranch on Sand Creek had been flooded by Pathfinder Reservoir, and they had moved to the town of Alcova. Courtesy of Jack E. Atzinger Collection, Casper College Library.

And there it still stands, and may be admired, as much for the elegant blocks of its tall stone face as for the job it has done, doling out water on an irrigation-convenient schedule for nearly 100 years. Pathfinder used to look a great deal like its contemporary, the Theodore Roosevelt Dam in Arizona, located on the Salt River just below its confluence with Tonto Creek, until that dam was strengthened and cased in a layer of modern concrete in the 1990s. Both were completed in 1911, and were the first two dams of the fledgling Reclamation Service. The service, and its successor the Bureau of Reclamation, would become an engine of New Deal propaganda and national self-esteem in the 1930s, with the construction of the massive Hoover Dam on the Colorado and Grand Coulee on the Columbia. Wyoming kept its allies at reclamation's top levels, with Warren in the Senate until his death in 1929, and Elwood Mead, who served as the bureau's top officer from 1924 to his death in 1936. The bureau built dozens more dams around the West—including a few more on the North Platte—changing the western rivers forever and forever shifting the political balance between Washington and the western states. Federal water systems and federal land are still the two big, silent gorillas in the statehouse chambers of western politics, and the birth of the Reclamation Service is often pointed out as the start of a new kind of federal power in the West that has continued to grow since. What is often forgotten, however, is that the two gorillas have been quietly dispensing cash, all along. And right at the front of the line, at the front of the twentieth century, stood Albert Bothwell with his hand out.

The Bothwell who had shown Chittenden such hospitality and intellect had a reputation among some of his neighbors as a mean man—a reputation that dated from well before the Watson-Averell lynching. In 1886, when he ranched upstream from Sun as well as downstream, Bothwell stretched a fence across the old Oregon Trail, infuriating neighbors and travelers. In 1888, he shot a horse out from under its rider in a dispute over ownership of a pair of draft horses. In 1894, he tried to derail Boney Earnest's candidacy for the legislature by having him arrested for killing a steer—but the steer turned out to belong to a man Earnest was in business with, and the case was quickly dropped. Bothwell also kept wolves as pets, and at least once, in 1903, the wolves attacked a ranch hand who was trying to feed them, tearing up the man's left arm and shoulder. Bothwell's neighbors remembered the wolves a long time, and recalled that when they howled in their pens, wild wolves and coyotes would answer back from the ridgetops.[18]

Once the dam was designed and construction began, the Reclamation Service began buying up the land that would be flooded along the Sweetwater and the North Platte. Thirteen landowners sold plots ranging from 160 acres to Bothwell's holdings nearly twenty times that size. Most of the landholders sold out early in 1906. Oddly, the ranchers with the smallest plots sold for the least amount per acre. Prices ran as low as $4.38 per acre for one 160-acre piece;

most were in the $10- to $20-per-acre range. The larger landowners did much better. William H. Weaver sold his 1,400 acres for $36,400—$26 per acre—and Boney and Mattie Earnest sold their 1,120 acres for $28,000, or about $25 per acre.[19] Bothwell held out.

In February 1905, he asked $169,800; when the government wouldn't bite, he hiked the price further, offering in September "to cede to the United States all my lands and water rights" for $183,250. He valued his deeded acres at $50 each, priced 320 acres of a state lease he held at $40 each, and 485 acres of public land he irrigated but did not own at $30 each. "[A]nd not a postage stamp less," he added. Government estimates of his ranch's value, by contrast, ranged that year from about $44,000 to $53,000. The ranch would be "dear at $60,000," a Reclamation Service field assistant wrote to his boss in Casper. Already, however, it looked as though Bothwell was so determined and his price so high that the government would have to sue to condemn the property under public-domain law. If the suit didn't move fast enough, Bothwell could countersue, once his lands were damaged by the rising floods. The threat of rising water put a steadily upward pressure on the price.

In 1907, the Reclamation Service offered Bothwell $65,000 for the ranch. He didn't respond. Near the end of 1908, engineer I. W. McConnell sent a report back to Washington offering three different values for the Bothwell Ranch, ranging from $98,100 to $114,585. By this time the engineers believed Bothwell's claim to the half-section he'd bought from Florence Kelly in 1903 was fraudulent, but realized that matter, too, would probably end up in court. McConnell suggested the government now offer $80,000. Approached in February 1909, Bothwell refused to budge. He'd been treated in bad faith from the start, he said. The government could meet his price or meet him in court.

Snow was heavy that winter and spring. In March, the government hired a Cheyenne law firm, as the regular U.S. attorney for Wyoming had long had Bothwell for a private client. In May, the government sued in federal court in Cheyenne. In June, the court appointed a three-man arbitration commission to visit the ranch and set a value. The commission found the country along

Albert Bothwell. Shown here with unidentified friends and relatives, Bothwell, second from left, began ranching at the mouth of Horse Creek about 1884. He profited enormously after 1909, when the U.S. Reclamation Service dammed the North Platte River and flooded his land on the lower Sweetwater. Courtesy of David Historical Collection, Casper College Library.

the Sweetwater as green as it ever gets. Two commissioners—one a friend of Bothwell's from Casper, the second Bothwell's banker from Cheyenne—set the value at $193,890, including $16,000 for the Kelly tract, an average of $68.76 per acre. The third commissioner refused to concur. The government sought and was granted a jury trial.

Dam construction was finished in June. By July 3, the water was running so high that only slightly more than half of it could be let through the dam while the rest backed up the two rivers. Most of Bothwell's land flooded. In a different year, engineer McConnell wrote his boss, it might have been possible, by keeping the sluice gates open, to hold the water "below the level of Bothwell's land and eventually to wear him out on the proposition." But now, it was clear, the sooner they could get into court, the better for their case.

The case finally went before a jury late in November. The trial lasted four days. Bothwell's lawyer called fourteen prominent witnesses, "state senators, as a general thing, being his long suit," one of the Reclamation Service men reported. On the stand, Bothwell's witnesses valued his property between $72 and $125 per acre, with $100 being the average. Bothwell's lawyer called for a total price of $250,000—well supported by those estimates. Bothwell himself believed he'd get at least $200,000. The government called just five witnesses. All had inspected the land closely, and spoke specifically to its fences, hay land, alfalfa land, alkali land, buildings and corrals, little grove of pole-sized trees, acres irrigable, and acres dry.

The jury apparently was swayed more by hard information than by the social stature of witnesses, and went for a valuation very close to what McConnell had come up with a year before. The ranch proper was worth $108,250, the jury declared, which came out to $42 per acre. The Kelly acres, should a different court uphold Bothwell's title to them, were worth another $9,600—only $30 per acre but representing, if ever paid, a $9,100 profit over what Bothwell appeared to have paid for them in 1903. Though the judge was the uncle of one of the government's lawyers, he seems to have come down fairly evenly between the two sides on various motions and points of law. The Reclamation Service men had expected the jury would come down no lower than $150,000. The verdict was "a signal victory for the government," one wrote. The lawyers, pointing out the $76,040 savings for the government between the commission's valuation and the verdict, billed their client for $15,000.[20]

A price tells a kind of story, in that it represents the reaching of a consensus, voluntarily or not, between seller and buyer.

The price the federal government paid for Bothwell's 2,500 acres tells, first, how money flows to power. To buy land that two and a half decades earlier had not even been surveyed, the government spent $250,000, a third of what it spent to build the dam proper. More than half the money went to Bothwell, though he owned just over a third of the acres in question and his land, by all accounts, was not particularly better or worse than his neighbors'. But he had more of it, he was richer than they, perhaps greedier, perhaps angrier, and certainly more stubborn, and so he could make big trouble by refusing to sell. He got a much better price.

Still, he felt defeated, and the government felt victorious. The price tells another story, too: sometimes there are limits on how much money will flow to power. The same rising water that inflated Bothwell's power and asking price brought with it a new story, the government's version of what the land was really worth. The government's argument gained strength from appearing to have public welfare on its side. As the members of the jury watched the case unfold, they must have felt the new, government version of land value flooding smoothly over Bothwell's. Yet another layer of land ownership now was coming up the Sweetwater. As in the past, and as would continue to be the case into the future, control of the land meant control of the story.

Bothwell did not appeal, nor did he appeal the General Land Office decision that the Kelly tract should revert to the government. He did claim $125,000 in damages, however—$10,000 for his ruined hay crop and $115,000 for his lost cattle business. The federal Court of Claims was unimpressed. It ruled in December 1918 that Bothwell was due $5,150. He appealed. The Supreme Court upheld the Court of Claim's judgment on December 6, 1920. Meanwhile, in 1916, Bothwell had sold his remaining holdings on Horse Creek and the Sweetwater. He died in Santa Barbara, California, in 1928.[21]

# CHAPTER 13

# Story Spots

My father . . . had two little daughters, one of whom was buried on the plains here in Wyoming. He promised his wife that he would come back and take that body to the valley and bury it there, but when he came back for it with a number of chosen men, he found that the wolves had dug it up.

—*Heber J. Grant, 1931*

When he was ninety-five years old, the Oregon Trail booster Ezra Meeker published a novel, *Kate Mulhall*, in which the heroine crosses the plains with her family by ox team and wagon in the 1850s. On the way, Kate's mother dies near Devil's Gate, and the grieving family buries and leaves her there. The travelers mark the spot with a wagon tire, and with a wild rosebush and a small pine they transplant from a hillside to the head of the grave.

Many years later, Kate and other family members return in automobiles driven by her grandchildren. A sheepherder directs them to what he calls "the lone pine tree," and adds that he's always wondered how it came to grow by itself like that, out in the sagebrush. The family drives around a ravine and back toward the base of the tree. It stands 100 feet tall, in sight of both Devil's Gate and Split Rock and dominating everything around it. Wagon ruts, worn into the sandstone, pass nearby. The iron tire remains, arcing out of the ground in a half circle at the foot of the tree, and the rosebush is in bloom. In the illustration, the tree trunk rises straight as an obelisk. It's a monumental tree, a tree from the Adirondacks or the Cascades perhaps, but nothing like the tough scrub cedars and pitch pines that grow in the rocky hills along the Sweetwater.

Kate, her children, and grandchildren leave the cars and walk to the grave. They feel lightened, relieved. They've closed a circle. They've found an important part of their past and, to their comfort, they've found it thriving.[1]

Such a tree could never grow in such a place. But Ezra Meeker, who imagined it, was a visionary, which meant he could turn facts into symbols that glow with meaning. He walked into the national limelight in 1906, already an old man, when he, his two oxen Twist and Dave, their covered wagon, and a driver walked from Washington State to Washington, D.C. His white hair and beard were long and thick, his suits were rumpled, his hat original, and his eyes alert behind wire-rimmed glasses. He looked like an American Father Time, and he knew it. If anyone could make the nation believe that its pioneer past was an inspiration and a comfort to the living, he was the man for the job.

He had first crossed the trail in 1852, with his wife and their infant child, his brother, and his mother. His mother died somewhere along the Platte and another brother, crossing two years later, drowned at Devil's Gate. But the rest of the family settled in a temperate valley southeast of Seattle, founded the town of Puyallup, and prospered; Meeker made and lost at least two fortunes before setting out on his long walk at age seventy-five. He repeated the stunt twice more, selling his book, *Ox-Team*, and souvenir postcards to pay expenses. He crossed the continent a fourth time by automobile in 1916 and a fifth in 1926, by open-cockpit airplane, with his false teeth in his pocket for safekeeping.

He stopped in newspaper offices, met with commercial clubs, spoke to crowds in parks. His message was the same, time after time: something important happened here; raise the money and put up a monument before the world forgets; civilized people remember the past with an eye toward a better future. Sometimes the reception was warm, sometimes not. On his first trip he met President

Oregon Trail booster Ezra Meeker, shown here in 1925 with sculptor Avard Fairbanks, was keenly aware of his image as an American Father Time. Photograph
by Martin Studio, Eugene, Oregon, courtesy of Eugene Fairbanks.

Theodore Roosevelt. He lobbied Congress for federal funds for
trail monuments. He and his ox team were mobbed in New York by
men in boaters and bowler hats. He was a publicity machine.

In the final decade of his life, Meeker founded the Oregon Trail
Memorial Association, which institutionalized his desires.[2] By 1926
it had a headquarters in New York, with offices provided by the
American Highway Association, and links with big-money names
like Rockefeller, Morgan, and Eastman. In 1926, the association
successfully lobbied Congress to approve the minting of six million
Oregon Trail memorial half-dollars. The coins were sold by the
association for a dollar each. Profits were to go to build trail monuments, and to other, less well defined efforts at memorializing. On
one side of the coin, a pioneer family walks with ox team and prairie schooner toward the setting sun. On the other, an Indian man,

naked but for a breechclout, holds up a hand as if to stop the traffic coming from the East.[3]

Meeker made a last attempt to cross the country in 1928, again by automobile. This time, Henry Ford provided him with a brand-new prairie-schooner-topped Model A, with "Over the Old Oregon Trail" painted on the canvas. Meeker traveled to Detroit to see the vehicle, but fell ill before the journey could start. Ford put him on a train back to Seattle where, a few days later, he died, just short of his ninety-eighth birthday.[4] More than any other single person, Meeker had rolled the prairie schooner to full stop in America as a symbol of pioneer virtue and hope. But he also set other forces in motion that would continue to roll with the times.

Utah, late in the nineteenth century, was an isolated and parochial place, run by men with many wives and women with many children. The families that succeeded cooperated with other families and submitted to church authority, and the result was the West's most stable, consistently prosperous, and conformist society. This is not to say that Mormon Utah was the only Utah—it was not; there was a vigorous, parallel, boom-and-bust, mining-and-smelting Utah that was largely non-Mormon. Nor was Utah the vast, separate Deseret its founders dreamed of, tucked away forever from a nation that despised it. For better and worse, it was part of the West and part of the world. People came and went. Many of its earliest settlers suffered the difficult crossing only to find, once they arrived, they could not stand the conformity demanded of them, and left again.[5] And in later generations, plenty were born Mormon who did not stay Mormon—or did not stay very Mormon. But even when they fell away from religion, they often clung to the Mormon habit of enshrining an official past.

One not-too-Mormon Mormon was Howard R. Driggs, born in Pleasant Grove, south of Salt Lake City, in 1873. He would spend a long career as a teacher of teachers, first at normal schools in Utah and eventually as a full professor in the education department at New York University. He wrote many books and edited, co-wrote, and collaborated on many more. A few were about teaching; most meant to entertain and instruct young people about the western past. As a teenager, he often worked summers on family ranches around Driggs, on the Idaho side of the Tetons. We may imagine him alone with his uncles' cows in the lush meadows left by drained-out beaver ponds. As a boy, he knew old men who had been among the first whites to come into that country, and through them felt linked to a vivid past. "I reconstructed that almost primeval world and in my imagination lived in it," he wrote in his eighties. For him, the pioneers were "the men who had turned the great American West from a wilderness to a mighty storehouse of historic lore." The wild had been reduced to an archive in the space of a lifetime, and he elected himself archivist. He would see to it that the proper information was kept and cared for, and, when necessary, delivered into the proper hands.[6]

Driggs took a leave of absence from his job at the University of Utah in 1918, and came to New York. Soon he was writing boys' books that retold old men's stories. In 1919, he collaborated with Nick Wilson, whom he had known as a boy in Idaho, on *The White Indian Boy*, tales from Wilson's youth living among the Shoshones, riding for the Pony Express, driving a stagecoach, scouting for the army against his old friends the Gosiute Indians. In 1920, Driggs traveled to Puyallup and met Meeker for the first time; the result was *Ox-Team Days on the Oregon Trail*, which streamlined and recycled many of Meeker's tales from earlier, self-published books. Nineteen twenty-four saw publication of *The Bullwhacker: Adventures of a Frontier Freighter* by Bill Hooker, who had driven freight wagons across the Laramie Plains on the Medicine Bow-to-Fort Fetterman road in the 1870s, with Driggs listed as editor. Subsequent titles included *The Texas Ranger: A Story of the Southwestern Frontier, Rise of the Lone Star, Longhorn Cowboy, Jacko and the Dingo Boy, Deadwood Gold*, and *Hidden Heroes of the Rockies*. Many of these were published by the World Book Company in New York, in its Pioneer Life series of frontier biographies. Driggs was listed variously as co-author, collaborator, and editor. The books had a kind of wool-socks-and-desperadoes enthusiasm, and sold well among boys looking for adventure.

Through Meeker, Driggs linked up with the Oregon Trail Memorial Association from its earliest days. Where Meeker was valuable mostly as a public face and figurehead, however, Driggs soon became the real organizer, a position that would employ all his talents. Like Meeker, Driggs had an instinct for marking the best spots to imagine the past. "America has a heart[y] interest in this movement," he would tell the *Casper Daily Tribune* in 1930. "People go to Europe for its story spots, where history has been made and where literature has been created. We have our own story spots and they should be preserved, transformed into historic shrines."[7]

Driggs understood even better than Meeker the link between past drama and present commerce: historical monuments drew tourists. The same people who drove to mountain lakes for Sunday picnics would enjoy their scenery even more with a dash of story from the past. Local business and service clubs could be made to see the cash value in nostalgia, and would come up with funds for markers. Driggs also understood the larger changes that automobiles were bringing to the nation—both to the people who drove the cars and to the destinations they invaded. More cars needed more and better roads, and as better roads were built, more people went touring farther and farther from home. The trail association came to be as much about automobiles as about covered wagons. It became a club of mobile history buffs who caravanned along trail routes, with camping and campfire talks provided. Driggs was one of the club's best talkers, along with another living relic he revived—William Henry Jackson, the photographer.

In 1918, the same year Driggs left Utah, Jackson's wife died and Jackson moved back to Washington, D.C., to live with his daughter, Hallie. He had followed his years with the Hayden Survey with a long and successful career as a landscape photographer, commercial photographer, and photograph-company executive in Detroit. The Detroit Publishing and Detroit Photographic companies marketed photographs to millions. After World War I, however, with competition from cheaper postcard-printing techniques, the businesses collapsed. Jackson collected some back wages, but otherwise had little more than his Civil War pension. In Washington, he looked forward to a comfortable, scholarly retirement, attending meetings of the Cosmos Club, updating his old journals, writing, and painting again.

Then in June 1924, Jackson got a fan letter from the West. Robert Ellison, president of the Midwest Oil Refinery in Casper and officer of the Natrona County Historical Society, had acquired a folio of survey photographs from the 1870s. He was an amateur historian with money to spend, and he was a friend of Howard Driggs.

Within a few months Ellison put Jackson in touch with patrons looking for paintings of western subjects. Ellison was also in touch with Driggs, and in March 1925, Driggs, looking for a new book subject, contacted Jackson. Jackson doubted that his life had been exciting enough for a book. In his western travels through the strife-torn 1860s, he wrote Ellison, he had never seen any shots fired or fired any himself. Would the World Book Company really be interested in so tame a past? Ellison suggested spicing it up: "I do not see any reason . . . why you should not draw on your imagination a little in writing a boy's book," he replied.[8]

Ellison invited Jackson to come visit, look over the portfolio, and tour some old haunts. The old man—Jackson was eighty-one—was uneasy, but Ellison and an entourage of family and oil-company associates whisked him off on an auto tour to Yellowstone, by way of the Shoshone Reservation and Jackson Hole. Jackson was feted and photographed, and took photos of his own. Back in Casper, Ellison persuaded him to write out some autobiographical notes. Ellison revised the results and published them himself over his own byline in a pamphlet, *William H. Jackson: Pioneer of the Yellowstone.* Jackson was beginning his final career—as an artifact of western heritage, a new invention of men like Ellison and Driggs.

That same year, Jackson agreed to work with Driggs on an autobiography. He began retyping his early western diaries into more condensed narrative, and at the same time began painting steadily for the customers Ellison was finding for him. They were interested primarily in original drawings left from the early days, of which

Painting the Past. Myth, memory, and history overlap in William Henry Jackson's 1936 painting of wagons approaching Independence Rock. He's simplified the land forms, and opened Devil's Gate wider than it really looks from there. Courtesy of Scott's Bluff National Monument collection.

Jackson had very few. Their second preference was for pictures he made from memory, often based on his own early photographs. Third, they wanted paintings of famous western events, particularly Indian fights. Ellison and Driggs began using new Jackson pictures to illustrate their publications, gaining extra cachet by the connection, and funneling to Jackson money he badly needed. No one seems to have been much interested in the empty or near-empty landscapes Jackson had painted and photographed so evocatively in his youth. People wanted incident; they wanted action. Places didn't mean much to them unless there was a story going on in the foreground. Jackson, buoyed by Ellison's and Driggs' kibitzing enthusiasm, was happy to provide what they wanted.[9]

After Meeker's death in 1928, Driggs, clearly the heir apparent, was named president of the Oregon Trail Memorial Association. Now all his writing, speaking, and organizing talents could be unleashed, to enshrine the kind of West he wanted remembered.[10] In 1929, the World Book Company published Jackson's autobiography as *The Pioneer Photographer: Rocky Mountain Adventures with a Camera*, with Driggs listed as collaborator. Soon afterward, he hired Jackson as "research secretary" for the Oregon Trail Memorial Association, and Jackson moved to New York. The old man checked historical facts for association publications from time to time, and continued to paint historical pictures. His real job, however, was to succeed Meeker as pioneer-in-residence. If Driggs was the association's great speaker and organizer, Jackson was its totem. Year after year until his death in 1942, often with Driggs, he rode in parades, dedicated new monuments, gave campfire talks, slide talks, and told stories at Driggs' story spots.

In August 1929, Driggs and other trail association directors visited Ellison in Casper, and they began planning an event at Independence Rock that remains unsurpassed. Ellison wrote another pamphlet, this one on Independence Rock, and again it was published by the Natrona County Historical Society, and included reproductions of Jackson's history-pageant paintings. By this point Ellison represented not just local but also statewide interests in the public marking of historical places and times, as by now he was chairman of the Historical Landmarks Commission of Wyoming. He'd founded it in 1926—writing the legislation that established it and lobbying for it successfully. The three commissioners served without pay, charged with acquiring threatened historic sites and with marking and commemorating many more. By 1929 the commission had acquired Fort Bridger for the state, and inside of a few more years would acquire Fort Laramie too, and eventually turn it over to the National Park Service. If Ellison hadn't taken up the banner of historical preservation during the twenties in Wyoming, someone else almost surely would have. It was part of a growing sense of self-awareness in the West, made up, in about equal parts, of a desire to preserve the past and a desire to draw more tourists.[11]

Driggs, meanwhile, was moving on the national level. First, he got President Herbert Hoover to declare 1930 the official centenary of the Oregon Trail, and governors in trail states issued similar proclamations.[12] Besides a gathering at Independence Rock over the Fourth of July, there would be other gatherings, too—at Fort Laramie in August, at St. Louis in April, and, oddly enough, on Governor's Island in New York harbor in June.[13] But the gathering at Independence Rock was the biggest—somewhere between 3,000 and 15,000 people were there, depending on who was counting—the longest, and the only one, thanks to the Boy Scouts, with an entire book written about it.

*Boy Scouts and the Oregon Trail*, published that fall by Putnam's Sons in New York, was one of dozens of such titles that sold steadily in the 1920s and '30s.[14] Scouting was still quite young—the Boy Scouts of America was just twenty years old in 1930—and its two main strains, love of nature and love of the flag, were held in a kind of rough equilibrium by the martinet James E. West, chief scout executive.[15] The national offices, under West, were located in New York, and, perhaps unsurprisingly, there were close connections between the scouts and the Oregon Trail Memorial Association. Lorne W. Barclay, Driggs' executive director at the association, had worked for many years in state, national, and overseas Boy Scout efforts. The philanthropist George D. Pratt, chairman of the Oregon Trail board, was treasurer of the Boy Scouts of America.

The Independence Rock event is still remembered primarily as a scout rendezvous. More than 600 Boy Scouts from fifteen states and their scoutmasters made the trek that summer. Nearly two-thirds were from Wyoming, but Utah and Nebraska sent large contingents, and good-sized groups came from Texas, Pennsylvania, Idaho, and Missouri. Most glamorous were the five scouts from New York City, one from each borough, who met with a mounted Governor Franklin Roosevelt before they left, and carried a letter from him to Governor Frank Emerson of Wyoming. They traveled in Ezra Meeker's oxmobile at Henry Ford's expense, and were greeted by Mayor Jimmy Walker on their return.

Most tidy were the scouts from Utah, with the Denver contingent a close second. Most single-minded, probably, were Eagle Scouts Eugene Crawford and Chester Kowalski, who hitchhiked

Wyoming-bound Boy Scouts. New York Governor Franklin D. Roosevelt hands a message for Wyoming Governor Frank Emerson to Clinton S. Martin, leader of the most glamorous of the Boy Scout contingents to drive to Independence Rock for the Fourth of July, 1930. They traveled in the canvas-covered "oxmobile" that Henry Ford had orginally customized for Ezra Meeker. From Martin, *Boy Scouts and the Oregon Trail.*

separately from Chicago.[16] Most history-minded may have been the contingent from Kansas City, whose route most closely followed the Oregon Trail. Best-named were the Bull Dogs, a troop from Pittsburgh. In their excitement before leaving, their scoutmaster wrote later, the boys "probably saw flitting through their dreams a confused pageant of Indians and cowboys and pioneers fighting for the right to the west and a group of Allegheny County Boy Scouts arriving on the scene of action just in time to save the day for the white man."

Feelings among the Shoshone Boy Scouts from Fort Washakie, on the Wind River Reservation in Wyoming, may have been more complicated. They got to play "Indians" in the second night's pageant: a wagon train circled, the Indians attacked, and a troop of mounted scouts in uniform rode to the rescue—an event as complicated, culturally, as black musicians of the same era wearing blackface to imitate white minstrels wearing blackface to caricature blacks. Afterward, Chief Tecumseh, a singer from Omaha, sang Indian songs solo from the top of the Rock, while the sun set and a big bonfire burned below. Many were moved by the singing and the setting. Afterward, the chief, "a full-blooded Indian," the Pittsburgh scoutmaster remembered, put his arms around the Shoshone boys "and made a moving plea for the Indian race." Like the setting sun, he went on, the tribes were passing away, and it was beautiful. "And as one looked at the Indians in the Boy Scout uniform," the scout master continued, "one felt happy to know that the organization was doing its part to take these boys, with their sacred traditions and closeness to nature, and help mould them into true Americans."[17]

Such ironies, if noticed, went publicly unremarked during three days of heat, dust, crowds, and speeches. Anticipating the traffic, the Wyoming Highway Department graded, graveled, and oiled the road from Casper to Rawlins. A big campsite had already been prepared—the sagebrush bulldozed off, latrines and a well dug, a speaker's stand built against the steep north wall of the Rock, and its railings draped with bunting. Most scouts camped in Casper or Rawlins the night before, and traveled the last leg to the Rock the morning of July 3. There they pitched pup tents and a few teepees on the northeast side in two large, crescent-shaped encampments, leaving an open space in the middle for pageants and parades.

Probably it was in that open space the first morning, where some local cowboys, just done with branding, staged a quick rodeo. That afternoon the scouts swam in the river, and as evening came on they were entertained first by a troupe of dancers from an Indian school in Colorado Springs, then the wagon-train attack, Chief Tecumseh's songs, a bonfire, and a big fireworks display. By midmorning Friday, the glorious Fourth, at least 3,500 people were on hand. Ceremonies opened with a long speech by Driggs, and shorter remarks from treasurer Pratt and executive West of the Boy Scouts, dedicating a bronze plaque to Ezra Meeker. There was a speech by the governor. After lunch came the Catholics—the bishop of Wyoming and a Jesuit from St. Louis University—dedicating a plaque to Father De Smet. Next the Masons met on top of the Rock, only Master Masons invited, to commemorate the first Masonic meeting in Wyoming, on the same spot in 1862. Late in the afternoon, ceremonies moved over to Devil's Gate, where Casper's Business and Professional Women's Club dedicated one monument to unknown pioneers, and a second to unknown pioneer women who died on the trail. They were near the Sun Ranch gate. Across the road from the ranch, little American flags fluttered in the breeze, marking otherwise unmarked graves on a hillside.

By afternoon, the *Casper Daily Tribune* reported, the crowd had swelled to 6,000, many of whom appear to have spent a night or two. The American Legion sold refreshments at a commissary tent; cold drinks sold briskly. There was a telegraph office, a tire repair service, and a press tent, where reporters dispatched stories to the *Natrona County Tribune*, the *Rawlins Republican*, the *Denver Post*, and the *Deseret News*. The city of Casper ran busses to the Rock intermittently Thursday and Saturday, and all day on Friday, the Fourth. People swarmed the Rock like ants on an anthill, the Casper paper reported, and the cars stretched toward Casper and Rawlins looked like a solid line of ants, going and coming.[18]

And, of course, the Mormons were on hand with a large, enthusiastic, and always slightly separate contingent. The *Deseret News*, owned then and now by the Mormon Church, advanced the event in a long article six days early, and then dispatched a reporter with the car caravan of 200 faithful on their pilgrimage to the Rock. The paper's coverage was careful, thorough, and written as if the Mormon past at Independence Rock and Devil's Gate was the only past that mattered—which, as far as its readership was concerned, was mostly true.[19]

The caravan camped its first night out at Fort Bridger, in the heavily Mormon Bridger Valley in southwest Wyoming. There, joined by local Saints around a big campfire, they sang the songs and danced the dances of 1847, "all bringing back the color and picturesqueness of a pioneer encampment," the *News* reported. Then there was time for serious talks from the senior men.

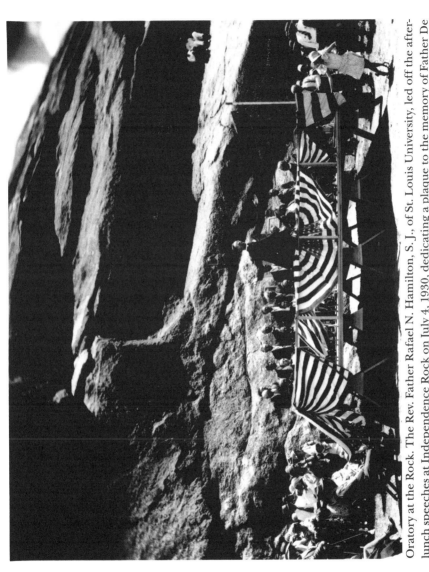

Oratory at the Rock. The Rev. Father Rafael N. Hamilton, S.J., of St. Louis University, led off the after-lunch speeches at Independence Rock on July 4, 1930, dedicating a plaque to the memory of Father De Smet. Courtesy of Wyoming State Archives.

Master of ceremonies that evening was the bespectacled, sickly—eventually he was diagnosed with a kind of lupus—George Albert Smith. A direct descendant of a first cousin of Joseph Smith, the prophet, George Albert Smith was a member of the Quorum of the Twelve Apostles, the top advisors to church President Heber J. Grant, and would succeed Grant as president fifteen years later. Smith liked to stay in the background of things and seems to have settled disputes by his very mildness and loveableness, according to church accounts. And he was Mormonism's strongest advocate of scouting. In 1911, the Church of Jesus Christ of Latter-day Saints had become the first denomination to adopt scouting as a permanent part of its ministry. Smith had brought that about, and it is fair to assume that it was through him that the Mormons were included in the planning of the entire Independence Rock event.

After Smith spoke, Andrew Jenson read out selections from the earliest Mormon emigrant diaries. Jenson, now seventy-nine, had crossed the trail in 1866, coming from Denmark with his parents. Supplies ran short; Indians ran off half their stock, and a September snow at South Pass could have killed them had their church train been led by less experienced men. Jenson had worked as assistant church historian since 1897, but had been passed over for the office's top position, church historian, in 1921, reportedly a great disappointment in his life. He was not a big thinker. His autobiography shows he was a careful and thorough recorder of facts, unconcerned with their implications.[20]

Quite the opposite was Brigham H. Roberts, who told tales of his own covered-wagon crossing that night at the campfire. Writer, politician, historian, theologian, and the oldest U.S. Army chaplain in World War I, he had been husband of three wives at once and fathered fifteen children. In 1898 he was elected as a Democrat to the U.S. House of Representatives, but Congress refused to seat him because of his polygamy. He was the greatest Mormon thinker of his generation, or perhaps any generation, he was the faith's ablest defender, and yet late in his life, he was torn by doubt. He worried, for example, about the many pigs, asses, cattle, and horses in the Book of Mormon's ancient America, all animals that, he knew, showed no evidence of having existed in the Americas before the Spaniards came. In an attempt to face his doubts honestly, Roberts wrote out a pair of long manuscripts and took them before the church president and apostles. He was met first with a blank silence, then by simple declarations that the Book was true, instead of the argument and engagement he had longed for. Roberts's *Book of Mormon Difficulties: A Study,* and *A Book of Mormon Study* were not published until 1985, fifty-two years after his death, and the autobiography he dictated during the last nine months of his life was not published until 1990. His doubts, he knew, were too dangerous for publication during his lifetime, and so he kept them to himself. He remained in the upper levels of church authority as a member of The Seventy, but never rose higher. If Jenson's advancement was stalled by his lack of intellectual equipment, Roberts's was stalled because he thought too deeply.

Like Jenson and William Henry Jackson, Roberts had crossed the trail in 1866. He was something like an orphan; he and his sister had been left behind in England with a semicriminal foster family when, newly converted, his mother left her husband, took one child and headed for Utah. When Roberts and his sister were able to follow, they were robbed and cheated by fellow Mormons along the way, and on the trail slept under wagons without tents or blankets. For much of the journey, he had no shoes. All his life, he would remember his sister's care for his chapped, cut, and cactus-punctured feet each night. Once, hoping to get a forbidden ride in a wagon by hiding in a barrel, he was surprised to find his feet sinking into four inches of molasses as he lowered them to the bottom. The black goo stung his cracked feet terribly, but he kept quiet, fell asleep, and woke up sticky. He was nine years old. Whether he told these stories that night at the campfire went unrecorded by the *Deseret News.*[21]

On July 3, the caravan arrived at the Rock late in the day and arranged their tents on the flat in the shape of a large beehive. That night again, Smith emceed and Jenson and Roberts were principal speakers at a separate Mormon program that attracted hundreds, the *Deseret News* reported, away from the main festivities.[22]

On the Fourth, when the crowds were at their largest, Driggs introduced all the pioneers—his entire stable of codgers—to the multitude. Jenson, Roberts, and William Henry Jackson, the 1866 trail-crossers, were given special status, as was Ruth May Fox, an early Utah suffragist, now president of the Young Women's Mutual Improvement Association, one of the main engines of getting things done in Mormon Utah. Fox, too, had crossed the trail in her youth. Also on hand were locals Finn Burnett, who had served in General Connor's 1865 Powder River campaign, and Tom Sun's old hunting partner, Boney Earnest, still living at Alcova since his ranch had been flooded by the reservoir. Driggs also introduced a couple of his World Book Company cohorts: ex-bullwhacker Bill Hooker and ex-cowboy Jim Cook.

Odd as the combination of people seems now, and mixed as Driggs's motives may have been in assembling it, no one else would have thought to draw so many of the West's diverse strains together. Driggs was a politician of the past; he knew the Oregon Trail Memorial Association needed a broad base if it was to look legitimate and thrive. The Boy Scouts alone wouldn't provide that, nor would just the Rock, nor local ranchers, nor Mormons. But mix together everything the Rock's past could offer—Mormons, Catholics, Masons, stir it up with Boy Scouts for mortar, add a few Indians for color and sprinkle in some codgers for an authentic smell—and you'd have something worth talking about. You'd have a story spot with a whole new generation of stories.

Seven decades later, Thad Walker of Casper remembered the gathering as hot and dusty, with no shade at all. The speeches had seemed endless, and the open latrines stank and frightened a young boy. He would have been too young to appreciate the sheer ambition of what Driggs had done. Driggs the promoter was also Driggs the educator, Driggs the teacher of teachers. He believed schools needed to teach the American past as an inspiration to schoolchildren. That meant smoothing off the West's sharp edges, treating it as though it were a place of ennobling successes, only. It also meant taking a bigger picture, a longer view, making popular a new comprehensiveness, accurate or not. He did all this at Independence

Rock, in 1930, at the start of the Depression, before anyone called it that or sensed the hard times coming.

Later on the Fourth, some of the Utahns set off to put up a marker a mile south of the Rock, where the Mormon geographer and astronomer Orson Pratt, counselor to Brigham Young, had measured longitude and latitude in 1847. And when the ceremonies moved to the Sun Ranch late in the day, to dedicate the marker to the unknown pioneer women, the Mormons were certain the graves were their own. "According to the leaders of the Utah party," reported the *Deseret News*, "all information indicates that the graves were those of 'Mormon' handcart veterans, who died in 1856 of exposure after having been overtaken by early October snows."

The following day, Saturday the fifth, the Utahns again visited the Sun Ranch, this time Martin's Cove itself, to put up a marker and conduct a short service. Then they took a rougher, slower route home, up the Sweetwater and over South Pass, following the old route closely in their cars—Jenson would remember riding in his son Parley's "splendid automobile"—stopping and studying spot after historical spot.

The Mormons weren't finished. They had more marking to do. In 1930, when the various Driggs constituents had dedicated strong bronze plaques, the Mormons had managed only a big square of white paint, with black lettering on it commemorating the 1847 passage. This may indicate that Driggs and Ellison included them only late in the planning process, and they hadn't had time to get a plaque made. The next year, in any case, they returned to finish the job, and this time had the place and the past to themselves.

A crowd of a few hundred, nearly all of them Saints, gathered Sunday morning June 21, 1931, the eighty-fourth anniversary of the first Mormon wagon train's noon stop at the Rock, to hear church President Heber J. Grant dedicate a permanent plaque. Grant spoke for a long time, mostly in praise of Brigham Young, whom he had known as a boy and some of whose wives had been close friends of Grant's mother all the way back in Nauvoo. Grant himself had been born on Main Street, he told the little crowd, by which he meant Main Street, Salt Lake City, when downtown was still quilted with orchards and cabbage patches. His family's house was just a block from Brother Brigham's many-gabled Lion House, where the president lived with twenty or so of his wives. Grant's own father had lost one of his wives on the trek west, and two of her daughters had also died on the trail, one of them in Wyoming. Years later, when Grant's father had returned to look for the spot, there was no past left to find. Wolves, he assumed, had scattered the remains.

Like all of his Mormon listeners that day, Utah-born or not, trek veterans or not, Grant kept the trail at the center of his understanding of who he was. Stories like the one told by Grant's father bound them together; now they were celebrating a strictly Mormon anniversary, with a largely Mormon crowd. A small auto caravan, just fifty people this time but led again by George Albert Smith and Andrew Jenson, had left Salt Lake City the morning of June 19. They stopped at trail sites in Utah, ate lunch in Evanston, Wyoming, and drew a crowd of five hundred Mormons that night for another big campfire at Fort Bridger. The next day, they stayed on roads close to the old trail—across the Green River, past Pacific Springs and South Pass, and on down the Sweetwater. It was the route of the handcart rescuers of 1856, and the route of fictional Kate Mulhall, late in her life, on her auto pilgrimage back to her mother's grave.

They arrived at the Rock late in the afternoon of Saturday, June 20, in time for a big picnic supper. By Sunday morning, the crowd had swelled to several hundred, mostly Mormon families from Casper and Rawlins. Grant had traveled to Rawlins by train and arrived at the Rock that morning by car. Speeches started at 10. Besides Grant, there were a number of Mormons, including, to represent Wyoming's governor, Wyoming Senate President Clarence Gardner, who also happened to be president of the Star Valley Stake. There was a sprinkling of non-Mormons too, among them former Wyoming Governor B. B. Brooks, the new chairman of the Historical Landmark Commission. Driggs was on hand again and said a few words on behalf of the Trail Association. But he was not the main attraction this year. Nor, even, was the new plaque, nor Heber J. Grant's long speech about it. As far as the *Deseret News* was concerned, when all was said and done the biggest story was Martin's Cove.

"PIONEER TRAIL GROUP LOCATES TRAGIC REFUGE," the *News* announced when the caravan returned to Salt Lake City. George Albert Smith said the matter was settled—a cove about two and a half miles west of Devil's Gate was where the suffering members of the Martin Handcart Company had camped to wait for rescue or death. Members of the auto caravan had visited the site, and searched it thoroughly for physical evidence of the handcart-ers' presence, seventy-five years before. They had found nothing, the paper reported. No bones, no buttons, no tools. Still, Smith's examination of the land, together with his reading of Dan Jones's account of the rescue, made it clear the cove was the place. While survivors of the 1856 handcart disasters were still alive, church officials had never managed to travel back to the cove with any of them and mark the spot, the paper noted. Now, after looking for the place for many years, the officials were convinced they had it right. This was the place. The paper ran a photo of church leaders at the cove. They stopped also at a site on Rock Creek where they believed many members of the Willie Company had died, placed a marker there, and then camped near South Pass. On Monday, they returned to Salt Lake, Smith made his announcement, the paper ran it Tuesday and that, as far as everyone was concerned, settled the matter.

No one seems to have had a copy of Jones's book handy to check what he actually wrote. In *Forty Years among the Indians*, published in 1890, thirty-four years after the disaster, he noted only that "The hand-cart company was moved over to a cove in the mountains for shelter and fuel; a distance of two miles from the [Seminoe] fort."[23]

Smith was an apostle, a member of the Quorum of the Twelve and it would have been unseemly for the *News* to have questioned his authority. Jones's geography, vague as it was, was more specific than anything the rescuers' primary journal keeper—Robert T. Burton—had written at the time.[24] For George Albert Smith to announce that Jones's account settled the matter seems, in retrospect, too hopeful. He was driven, of course, by the same desire that drove Kate Mulhall in her search for her mother's grave: the need to find the place where the past could be located. Once located, the past can be kept alive and cared for, in ways that meet the needs of the living.

# CHAPTER 14

# Perfect Balance

Those who served in this project have been blessed—every one of you. And those on the other side have been blessed as you have done for them that which they could not do for themselves.

*—Gordon B. Hinckley, first counselor*
*in the LDS First Presidency, 1992*

Scott Lorimer is a round-faced, thickset man in his early fifties, with a friendly smile, intelligent eyes, and a long memory. He is chief financial officer of U.S. Energy, based in Riverton, Wyoming. One Friday in December he made time for me and I interviewed him there, in his roomy corner office. It was a mild, dress-down, Christmastime Friday; Scott was off doing errands when I arrived and a secretary in jeans and a sweater showed me into his office to wait. The building was modern and comfortable, lots of plate glass, plants, and sandstone; his office included a main desk with a lower desk teed off it. I sat there and looked through notes of a previous conversation; he arrived shortly, also in jeans, also smiling, and sat across from me at the lower desk, leaving his main chair empty.

I had met him only once before, a month earlier when he'd driven over to Casper to talk to our little group of Oregon Trail buffs. That time, as is proper for a Mormon in public representing

Mormon interests, he had worn a suit and tie, and so at this second meeting I was caught off guard by the informality of his attire.

Besides his corporate position, he has held important ecclesiastical ones. He is a former president of the Riverton Stake, more or less a Mormon diocese, with about 2,800 members. In 1991 the stake presidency—that is, the president and his first and second counselors—received an inspiration, as the stake tells it, that there was a great deal of spiritual effort left to be performed on behalf of the dead Willie and Martin handcart company pioneers. "We didn't hear any voices or see anything, or anything like that," Lorimer said. "But you know how you get an idea in your head?" He was more explicit when he talked to the *Church News* at the time, a weekly section in the *Deseret News*, the daily paper owned by the Mormon church. He felt the spirit of the Willie people resting on him, he told the paper, and first interpreted the pressure as an inspiration for the church to acquire one of the sites of their suffering, at what the Mormons now call Rock Creek Hollow. Later, he came to understand the pressure as something more complicated, more diffuse, and more demanding of labor.

The Mormons call it temple work. Nearly all the handcarters in 1856 were recent converts. Most were baptized during their lifetimes, but many were not. In the Mormon world, it's never too late to baptize people, even long after they're dead, and to seal them for all eternity to a spouse or to parents or children. This ensures that families can stay united, and that the advantage of one family member will benefit all as they advance to higher and better planes in the afterlife. These ceremonies, or ordinances, are time-consuming, and are too important to be performed in ward house or stake house; they must be performed in a temple. The Riverton stake lies in the bailiwick of the Ogden, Utah, temple, a six-hour drive away.

President Gordon B. Hinckley, then eighty-one, first counselor to church President Ezra Taft Benson, ninety-two, was surprised to learn the temple work for such legendary Saints was still incomplete. "President, don't you stop until it's finished," he told Lorimer. So Scott and his counselors asked for volunteers. There were around

1,300 Saints altogether in the Willie and Martin handcart companies and the two wagon trains close behind. All had to be sealed to their parents, sealed to their children, and if necessary baptized; most had had this work performed before by family members, as is customary, but many had not. The volunteers stepped up, nearly 1,200 strong. First they researched the names and relationships on new computers linked to the church's vast genealogical records, and then made the six-hour drive each way to perform the ceremonies in the Ogden temple. There were 4,007 ordinances to perform, at two hours per ordinance. It was an enormous investment. "This project has lit our stake on fire," Lorimer told the *Church News* later. "We know these people. . . . I have a testimony of life after death. We love them. They are our friends."

In August 1992, President Hinckley came to Wyoming for the dedication of three new monuments. One was on Rocky Ridge, a high point on the trail east of South Pass that the handcarters crossed with great difficulty. The second was at what Mormons call Rock Creek Hollow, east of Rocky Ridge at its base, at a spot where the Mormons are convinced the Willie Company had stalled, and many died. And the third was at Martin's Cove. Where the first rescue had saved many pioneers from freezing and death, now the Second Rescue, as the Riverton Saints call it, saved their souls from stalling in the afterlife. Non-Mormon historians continue to point to a variety of good reasons to doubt church versions of who and how many died where. But for Mormons, the three sites are sacred ground, and of the three, the cove is holiest of all. "It's a lot more," Lorimer told me, "than just a place where the people died."[1]

Not far from Martin's Cove, a local carpenter built a gate for Tom Sun sometime before 1900, across the entrance to the ranch yard from the public road. The gate was perhaps twenty feet long, from the post it pivoted on to the post it closed against. The top beam was a foot thick and a man's height above the ground; it and the other posts and rails were all strapped together at their intersections. The gate was literally bound with the past, tied together with lengths of transcontinental telegraph wire still cluttering up the

The Gate of Perfect Balance. Five-year-old Adelaide Sun sits on the gate at the entry to the Sun Ranch yard, about 1940. It was so well balanced that a person could push it open with a finger. Courtesy of Adelaide Sun Reinholtz.

ranch at the time; later repairs were made with strips of hide. A cow skull hung at the middle of the top beam, with the Suns' hub and spoke brand between the eyes. Beyond the pivot post, the top beam extended some distance and slanted down at a slight angle. Here a wooden trough was attached, and filled with rocks from the Sweetwater Valley to the exact weight of the rest of the gate. The counterweight was so true, everyone said, that a child could move the gate with a single finger. It was called the Gate of Perfect Balance.[2]

Sun died at a hospital in Denver in 1909, of Bright's disease; he was about sixty-four. The ranch passed to his only son, Thomas E. Sun, generally known as Tom Sun, Jr. He and his wife, Nellie, had five children: Tom Sun III, known as Thomas; George; John Hugh; Bernard; and finally Adelaide, born in 1937 and thirteen years younger than Bernard. The four boys were all old enough to be on hand for the 1930 scout rendezvous and speechfest at Independence Rock, where the Boy Scouts presented them with the American flag that had flown over the encampment.

Unlike many neighboring ranches, the Sun Ranch survived the droughts and Great Depression of the thirties intact, and survived as well the advent of the new public-land grazing-lease system that came with the Taylor Grazing Act of 1934. A rancher still had to own only a small fraction of the land he actually grazed his cattle on, but now he paid a fee for the grass he'd grazed free for generations. The leases came up for renewal on ten-year cycles, and the system of who grazed what moved formally from custom into law.[3] The old General Land Office was absorbed into the new Bureau of Land Management, and the government, in the wake of the New Deal, was charged with protecting and managing the rangeland it had never been able to give away or sell.

The Hub and Spoke, as the home ranch was called, was still headquartered on the Suns' original Desert Land claim on the Sweetwater, just upstream from Devil's Gate. A person who pushed open the Gate of Perfect Balance would see a log bunkhouse on the right, a big log barn straight ahead to the north, and off to the left a low, L-shaped, whitewashed log house with a porch along the inside limbs of the L. Poppies grew by a garden fence in front of the house, and cottonwoods arched above it.

The ranch house was built from several cabins skidded or disassembled and moved off other homestead claims as the Suns acquired them over the years. Mary Hellihan Sun, the senior Tom Sun's widow, lived until 1936 and kept a sitting room and bedroom in the toe and foot of the L. Around the heel, Thomas and Bernard had a couple of rooms. Along the long limb were a kitchen and dining room big enough to feed and serve the whole ranch, then a storeroom tacked on to the west side, and on the south end, another bedroom. It was here, Kathleen told me, that she and John Hugh lived the first few months of their marriage, right after World War II. At other times the room was lived in by various ranch hands. By then Tom Sun, Jr., and Nellie lived in another, smaller house just west of the main house.

Scattering away from the main ranch yard were an ice house, a meat house, shops, sheds, and a jumble of corrals. Devil's Gate itself was and still is on a piece of state land just north of the Hub and Spoke corrals. By the thirties, the Suns' deeded land ran several miles west up the Sweetwater; cattle grazed there and on leased land running north to the rocks and south a much greater distance.

Early on, the Suns acquired a little 160-acre piece many miles to the east, near the Buzzard Ranch, near Sand Creek. For decades they swapped use of the piece and the grazing land around it for a Buzzard 160 much closer to them, across the public road east of the Hub and Spoke and up against the Sentinel Rocks, south of Ind-pendence Rock. This piece brought with it the grazing on the Beef Acre, a big surrounding pasture of government land. Early in the 1920s, Tom Sun, Jr., acquired Savage Pocket, an eighty-acre piece in the rocks north of Devil's Gate. Late in the 1920s the Suns bought the Bucklin Ranch, just south of the Hub and Spoke towards Muddy Gap, after its owner was killed in a gruesome tractor accident.[4] With the Bucklin Ranch came water rights in Whiskey and Muddy creeks, flowing north out of the gaps of the same names. Finally, during these years, the ranch acquired a forty-acre piece near Lost Soldier, south of Whiskey Peak and Green Mountain, bringing with it, for the first time, grazing rights on the surrounding desert land.

Tom Sun, Jr., may have felt like expanding once the price con-trols on beef were lifted after World War II, though family tradition says he kept buying more ranches just to keep his sons busy. After the war they leased the Bar Eleven, east of the new highway to Rawlins and south of the Beef Acre. John Hugh married Kathleen Douglas in 1946 and they ran the place out of its drafty log house. The family bought the Bar Eleven in 1949, and began leasing the Turkey Track, the next ranch west up the Sweetwater from the Hub and Spoke, where the Durbins had headquartered in the 1880s. In 1951 the fam-ily formed the Sun Land and Cattle company, and bought the Turkey Track. With it came more grazing rights south of the mountains.

Still the ranch and the family kept growing. Thomas never married, and made his life on the ranch, usually spending summers with the cattle around Lost Soldier, and the cold months with them on winter range on the Turkey Track. George married Dorothy Boyles in 1944, worked as a surveyor in the uranium industry, and eventually moved to Dorothy's family's ranch on Poison Spider Creek, west of Casper. George and Dorothy's children—Dennis, David, Maureen, and Margaret—grew up mostly in Casper, though they often spent time at the Hub and Spoke in summers and Dennis would work there much of his young manhood. On the Bar Eleven, meanwhile, Kathleen and John Hugh had three sons and a daughter—Jess, Steve, Janet, and George. Back at the Hub and Spoke, Bernard took on more of the responsibilities as his parents aged. In 1955 he married Noeline Esponda, from a longtime sheep-ranching Basque-American family in Buffalo, Wyoming. They eventually would have three children—Tena, Tom and Joe. Bernard and Noeline built a new house—it looks like a regular ranch-style suburban house—on a rise just across the old highway from the ranch yard. Adelaide, youngest of the children of Tom Sun, Jr., and Nellie, was sent away to school at age ten and, except for summers, never entirely returned. She married Larry Reinholtz in 1960, and they have recently moved from Rawlins to Cheyenne. When they first visited the ranch as a couple, Larry remembers now, the Gate of Perfect Balance was tied back and propped up, no longer swinging. It gradually disintegrated during the 1960s.

In 1961 the family corporation bought the Separation Ranch on Separation Flats, well south of the mountains and west of the highway to Rawlins. Kathleen and John Hugh moved to Rawlins and bought a house there, where their children could more easily go to school, and began running the southern end of the empire from town. Late in the 1960s, the Suns bought the Jawbone Ranch farther west on a corridor of the checkerboard lands, extending south now from Separation Flats to within six miles of I-80 and the line of the Union Pacific. The midsection of the ranch was bought last, in the 1970s—the Diamond Hook, and two ranches belonging to the Grieve and Stratton families at the foot of Whiskey Peak and Green Mountain, south of the Muddy Gap–Lander highway.

With that, the empire reached its greatest extent—more than 725 sections, important scraps of it deeded, the overwhelming majority leased—nearly half a million acres.[5] Contiguous pieces ran from Devil's Gate all the way to a point six miles north of Rawlins, nearly sixty miles. But like any empire, the forces that made it grow strengthened new forces that pulled it apart. The decision to expand so far south was probably a mistake.

Thomas died in 1981. George's brothers, Bernard and John Hugh, eventually bought out George's share; he died in 1988. For many years before that they had been running things, with Bernard at the power center and John Hugh on the rim.

When Kathleen and John Hugh moved to Rawlins, they had assumed they would continue running the south end and Bernard the north, and that they would someday divide it that way. The south end, however—big, dry, and barren even for ranching purposes—wasn't as good a piece of land. Kathleen and John solved their winter feed problems not with hay, as most ranches do, but the old-fashioned way, with space and distance. If the snow got too deep or the land too drouthy, they moved the cows somewhere else. By their fourth year down there, Kathleen and John Hugh understood what the country lacked. Some years they could run cattle on the ground through January, but not every year. "We didn't have any winter pasture," Kathleen told me, adding: "John said, 'This won't work.' And it didn't."

Still, they stayed, moving to a house at Willow Hill north of Rawlins once their children were out of school. The crunch came in the eighties with low beef prices and high interest rates; the Suns were paying 16 percent on their annual operating loans and 12.75 percent for long-term money. The family sold the Jawbone on the checkerboard lands first, and then after a few years sold the Separation Ranch, further upsetting the north-south balance that had never balanced all that well to start with. Relations between John Hugh and Bernard deteriorated. Then one day in 1994, Scott Lorimer happened to be on the ranch when the balance broke down completely. Through Scott, the Mormon Church was on hand too.

About a mile and a half west of where the Gate of Perfect Balance once swung so easily, a rock monument stands by the old highway. It is a spot with a good view across the river toward Martin's Cove. George Albert Smith returned to the area again in 1933, to put up this monument and another at a Willie Company site near South Pass. The plaque tells of the sufferings of the Martin Company, relates that they were caught by an early winter, and notes (incorrectly) that fifty-six died at the cove. For a century or more, this was as close as most non-Suns ever got to the place. It's an ideal view. The cove rises into the naked rocks. A sand dune, covered with sparse grass and sagebrush, rises up through the middle of the cove.

Many Mormons, without archeological evidence to back them up, are convinced the Martin Company members huddled mostly in a gully high along the cove's east edge. Some non-Mormon historians, likewise without archeological evidence, but arguing from geography and the pioneers' exhaustion, say a pocket against the rocks at the southwest corner of the cove seems more likely: the sufferers wouldn't have had to climb so high.[6] And from the vantage point of the George Albert Smith monument, as Lorimer calls it, it's quite clear there's another, very similar, slightly smaller cove in the granite face just to the east, and a third, larger, but still very similar cove just to the west. George Albert Smith, that sober guesser, may have been hedging his bets against the eventual appearance of artifacts. The monument doesn't say which cove it's talking about. Still, Mormons are positive they know.

In the spring of 1992, the Riverton Stake, fired by its temple work and newfound affection for the dead, hoped to put up a new monument at Martin's Cove. Deeded land runs along the river, but the land in the cove is public. Lorimer first approached Dennis Sun, George's son and Bernard's nephew, who at that time was ramrod on the north part of the ranch. The stake members wanted to build a monument on top of the sand dune—big enough to be seen from the George Albert Smith monument. This made a kind of sense. There was no way to get there but to cross the river and the

Sun land beyond. A monument on the dune top, however, would pinpoint the story spot for anyone who stopped by.

Dennis, who may also have been hoping for some kind of access deal with the church, was fine with the idea, as was the rest of the family. But the Bureau of Land Management wouldn't go along. The monument, it said, would ruin the view and risk too much erosion on the fragile dune. So all parties agreed on a smaller monument, out of sight of the old highway and sheltered in scrub cedars near the top of the dune and the gully.

On August 15, 1992, President Hinckley, Stake President Lorimer, and a small crowd of the faithful dedicated new monuments at Martin's Cove. Then they moved up toward South Pass and dedicated two Willie sites before much larger crowds. Afterwards, Hinckley asked Lorimer to see if he could work out a permanent easement with the Suns, to allow people to cross from the George Albert Smith monument to the river and the cove.

So Scott Lorimer and Bernard Sun began to get to know each other. Lorimer liked the old man: "He was the patriarch. He didn't talk much, but when he did, you'd better listen." And Bernard was ready to deal. He and Lorimer agreed, finally, on a one-mile-wide easement, from the old monument across the Suns' land and into the cove. The church would fence it, build underpasses for the cattle under an improved road, build a new footbridge over the Sweetwater, and pay a fee, the amount of which Lorimer wouldn't disclose.

Lorimer wrote church headquarters, spelling out the deal. He got no response. In the meantime, the Suns were already working out the access question on an ad-hoc basis. The *Church News* had first run a big story on the Riverton Stake's Second Rescue in October 1991. There was a picture of Lorimer and his two counselors, President John L. Kitchen and President Kim W. McKinnon, standing in suits and ties at Martin's Cove, and a map vaguely locating the cove and Rock Creek, where supposedly fifteen members of the Willie Company died. Ten months later, after the 1992 monument dedications, the *News* ran an even bigger story, with many more pictures, and a detailed map of both sites. Many Mormons assumed, not unreasonably, that the church now owned both spots. This was not the case and the stories did not say so, but people began showing up at the Sun Ranch, looking for Martin's Cove.

Some asked permission; some didn't. Some walked, some drove, some got stuck by the river. When they did, the Suns pulled them out, and before long were charging $10 per vehicle to cross their land. Still, Lorimer heard nothing from Salt Lake City.

Meanwhile, the church continued negotiating for other sites. In September 1992, a month after the three new monuments were dedicated, the church bought 120 acres from a rancher named Ken Ballard in what they call Rock Creek Hollow. This was the site where, most Mormons are convinced, thirteen members of the Willie Company died in a single night and two more died the next day. Church officials dedicated a monument there in July 1994.

After *that* ceremony, Lorimer was riding with Hinckley in the first counselor's vehicle over the rough roads up to South Pass, when the conversation again circled around to Martin's Cove.[7] Scott's two counselors were following along behind in a separate vehicle. How were the negotiations going for the easement? Hinckley asked. Going nowhere, Scott answered, and explained how he'd heard nothing from Salt Lake City once he thought he'd worked out a deal. The first counselor asked the stake president who he thought was causing the problem, and Lorimer answered that he had no idea. "Then I said, 'Let's drop it. *We're* becoming the problem out there.'" The Suns were feeling badly toward the Mormons; the Mormons who showed up unannounced didn't like being charged by the Suns. There seemed no way out of the mess. Hinckley agreed the matter was best dropped, though he seemed surprised.

Then, Lorimer says, there in the car, he got another idea. "I said, let's just buy the whole ranch," he told me during the interview in his office. "I said, the reason we need to buy it is, it's not a ranch, it's a group of historical sites that go all the way from Independence Rock to Split Rock." If the church had to buy a million acres to get a thousand they cared about, it seemed worth it if it could really be theirs, once and for all. Hinckley agreed, a second time, though perhaps this was what he had been waiting to hear all along. "On behalf of the church," he told Lorimer, "I authorize you to go buy the ranch." Then he dropped him off at windswept Farson, on the far side of South Pass. Lorimer's counselors picked him up and drove him back to Riverton.

Two weeks later, in early August 1994, Lorimer was asked to come speak at the cove to a group of several hundred Mormon youths from Colorado. Scott was nervous; he still hadn't said a word to Bernard about a purchase, and was embarrassed by the church's eighteen months of silence. He didn't really want Bernard even to know he was there.

Then, from up in the cove, he saw Bernard's old dust-colored Toyota Land Cruiser roar down the road from the ranch gate, and pull up at the George Albert Smith monument in a spray of gravel. Bernard only drove like that when he was upset. The gathering was breaking up; Scott and the others made their way down the slope, out of the cove, and some of them waded the river. Bernard waited a moment, and then when he could get close to Scott, he poked him in the chest. "Scotty, you and I have got to talk. But not here around all these people." They started walking down the road toward Bernard's house. After a time, Scott looked over. Bernard, an old man in an old hat, was staring at the ground with big tears rolling down his face.

"What's wrong?" Lorimer asked.

"Wrong? They threw me out, that's what's wrong."

"What? Who threw you out? What do you mean?"

"Those nephews of mine," Bernard said, and explained that there had just been a shareholders' meeting. Though George had sold his share to his brothers decades before, Nellie, their mother, had felt George's line of the family needed still to be represented in the family corporation, and so she had given some shares to Dennis. Before this point, Dennis had always voted with Bernard. But on this day, Dennis had voted his shares with Steve—John Hugh's son—and now Steve was president of the Sun Land and Cattle Company. The balance had shifted. Bernard was no longer in charge.

Within a matter of weeks, Bernard contacted Lorimer: "Would you like to buy this ranch?" Despite the power shift, Lorimer assumed Bernard meant the whole thing, and that he was speaking for the whole family. In hindsight, neither seems certain.

Ten years later, Steve Sun told me that there comes a time after a few generations when one family member will be living his dream on the ranch and the rest will feel stuck—and there's never enough cash around for one side to buy out the other. He declined to get more specific, but he meant that it was his uncle Bernard who was living his dream. Bernard had been so deep in the life for so long that it had never occurred to him there might be entirely other reasons than his own for wanting the ranch, or reasons for no longer wanting it at all. He was blindsided.

It was clear the ranch would have to be formally divided. They called lawyers and accountants together, and worked out an I-cut-you-choose arrangement. Half the family would draw the line that would divide the ranch, and the other half would get to choose which side of the line it would take for its own. Bernard, Steve Sun told me, very much wanted to be the one to draw the line. Bernard's daughter Tena, Scott Lorimer told me, was the one who actually drew it. Her line left just the Hub and Spoke, the Beef Acre and the Bar Eleven on one side, and all the rest—about four times as much country, about twice as much deeded land—on the other.

Unlike her cousins, who'd grown up in Rawlins, in Casper, and on various parts of the ranch, Tena and her brothers had always lived on the Spoke, as they still call it, when they weren't away at school. She hoped very much that by drawing her favorite half small, her cousins would settle for the larger, drier share. She still regrets, she told me, that she didn't draw it smaller still.

Lorimer happened to be there that day, too. Dennis came out of the house giggling, Scott told me, and said to him, "Bernard doesn't own what you want anymore."

John Hugh and his sons took the small half—the Hub and Spoke, Bar Eleven, and Beef Acre—leaving Bernard and Noeline the rest, along with the right to live out their lives at their house across the old highway from the ranch yard. John Hugh and Kathleen had the balancing right, if they'd wanted it, to keep their house at Willow Hill. But they and their sons wanted to sell. Dennis, who had put up part of his mother's family land as collateral when the Diamond Hook was first purchased in the 1970s, got the Diamond Hook as his part of the division.

Lorimer reported developments to the church, and after that, events left his hands. John Creer, president of the Farm Management Company, the LDS Church's wholly owned agriculture and landowning corporation, took over negotiations with the Suns. The last details were worked out in 1997. For the Spoke, the Bar Eleven, and the Beef Acre, a total of 113,000 acres, 13,000 of them deeded, the church put the money in escrow while Steve and Jess looked for a ranch they'd like to have instead. They found two—one near Oshkosh, Nebraska, and a second near Goodland, Kansas. The church took the money out of escrow and bought the two ranches, and the swap went straight across: No money changed hands between the church and the Suns. Such arrangements are not uncommon in the ranching world, as they protect the sellers, at least for a time, from having to pay income taxes on the ranch's gain in value during the time it was owned. Steve, Kathleen, and Scott all declined to say how much money the church put into the escrow account. Tena, in passing, mentioned five million dollars, though she admitted she doesn't know for sure. No one mentioned 124 years—the time between when Tom Sun supposedly first built a cabin at Devil's Gate, and the sale. That century and a quarter continues to swing like a gate, balanced between the millennia before it and the short years since. Sun ownership and its stories held sway for a long time.

For some time after the sale, there remained a large Sun Ranch sign at the turnoff on the state highway. Church officials had told the family the ranch would always remain the Sun Ranch, and Steve and his mother Kathleen, when I talked with them at their new ranch in Nebraska, said they were glad at the time of this assurance. But after a while the sign disappeared; the Mormons put it up again, and it disappeared again. "They would have kept putting up signs forever if we hadn't told them not to bother anymore," Kathleen told me.

A second road leads off to the right a few miles farther south-west. There are no signs; just mailboxes. One reads SUN on the side, with the *U* faded more than the other letters. This is the turnoff to the Turkey Track, where Tena and her husband and her two broth-ers and their families live. After the division, she told me, having the big Sun Ranch sign by the Mormon turnoff caused problems; deliveries meant for the Turkey Track went to the wrong place. It wasn't the Sun Ranch anymore.

The Gate of Perfect Balance disintegrated long before the Suns divided and sold, and the new owners have felt no need to replace it at its old location. Out at the highway turnoff to what used to be the Hub and Spoke, however, there's now a fine new ranch gate over the cattle guard, and people are welcome to drive through. The new gate, made of black steel, tall, squared across the top, tells a story of its own. On either side of the gate are iron silhouettes of hand-cart-pulling pioneers, and in the top in the middle, an accurately rendered, full-color, three-dimensional metal handcart, probably three feet long. The lettering across the top reads, Mormon Hand-cart Historic Site. Underneath, arching above the handcart, the lettering adds: Martin's Cove.

# A Drying Wind

A smooth, sandy parking lot, often filled on summer days with Utah vehicles, covered the Hub and Spoke's old ranch yard for several years after the church acquired the property. In the summer of 2005, the sand was replaced by a landscaped hummock, and most of the parking moved elsewhere. The bunkhouse is still there; the same big old log barn is there, half again as big. On the far side of the parking lot from the ranch house, where the old highway winds past, there's a picnic table. Ranked nearby are sometimes as many as 100 brand-new handcarts, tipped back on their boxes with their pull-handles up. Beyond the barn, a new white chapel points a sharp spire at the sky. From the outside, the ranch house looks the same, though the paint is fresh.

Two small log buildings stand to the right. These are new. One bears a modest sign: People of the Sweetwater Museum. Inside, it's packed with interesting stuff. There are pictures of various Suns; a book with laminated pages of historical accounts, including Boney Earnest's memoir and some historical accounts Noeline and Kathleen have written over the years; Indian blankets, weapons, backrests, and rattles; a .45 automatic used in a murder in Rawlins and found under the floor of a grocery store; a framed copy of a *Denver Post* story from 1931, advancing the Mormon gathering at Independence Rock that year; and the final patent to the Suns' original Desert Land claim, signed by President Benjamin Harrison.

A person still enters the ranch house through the toe of the L, and comes on what once was Mary Hellihan Sun's sitting room, which Nellie Sun turned into a family museum after her mother-in-law died in 1936. Its best feature is its fireplace of river rock and Indian manos, with a mantel of flat, smooth metates. Over the fireplace is still the silver-mounted little 32-shot carbine inscribed on its butt plate from Buffalo Bill to his friend Tom Sun. Pictures of various Sun families as they looked around 1985 hang on the walls, also a horsehair headstall, supposedly braided in jail by Tom Horn in the months before he was hanged, and some interesting pistols. On a shelf in the corner is a copy of the Book of Mormon inscribed to Tom Sun, Jr., from George Albert Smith in 1930. Next to it is a copy of a biography of Joseph Smith, also inscribed by George Albert Smith "To the Tom Sun family as a small token of appreciation of the hospitality and kindness extended to the Utah Pioneer Trails Pilgrims" in June 1933, when the Martin Company monument went up a mile down the road. And nowhere, of course, is there a word about the Averell-Watson affair.

The rest of the house, five times as much space, is a shrine to the handcart story: big, clear maps of the route, a full-sized handcart, and compelling murals of scenes from the docks of Liverpool to the snows of South Pass. The exhibits change, from time to time. Among the more compelling have been a small pile of goods inside a glass case representing the seventeen allowable pounds of personal items a handcart pioneer might have brought along: a Book of Mormon, a Bible, a sewing basket, a blanket, some spare socks, and not much else. Inside another case, on a pedestal, is a little pile of flour—the daily quarter-pound each person in the Martin Company was reduced to after Deer Creek. At the end one or two missionaries will ask if you'd like to see the video too. They are cheerful and kind, and interested in where you're from. They are careful not to pry further unless asked, but eager to know if you'd like to know more of the story.

Outside, a main path leads away west from the ranch house and up a low rise, past a pair of excellent restrooms in their own new building opposite the house where Tom Sun, Jr., and Nellie lived, and where now the Handcart Center has its offices. Farther off to the left can be seen the big bus-parking lot, and closer in, a new replica of the Seminoe Fort, finished in 2003 and made of squared logs from Norway.[1]

The path continues toward the river, passing what appears to be a new meeting hall of milled logs. A stout new bridge of wide planks on steel girders crosses the river. On the bank is a granite monument marked Veil Crossing, celebrating the trials of the pioneers who crossed here on their way to the cove.

The path is broad, graveled, edged, nearly flat, and excellently maintained. It's wide enough that two handcarts can pass easily—sometimes necessary for large groups. Motorized maintenance carts putter up and down the path, and sometimes, if it is summer, a single family will pass with a handcart as well. It's a splendid walk in almost any weather: the granite rises steeply on the right in some places just yards from the right-hand edge of the path. On the left, the river reflects the sky. Far out to the south, the line of Whiskey Peak and Green Mountain makes the horizon. Straight ahead to the west, Split Rock rises, hazy, distant, and real.

At the mouth of the cove the path divides. One branch heads up the gully on the eastern edge, the other more directly up and over the sand dune. It's steeper now, and wide enough for only one handcart. The church has provided benches at little way stations—sometimes several benches, as if for a mini-congregation. Signs tell dramatic stories of the Patience Loader kind, implying that a person is standing right where the event occurred. There is no path along the west side of the cove. The two paths join at the top, where there is another rest room and benches for a larger congregation. These improvements are concealed from below by the gully and some cedar trees. It's another mile from the opening of the cove to the junction, and that mile, although it is entirely on public land, threads its way among all-Mormon stories. Or at least it did through the summer of 2005.

In 1997, the year after the ranch sale was final, the church and the Bureau of Land Management worked out a five-year, cooperative agreement to jointly manage the public land in the cove. Until then it was part of a Sun Ranch grazing lease, but there was no longer a reason to run cattle there; in fact, both sides agreed, it would be a bad idea because of the increased human traffic the new arrangement would bring. The church guaranteed free public access to the cove and Devil's Gate, and both sides agreed to contribute labor and materials toward building the paths and improvements on the public land. The labor, mostly, came from church volunteers; the materials, mostly, came from the government. The text of the signs—the storytelling—was to be coordinated among BLM staff, church representatives, and outside non-Mormon historians. The Mormons, of course, were free to write whatever they wanted on signs and monuments on their own lands. The BLM, theoretically at least, kept veto power over any language on signs on the public land.[2]

Church leaders soon made it clear they wanted the church to own Martin's Cove outright. There were feelers for a land swap, but the BLM stuck to long-standing policy that any trade would have to be for a piece of similar and equal historic value—that is, along the trail and inside Wyoming. With an eye toward a swap, the church bought land at what the Mormons call Sixth Crossing, the last pioneer crossing of the Sweetwater before the trail headed up toward South Pass. Once they'd bought it, they found they wanted to keep the most historic parts and swap only the less historic sections. No deal, said the BLM. So the Mormons went to Congress.

In the fall of 2001, Representative Jim Hansen (R-Utah) and six other Mormons in the House drafted a bill directing the secretary of interior to sell 1,640 acres of land at Martin's Cove to the church. Hansen had announced he was in his last term, and it was clear the bill meant a great deal to him. It was introduced and assigned to his House Resources Committee the following spring. As it was primarily of local interest, the bill stayed below House radar for national issues. It ran into intense opposition in Wyoming, however, where people across the political spectrum like having plentiful public

Handcart ranch gate. Access to public land at Martin's Cove now lies through the Mormon Handcart Historic Site, owned by the Farm Management Co., a subsidiary of the LDS Church. Photograph by the author.

land in their back yards, even when they don't use it much. Many doubted repeated Mormon assurances that the cove would always stay open to the public for free. Wyoming's lone congressional representative, the Republican and House Resources Committee member Barbara Cubin, found herself having to choose whether to displease her committee chairman or displease her constituents.

Hansen scheduled a field hearing on the bill in Casper. Opponents in Casper paid for an eight-page insert in the *Casper Star-Tribune*, Wyoming's only statewide paper, arguing against the sale in exhaustive detail, and comparing it to Teapot Dome. Rattled and angry, Hansen wrote a long letter to the paper accusing his opponents in Wyoming of mounting "a vicious, false attack . . . Mormon bashing, plain and simple. There is no other way to describe the innuendo and bigotry."

He didn't show up at the hearing in the Casper College gymnasium; the only committee members on hand were Eni F. H. Faleomavaega, a nonvoting representative from American Samoa—also a Mormon—and Cubin. Hansen had lined up four pro-sale witnesses and only two against. Local Mormons, loyal and up-to-date as always, outnumbered sale opponents in the crowd two to one. Some Sierra Club protesters stayed outside and carried signs.

Back in Washington, Cubin did her best to have it both ways. She announced she opposed the bill, but because its success seemed likely she said she would improve it. With Hansen's tacit support, she persuaded the committee to accept amendments reducing the sale size to 940 acres, guaranteeing protection for any archaeological artifacts that might turn up, and also guaranteeing permanent public access. Mormon leaders were comfortable with these changes. And Cubin, consistent with her earlier announcements, then voted against the bill as it came out of committee.

Neither Mike Enzi nor Craig Thomas, Wyoming's two Republican senators, liked the bill much at all. They were worried about access, they said, and they were particularly worried about setting a precedent that would encourage American Indians to press for purchase of sites sacred to them—Devils Tower, for example. Hansen promptly threatened to bottle up a Thomas bill then before his House committee, if Thomas didn't smooth the way for the Martin's Cove bill in the Senate. Thomas told the *Deseret News* that because he was so opposed to the cove sale, he was ready to let his own bill die.

By mid-June 2002, the bill, uncontroversial in the larger scheme of things, was slated for a quick voice vote on the House floor. Wyoming pressure on Cubin was more intense than ever, but on the day of the vote she was late getting back across Washington from a doctor's appointment with her husband, and missed the vote entirely. The bill passed the House unanimously. Hansen had saved face, Cubin had pleased no one, the Mormons looked as if they were on their way to victory, but the bill stalled in the Senate.

Hansen retired, and in 2003, Thomas, the church, and the BLM started work on a one-of-a-kind lease. The church hoped for a nonety-nine-year term; negotiations reduced that to twenty-five years. Thomas got the lease tacked on to a huge, irrelevant funding measure—the Energy and Water Development Appropriations Bill, which already had passed the House. Still below the general radar, the lease easily survived conference committee work, and President Bush signed it into law early in December.

The lease guarantees public access to the cove, while allowing, if anything, slightly more Mormon control of the site than the original five-year agreement with the BLM had provided. The law left the price unspecified. A Department of Interior appraiser recommended $16,000 per year, and BLM higher-ups went along. The price is quite high compared to a grazing lease, but extremely modest in light of the fact that the cove is the sole reason for the Mormons' multimillion-dollar investment in the first place.

Before 1990, there were probably only 200 people alive who had ever been in Martin's Cove. Now, something like 40,000 people visit the historic site each year, of whom as many as 30,000 walk out to the cove, many with handcarts. Similar human pressure on the Willie sites near South Pass—the two-tracks up there are not graveled, nor edged, and are far more vulnerable to handcart wheels than the path at the cove—has led the BLM to restrict trekker numbers there. The same opponents whose big ad drew Hansen's wrath have appealed the lease, but only on the grounds of the appraiser's methods, not the price. Their appeal is now in front of the Interior Board of Land Appeals, where it could stay for years. In the spring of 2005, the American Civil Liberties Union filed suit against the BLM in federal district court in Casper, charging that the terms of the lease compromise the religious freedom of non-Mormons who must pass proselytizing Mormons if they want to walk the graveled path to the cove. As this book goes to press, a settlement to the lawsuit looks likely. Since the main parking area will now be located south of the Seminoe fort, it will be simple for a person to go straight to the path to the cove, without having to pass close to the visitor center or proselytizing missionaries. New signs will make this "abundantly clear," one BLM official said. Other new BLM signs in the cove will emphasize the area's broad importance to the history of travel and emigration in the West, and show that the handcart disaster was only one important story out of many. Perhaps the Mormon version hasn't won a total victory, after all.[3]

Bernard died in 1999. John Hugh died in 2003. Steve Sun and his family, and Steve's mother, Kathleen, live in two modest houses on a place on the North Platte near the hamlet of Oshkosh, in western Nebraska. Steve likes to think his great-grandfather camped right along there at one time or another. They call the new place the Sun Ranch, too, and took the Hub and Spoke brand down to Nebraska with their herd. They couldn't register it, however, because another Nebraska rancher who bought Sun cattle decades ago had registered something very similar for himself. So the Suns no longer use the brand. Tena and her brothers now run the rest of the ranch from the Turkey Track.

The country along the Sweetwater looks pretty much unchanged. In January and February, cattle still graze the good winter range along the river, now on Mormon land. Pelicans still coast up the river in spring. Snowfall and rain finally reached average levels in the winter and spring of 2005 after many, many dry years. The drought could be over, though it's too early to say. A drying wind, as Kathleen wrote once, still blows at Devil's Gate almost continuously. Nothing can change the past, but how the past gets told, and who gets to tell it, will continue to change there and everywhere in the West—according to who controls the land.

# Notes

### Chapter 1: Pelicans on the Sweetwater

*Epigraph*: Beebe, *Reminiscing along the Sweetwater*, 55.

1. Flora, fauna, climate, and geology discussion is from Knight, *Mountains and Plains*, 3–107, and Lageson and Spearing, *Roadside Geology of Wyoming*.

2. Sun, "Ranch Management of Streamside Zones."

3. Wedel "Prehistoric Plains," 210–11.

4. Shakespeare, *Sky People*, 20–21.

5. Andrea Cerovski, Wyoming Game and Fish Department non-game biologist interview by author June 24, 2003; and Findholt, "Population Status,"

### Chapter 2: Tenantless and Forlorn

*Epigraph*: Parkman, *Oregon Trail*, 302.

1. Clow, "Bison ecology."

2. Muir, *Story of My Boyhood*, 174–75. See also Ekins, *Defending Zion*, 141–43, for a discussion of the Enlightenment idea, so dangerous to Indians, that people who cultivate the land have a natural right to it.

3. Parkman, *Oregon Trail*, 174. See *Journals of Francis Parkman*, 436, for a plainer description.

4. Fowler, *Arapahoe Politics*, 15–17.

5. Smaby, "Mormons and the Indians."

6. Washakie soon became a leader among the Shoshones. He was a big-picture thinker and he knew how to get white people to like him, skills that proved valuable to his people and his career. Little Fawn had two children with Bridger. He spent forty-nine years in the mountains before blindness drove him back to

Missouri, and was fond of saying he'd been around since Laramie Peak was a hole in the ground

7. Dorn, *Wyoming Landscape*, 39–44.

8. It may have made matters worse. When Parkman came a year later, the talk around Fort Laramie was that Kearny's failure to follow through on threats against the Arapahos had only emboldened them. But nothing had happened, and Parkman's Lakota friends told him the Arapahos were now "determined to kill the first of the white dogs whom they could lay hands on." *Oregon Trail*, 215–16.

9. Fowler, *Arapahoe Politics*, 24.

10. *Journals of Francis Parkman*, 456; Parkman, *Oregon Trail*, 170. Parkman, then only twenty-three, was putting Raymond in more danger here than he had any right to do and they were lucky to emerge unharmed. He was eager to spend time with the Lakotas—the Sioux—because to him they were the last free Indians. When he found them, they disappointed him because they lacked what he thought of as sufficient noble qualities. As he already planned to write books about the French and Indian War, the Indians whom Parkman really wanted to know were the woodland Iroquois from a century before. But he made do with the Sioux. See Wade's introduction to Parkman's 1846 journals, 385–404.

11. Trenholm, quoted in Thomas Johnson, *Enos Family*, 97.

12. Fowler, 23. Many scholars argue the Plains Indians were pastoralists—herders of horses—as much as they were hunters and gatherers. See Bennett, "Human Adaptations."

13. Kappler, *Treaties*, 594–96; Fowler, *Arapahoe Politics*, 29–32.

14. Morgan and Harris, *Rocky Mountain Journals of William Marshall Anderson*, 269.

15. *Missouri Republican*, November 9, 1851, cited in Fowler, 32.

## Chapter 3: The Pathfinder's Lost Instruments

*Epigraph*: Frémont, *Exploring Expedition*, 70.

1. Egan, *Frémont*, 54–56. Details of the activities of Frémont's first expedition during the summer of 1842 are, unless otherwise stated, from Frémont and Preuss's own accounts: *Exploring Expedition*, 9–79, and, *Exploring with Frémont*.

2. Even the Greeks had understood that the higher the angle of the sun at noon, the closer you are to the equator, where the sun always passes directly overhead.

3. Frémont, *Exploring Expedition*, 47.

4. Details on Frémont's instruments here and throughout the chapter are from personal communication with Bob Graham. See his excellent website at www.longcamp.com.

5. Williams, *Region of Astonishing Beauty*, 37–54, 61–68; Bryson, *Visions of the Land*, 3–31.

6. Only Preuss mentions the quarrel, p. 40. The voyageurs' names reflect a fact historians are only now coming to understand: the Rocky Mountain fur trade was carried out mostly by men of French extraction. Janet Lecompte estimates the ratio of French to Anglos at four to one, not one to four as H. M. Chittenden, Bernard DeVoto and others imply. Leroy Hafen, *French Fur Traders and Voyageurs*, 11.

7. Preuss, 43. One mountain in Wyoming and at least fifty in Colorado are higher than Fremont Peak. General consensus seems now to be that the men did, in fact, climb Fremont Peak and not Woodrow Wilson Peak, though scholars still argue the issue.

8. Frémont, *Memoirs of my Life*, 71, and Phillips, *Jessie Benton Frémont*, 62-63. Horace Day, the boat's inventor, was an early licensee of Charles Goodyear, whose first rubber patents were granted that same year, 1842. See Slack, *Noble Obsession*, 113–26.

9. Frémont, *Exploring Expedition*, 11, and Preuss, *Exploring with Frémont*, 6–7

10. Preuss, 51.

11. Frémont, *Exploring Expedition*, 72.

12. Descoteaux told it differently. Some years later, the voyageur more or less adopted Thomas Beausoleil, an eleven-year-old French-Canadian boy who turned up in St. Louis. The boy later anglicized his name, and as Tom Sun came to matter a great deal in the Sweetwater country. In the 1890s, Sun told a University of Wyoming geology professor that Descoteaux had told him that the rubber boat swamped on the lower Sweetwater, many miles before the party got to the rapids on the North Platte. This could be true, though Frémont's account is supported in its major details by Preuss, and Preuss was always quick to mock Frémont when he got a chance. The Descoteaux version more likely means that the boat dumped sooner than Frémont implies—Preuss's account appears to support that conclusion, too—and that in any case Descoteaux didn't much like being portrayed in Frémont's report as the only man to cry out in fear. See Wilbur Knight, "Wyoming Fossil Fields Expedition," 458.

13. Goetzmann, *Army Exploration*, 83, 101–6. See also the elegant reproductions of Frémont's and Preuss's maps in the map portfolio, vol. 4 of Frémont, *Expeditions*.

## Chapter 4: A Road to Somewhere Else

*Epigraph*: Amelia Knight, Diary, 1853.

1. Holmes, *Covered Wagon Women*. Goddell, 7:108; Mouseley, 7:184–85. Goodell was traveling in 1854 and Mouseley in 1857.

2. Field, *Prairie and Mountain Sketches*, 114–15. Field was traveling in 1843.

3. Upstate New Yorker Charles T. Stanton, traveling with the Donner Party in 1846, noted: "The river is a stream about as large as Onondaga creek." Dale Morgan, *Overland in 1846*, 1:616.

4. Hervey Johnson, *Talking Wire*, 203.

5. Munkres, "Independence Rock and Devil's Gate," 33.

6. Holmes, *Covered Wagon Women*, 7:108.

7. Frémont, *Exploring Expedition*, 71–72.

8. Field, *Sketches*, 116–17 and 174–75. Clay, of Kentucky, had first run unsuccessfully for president in 1824. Van Buren, of New York, was elected president in 1836 but failed to win a second term in 1840. By 1843 they were the two most likely presidential candidates for 1844.

Field made a detailed list of names he found on the Rock. It included many mountain men from the earliest years—Tom Fitzpatrick, Black Harris, Joe Walker—and many more whose identities are lost.

9. Many later regretted the trip. Cf. Parkman, *Oregon Trail*, 13: "Among [the emigrants] are some of the vilest outcasts in the country. I have often perplexed myself to divine the various motives that give impulse to this migration; but whatever they may be, whether an insane hope of a better condition in life, or a desire of shaking off restraints of law and society, or mere restlessness, certain it is, that multitudes bitterly repent the journey, and, after they have reached the land of promise, are happy enough to escape from it."

10. Of the 500,000 or more emigrants who traveled the road between 1840 and the completion of the transcontinental railroad in 1869, as many as 10 percent may have died in the most disease-ridden years. In all years, nearly nine of ten deaths were from disease, the great majority from cholera, the result of drinking water polluted by human feces. Accidents, mostly drownings and gun accidents, were the second largest cause of death. Deaths attributable to Indian attack were a tiny fraction of these totals, only 362 between 1840 and 1860; 426 Indians were killed by emigrants during the same period. Unruh, *Plains Across*, 185, 408–14; Mattes, *Platte River Road Narratives*, 2–3, and "Potholes in the Great Platte River Road," 10–11.

11. DeVoto, *Across the Wide Missouri*, passim.

12. By the mid-nineteenth century, the words "beautiful," "picturesque," and "sublime" had separate meanings on an aesthetic continuum from tame to terrific. The beautiful showed the effects of human handiwork; picturesque was wilder, but only the sublime implied the presence of the divine in nature; only the sublime inspired awe. See Hales, *William Henry Jackson*, 43, 46.

13. Field, *Sketches*, 122–24.

14. Delaware Indians had first encountered Europeans on the Atlantic coast. Two hundred years of war and disease reduced their population by 90 percent, and by the early nineteenth century they were scattered from Texas to Canada, with many near the confluence of the Kansas and Missouri rivers. Friction soon arose with Pawnee people who already lived there, and Delaware decisions in subsequent decades to work as professional hunters and scouts for the fur traders and emigrant wagon trains led to more friction with other Plains

tribes. See http://www.tolatsga.org/dela.html. Parkman, in *The Oregon Trail*, p. 3, notices Delawares "fluttering in calico frocks and turbans" on the streets of Westport (now Kansas City), Missouri. The French-named Delaware, Antoine Clément, served as Stewart's chief hunter, foreman, and trail boss on all the baronet's Rocky Mountain excursions. Later Clément accompanied Stewart back to Murthly Castle in Scotland, and spent the rest of his life there as Stewart's valet, waiting on table in a black wool suit and attending crofters' galas in a kilt (DeVoto, *Across the Wide Missouri*, 360). And about a dozen Delawares whom Frémont hired in Missouri in 1845 became a fierce and loyal bodyguard throughout the pathfinder's operatic career in California (Egan, *Frémont*, 332–40.)

15. The tribal boundaries we have seen described in the Treaty of 1851 roughly represented the status quo at the time. The Shoshones were closest to the Sweetwater, and many of the traders along this part of the trail took Shoshone wives and started families.

16. Sutton quoted in Holmes, *Covered Wagon Women*, 7:51.

### Chapter 5: Burning Bridges

*Epigraph*: Magloire Alexis Mosseau, interview by Judge Eli Ricker, October 30, 1906, Ricker Collection, tablet 28, 19–20, Nebraska State Historical Society. Mosseau was interviewed by Judge Ricker at Buzzard Basin, Pine Ridge Reservation, South Dakota.

1. Archambault, "Historic Document"; Mokler, *History of Natrona County*, 110–11; Mosseau interview, 24. Mosseau claimed to remember finding nuggets himself, and thereby starting the South Pass gold rush.

2. Sutton diary in Holmes, *Covered Wagon Women*, 7:45–53.

3. Ibid., 49.

4. Mosseau interview, 15–20; Archambault, "Historic Document," 229; Amelia Knight, Diary, 1853. Interviewed in 1906, Magloire Mosseau recalled that he had come as a clerk to Devil's Gate in 1852, though he sometimes got his dates wrong. Amanda Archambault recalled in 1907 that she and her husband, Alfred, started the post and built the bridge at Independence Rock in 1853. Mrs. Knight, in 1853, found the bridge rickety and expensive. She and her party swam their stock but paid three dollars per wagon to use the bridge.

5. Morgan and Harris, *Rocky Mountain Journals*, 83–84, 190–91, 334. Parkman, *Oregon Trail*, 95. Leroy Hafen, *French Fur Traders*, 239–52. Seminoe is now the name of a mountain range and reservoir in central Wyoming. Adding further to the confusion is the corruption to "Seminole," extending back at least to 1870, when Hayden called the range the Seminole Mountains.

6. Thomas Johnson, *Enos Family*, 93.

7. Mosseau interview, 16–17. There was also, recent archeology has shown, a foundation of sandstone rocks hauled all the way from Muddy Gap, twenty miles

southwest. John Albanese, personal communication. Tom Sun would choose the same spot twenty years later for his ranch headquarters; some of the same buildings may still have been standing when he first got there.

8. Sutton in Holmes, *Covered Wagon Women*, 7:42–44.

9. For an account of the Grattan fight that seems accurate in its details if suspicious of Lakota motives, see Hyde, *Spotted Tail's Folk*, 48–54. For a lucid discussion of the discrepancy between white and Indian attitudes toward property and food, see Skogen, *Indian Depredation Claims*, 3–15.

10. Mosseau interview, 19–20; Archambault, "Historic Document," 230.

11. McDermott, *Frontier Crossroads*, 15–16. Recent archaeology has shown the buildings at Devil's Gate did burn, and accounts today at the LDS museum on the site attribute the burning to Mormons retreating ahead of the advancing federal army in the fall of 1857. The post appears, however, to have been burned in the spring of 1862, by miners traveling from the played-out Pike's Peak diggings to new prospects on the Salmon River in Idaho. See Robert Taylor Burton's diary entry for May 21, 1862, ms. 1221 in the LDS Church Historical Department Archives, microfilm reel 1. For this citation, I'm grateful to Lyndia Carter.

12. Major I. Lynde, commanding post at Fort Laramie, to chief of the adjutant general's department, Headquarters of the Army of Utah, en route to Salt Lake, December 24, 1857. Records War Department, U.S. Army Commands (RGO 98), letters sent: Fort Laramie.

13. By the spring of 1858, the freighting firm of Russell, Majors & Waddell was employing 4,000 men and 3,500 wagons hauled by 40,000 oxen on the western plains. Spring, *Caspar Collins*, 23–25.

14. Glass, "Crossing the North Platte River," 35; McDermott, *Frontier Crossroads*, 16, 20–21. Parkman met Richard twice in 1846, near Fort Laramie and later at the Pueblo on the Arkansas River, and admired his "mingled hardihood and buoyancy." *Oregon Trail*, 93, 272–74.

15. McDermott, *Frontier Crossroads*, 21; Coutant, *History of Wyoming*, 365–67.

16. The bridge is described in detail in a claim filed years later by Louis P. Guinard, nephew of the first Louis Guinard, seeking government reimbursement after the bridge was burnt in the Indian wars. See Louis Guinard Indian depredation claim, number 1319, Record Group 123, National Archives, Washington, D.C. The case lasted at least twenty-five years and was absorbed into claims 8156 and 7860. In the latter, see especially an undated typescript of testimony, probably from 1898, by Louis P. Guinard, John Lajeunesse, Magloire Mosseau and others, pp. 5, 7, 23.

17. Burton, *City of the Saints*, 90–92. Parkman did not understand the meaning of similar stories, though he had some of them from the same source. Reynal, one of Parkman's three French-speaking guides, was running the post near Fort Laramie when Burton spent the night there fourteen years later. See also DeVoto,

*Across the Wide Missouri*, 374, for more on the cynical use of whiskey in the fur trade by the Richard brothers and many others.

18. Burton, *City of the* Saints: bad food and Arapaho war party at Guinard's bridge, 156–57; "a queer lot these French Canadians," 168; "hair like the ears of a Blenheim spaniel," 66; "the transverse diameter of the rounded skull," 115–17; "halfbreeds are . . . quasi-mules," 89–90; "a multitude of whitey-reds," 84.

19. McDermott, *Frontier Crossroads*, 61–76; John Lajeunesse, pp. 1–2, and Louis P. Guinard, pp. 8–9, 17–18 in the Guinard bridge claim, number 7860.

20. Guinard claim 7860, pp. 3–4; claim 1319, abstract of testimony May 3, 1898, p. 7.

21. Mokler, *History of Natrona County*, 110–11.

### Chapter 6: Brigham's Curse

*Epigraph*: Editorial quoted in Hafen and Hafen, *Handcarts to Zion*, 26.

1. Hafen and Hafen, *Handcarts to Zion*, 242–43.

2. Stegner, *Gathering of Zion*, 168.

3. Plenty of Indians already lived there, following game and gathering seeds and roots on a seasonal round that made them hard for the Mormons to see as occupiers, because they never exactly stayed in one place. See Smaby, "Mormons and the Indians."

4. Bagley, *Blood of the Prophets*, 48–53.

5. Hafen, *Handcarts to Zion*, 239–40.

6. Ibid., 46–48, 92–93.

7. John Chislett, "Mr. Chislett's Narrative," in Stenhouse, *Rocky Mountain Saints,* 317. First published 1872. Chislett does not say which speaker made the remark about eating snow. George D. Grant was a brother of Jedediah Grant, a member of the First Presidency, the church's top triumvirate, and William H. Kimball was the son of Heber Kimball, Brigham Young's best friend and closest counselor. As such both, in the emigrants' minds, represented the highest levels of church authority.

8. See Hafen, *Handcarts to Zion*, passim, Stegner, *Gathering of* Zion, 221–74, and forthcoming books on the Willie and Martin companies by Gary Long and Lyndia Carter, from the University of Utah Press.

9. Richards's report to Brigham Young, in Hafen, *Handcarts to* Zion, 219–21.

10. Chislett in Stenhouse, 319, says that when the returning missionaries and their "grand outfit of carriages" passed through the Willie Company, Richards again rebuked Savage for his earlier warnings, and assured the faithful that God would protect them. Food as well as bedding would await them at Fort Laramie, Richards promised. The buffalo robes Richards purchased were there, but no extra food, again suggesting more concrete plans of resupply that did not materialize.

Similarly, Martin's fatal decision at Deer Creek on October 17 to abandon most bedding and warm clothes may suggest that he, also, had been hoping to hook up with the three wandering supply parties that Richards mentions in his report to Brigham Young.

11. Stegner, *Gathering of Zion*, 249–50. Richards's report to Brigham Young is in Hafen, Handcarts to Zion, 219–21.

12. Journal of Robert T. Burton, leader of the first rescue party, in Hafen, *Handcarts to Zion*, 222–26 and reminiscent account of rescuer Harvey Cluff, 232–38.

13. Margaret Ann Griffiths in Carter, *Heart Throbs*, 6:369.

14. Hafen, *Handcarts to* Zion, 114; Stegner, *Gathering of Zion*, 252.

15. Burton, in Hafen, *Handcarts to Zion*, 224. The Mormons called Horse Creek Greasewood Creek.

16. Grant quoted in Hafen, *Handcarts to Zion*, 228.

17. Jones, *Forty Years*, 60–110.

18. Hafen, *Handcarts to Zion*, 119. Young's October 30, 1856, letter to Pratt was printed in the *Millennial Star*, the Mormon paper published in Liverpool, February 14, 1857. It was common for traders to travel east from Salt Lake City to meet incoming trains and sell them goods. The three small resupply parties that Richards encountered were probably such traders; they may have been hoping to meet the last handcart companies, as well a train of Mormon freight wagons led by A. O. Smoot, which Richards overtook east of Fort Laramie. The long-held version that no one in the Salt Lake Valley knew the Willie and Martin companies were coming does not seem to be borne out by the facts.

19. Brigham Young's and Heber C. Kimball's addresses in the tabernacle, November 2, 1856, Hafen, *Handcarts to Zion*, 239–47. Originally published in the *Deseret News*, November 12, 1856.

20. Hafen, *Handcarts to Zion*, 193.

21. See http://www. xmission.com/~country/reason/hicklhm.htm on Hickman's claims, and http://www.media.utah.edu/UHE/r/ROCKWELL.ORIN. html for more on Rockwell.

22. Bagley, *Blood of the Prophets*; Denton, *American Massacre* and "What Happened at Mountain Meadows?"

23. Mattes, *Platte River Road Narratives*, 2–3.

24. I am grateful for these insights to the historian Lyndia Carter—personal communication, December 3, 2003.

25. Stenhouse, *Rocky Mountain Saints*, 336, 337. The Martin Company story covers pp. 332–38.

26. Ibid., 338–42.

27. Jacques quoted in Whitney, *History of Utah.* 562–63.

28. Jones, *Forty Years*, 69–70.

29. See "Harvey Cluff's Account of the Rescue," in Hafen, *Handcarts to Zion*, 232–38. Cluff still hoped to recover his investment in the cattle, if only in heaven:

"Fifty-two years have passed since then and not one dollar has ever come into our hands. What will the principal and interest, at compound amount too in the next world? The Lord will judge the case."

30. Godfrey et al., *Women's Voices*. 222–42.

## Chapter 7: War

*Epigraph*: Hervey Johnson, *Talking Wire*, 210 (January 15, 1865).

1. Johnson, 45, 53 (September 20 and October 12, 1863).

2. Ibid., 114–16 (April 18, 1864).

3. Ibid., 195 (November 25–28, 1864).

4. Ibid., 197–98 (December 8, 1864).

5. Blight, *Beyond the Battlefield*, 63.

6. Mattes, *Great Platte River Road*, 217–29.

7. With Lot Smith in 1862 was Robert T. Burton—no relation the English travel writer—who had led the handcart rescue party in 1856, and who kept a journal this time as he had then. The post at Devil's Gate was not burnt when the Mormons passed through on their way east to Platte Bridge, but by the time they returned a month later, it had been, probably by miners. See chapter 5, note 11.

8. Spring, *Caspar Collins*, 31.

9. Ibid., 116–27. At South Pass, the Mormons presented one of the cavalry officers with a grizzly skin.

10. Hervey Johnson, *Talking Wire*, 147–50 (July 18, 1864).

11. Hyde, *Life of George Bent*, 164–222. As it had farther north, the withdrawal of regular troops from Colorado Territory had left a military vacuum. But Colorado was now a territory, populous enough to raise its own troops. Territorial politicians recruited a militia from the jails and saloon floors of Denver. They spent the summer of 1864 in inconclusive chases and skirmishes with various bands of Lakota, Arapaho, and Cheyenne Indians on the plains of eastern Colorado and western Kansas. Some Indians stepped up raids and reprisals; others, including Black Kettle's band, sought peace. After the fight, volunteers showed severed Indian body parts from theatre stages in Denver to loud cheers from crowds.

12. Hervey Johnson, *Talking Wire*, 198–99 (December 8th, 1864). Compare with similar language from Lt. Collins in a letter to his mother, April 15, 1865: "The object of Gen. Connor is to keep the Indians north until the Platte, Sweetwater and other rivers are past fording, when I think the intention is to exterminate them." Spring, *Caspar Collins*, 170.

13. Hervey Johnson, *Talking Wire*, 211 (February 1, 1865).

14. Spring, *Caspar Collins*, 172. Johnson notes that the Arapaho were camped "one sleep" to the north—more likely on the North Platte and out of the way of white traffic than by the road at Willow Springs or Horse Creek.

15. Hervey Johnson, *Talking Wire*, 223–26 (February 26, 1865).

16. Ibid., 227–28 (March 9, 1865).

17. Hyde, *Life of George Bent*, 164–222.

18. Fowler, *Arapahoe Politics*, 43.

19. Hervey Johnson, *Talking Wire*, 230 (March 9, 1865). Lt. Collins also noted the attackers "claimed to be Arapahoes." Spring, *Caspar Collins*, 169.

20. McDermott, *Frontier Crossroads*, 61–76. The fight at the bridge is often called the Battle of Platte Bridge; the fight at the wagon train is often called the Battle of Red Buttes.

21. Hervey Johnson, *Talking Wire*, 307 (January 20, 1866).

22. Madsen, *Glory Hunter*, 79–87.

23. Ibid., 98, 118–20.

24. Fowler, *Arapahoe Politics*, 65.

25. This story was told by Pius Moss, an Arapaho elder. Online as of 5/18/06 at http://www.wyomingcompanion.com/wcwrr.html#arapaho3

### Chapter 8: Hayden's Gaze

*Epigraph*: Hayden, *Preliminary report of the United States Geological Survey of Wyoming*, cited hereafter as *Fourth Annual Report*, 27.

1. Jackson, unpublished diaries, August 24, 1870, p. 23; William Henry Jackson Collection, Colorado Historical Society, Box 4, microfilm reel 7.

2. Jackson, *Time Exposure*, 198–99.

3. Cassidy, *Ferdinand V. Hayden*, 40–44

4. Ibid., 52–71.

5. Bartlett, *Great Surveys*, 3–4.

6. Goetzmann, *Exploration and Empire*, 489.

7. Ibid., 496–99; see also Bartlett, *Great Surveys*, 12–14.

8. This encounter is interesting in light of the fact that Hayden died in 1887, at fifty-eight, of locomotor ataxia, a kind of paralysis resulting from syphilis. Hales, *William Henry Jackson*, 42; Cassidy, Hayden, 290, 324–25, Bartlett, *Great Surveys*, 119. This discussion relies heavily on Hales for its biographical and aesthetic discussions of Jackson and his photographs.

9. Jackson, *Pioneer Photographer*, 73–74; *Time Exposure*, 188.

10. Hayden, *Fourth Annual Report*, 11.

11. Ibid., 27, 30, 31, respectively.

12. Hales, *William Henry Jackson*, 71–72. Appelgate, in *Hudson River School Visions*, 67–69. Gifford's sketching friends were the painters Worthington Whittredge and John Kensett.

13. Jackson, unpublished diaries, August 27, 1870, p. 25. Jackson, *Pioneer Photographer*, 83–84. Gifford also recalled the chase and remembered as well that Jackson's horse, high in the shoulders, was named Giraffe. See Gifford-Hayden,

January 6, 1871, National Archives, College Park, Md., RG 57, microfilm M623, reel 2, cited by Appelgate, 67 and n. 88, 72.

14. Hayden, *Fourth Annual Report*, 30–31. One of the exceptions was John Muir, who already by this time understood that Yosemite was in danger. But everyone was circling the question, even Pvt. Hervey Johnson five years earlier along the very same rocks: "Went hunting alone yesterday, on foot of course as I have no horse. I love the emptiness of it all, seeing something to interest me almost every step. . . . I could sit all day in one place and find amusement and pleasure in gazing on what is around and below me. I don't know how it would seem in a more civilized country to look down from the mountains on a plain dotted with villages, and farm-houses, and marked up with a perfect network of roads, along which pours the busy population, and see every where, the inroads science and art are making upon nature, but here to look upon the unbroken solitude from the dizzy heights, inspires one with emotions such as none but a true lover of nature can appreciate." *Talking Wire*, 235 (April 11, 1865).

15. "Report of Professor Thomas," in Hayden, *Fourth Annual Report*, 255.

### Chapter 9: Grazing in Paradise

*Epigraph*: Endlich quoted in Hayden, *Eleventh Annual Report*, 55.

1. "Passing of a Pioneer," *Carbon County Journal*. June 12, 1909, 1; *Annual Report* 146–47; *Carbon County Land Records, 1841–1920, index ca. 1871–1918*; U.S. Census Office, 10th Census, 1880, for Sweetwater, Carbon County, Wyoming Territory; "Married: Sun-Hellihan," *Rawlins Republican*, December 22, 1883, 2. All of the above preserved in a genealogical notebook prepared for the Suns by the Mormon Church in the mid-1990s. "Tom Sun's Ranch," *Cheyenne Daily Leader*, December 8, 1882, 3; "Out at Tom Sun's," *Cheyenne Daily Leader*, December 10, 1882, 3.

2. Boney Earnest, from typed copy of a manuscript of recollections written sometime after 1923, on display at the People of the Sweetwater Museum at the Mormon Handcart Historic Site, pp. 1–6.

3. *Laramie Sentinel*, May 6, 1872; July 19, 1872; September 28, 1872. Cited in Meschter, *Carbon County Chronology*, pp. 79–81, 92.

4. *Cheyenne Daily Sun*, September 3, 1875. Cited in Meschter, *Chronology*, 394.

5. *Laramie Sentinel*, August 22, 1874; September 28, 1874, in Meschter, *Chronology*, 271, 277.

6. *Laramie Independent*, September 11, 1874. Datelined September 2, 1874, in Meschter, *Chronology*, 274.

7. Earnest recollections in a separate section titled "True Story of Boney Earnest," pp. 1–2, also in the People of the Sweetwater Museum at the Mormon Handcart Historic Center.

8. *Laramie Sentinel,* May 25, 1875, in Meschter, *Chronology,* 360. Pope put it this way:

Lo, the poor Indian! whose untutored mind
Sees God in clouds, or hears him in the wind;
His soul proud science never taught to stray
Far as the solar walk or milky way;
Yet simple nature to his hope has giv'n,
Behind the cloud-topped hill, an humbler heav'n.

*An Essay on Criticism,* lines 99–104, Oxford Dictionary of Quotations, Second Edition. London: Oxford University Press, 1974.

9. Wilkinson, *Lammot du Pont,* 158–64. Wilkinson spells Graff's name with an extra "e": Graeff. But signing Tom Sun's land-claim documents in 1883, Graff spells the name as I've spelled it.

10. *Laramie Sentinel,* October 2, 1878, and August 23, 1879, in Meschter, *Chronology* 580, 612. Wilkinson, *Lammot du Pont,* 164.

11. *Laramie Sentinel,* July 17, 1877, in Meschter, *Chronology,* 497. Endlich in Hayden, *Eleventh Annual Report,* 35, 38; Endlich's full description of his summer in the Sweetwater country covers pp. 3–58.

12. Edwin C. Johnson, "Copy of the Hunting Diary of Edwin C. Johnson of his First Hunt with Tom Sun in the year of 1878." Sun Collection, American Heritage Center, Laramie, Wyoming.

13. Endlich in Hayden, *Eleventh Annual Report,* 31.

14. Edwin Johnson diary, 5.

## Chapter 10: Township and Range

*Epigraph:* Owen, Autobiography, in typescript, 18.

1. Owen, 53.

2. Ibid., 8.

3. Meschter, *Sweetwater Sunset,* 76.

4. Sakolski, *Great American Land Bubble,* 276–93.

5. Owen, Autobiography, 19.

6. Ibid., 29. Thomas Edison came to Rawlins to view the same eclipse at the invitation of the physician and amateur astronomer Henry Draper. A young railroad telegraph operator in Rawlins, Nute Craig, taught Edison how to shoot a rifle, and when Edison later went on a hunting trip guided by Tom Sun, the inventor dropped his buck from 300 yards, while Sun missed his doe. At least, that's according to Craig, who is more reliable for flavor than fact. See Craig, *Thrills,* 32–35, and *Laramie Sentinel* July 28, 1878, in Meschter, *Carbon County Chronology.*

7. Owen, Autobiography, 53.

8. William Holland, director of the Carnegie Museum in Pittsburgh, considered buying land scrip as a quick if expensive way to get title to a dinosaur quarry on public land in Wyoming in 1899. See Rea, *Bone Wars*, 59–67.

9. Meschter, *Sweetwater Sunset*, 76–81, includes a useful short discussion of American land law and the development of the township system of survey. See also http://www.publiclands.org/museum/story/story09.htm and http://www.publiclands.org/museum/story/story10.htm. And see Linklater, *Measuring America*, 48–88, for more on the politics of the early land ordinances.

10. Owen, Autobiography, 53.

11. Owen survey notes, on microfiche, Rawlins BLM office, p. 132.

12. 1880 census. Sun also told the historian Hubert Howe Bancroft he'd been born in Quebec. Bancroft, *History of Nevada, California and Wyoming*, 686n25.

13. Billy Johnson's account of the 1882 Oregon-Wyoming cattle drive, Sun Collection, American Heritage Center; Rollinson, *Wyoming Cattle Trails*.

14. Osgood, *Day of the Cattlemen*, 225. By 1892, cattle were down to 650,000 and now fluctuate between 1.2 and 1.5 million. See http://www.nass.usda.gov/wy/internet/livestock/hist-cattle.pdf.

15. Dunham, "Crucial Years of the General Land Office."

16. Worster, *River Running West*, 345–57.

17. Owen, Autobiography, 64.

### Chapter 11: Neighbors

*Epigraph*: Letter from Thomas Watson to the *Lebanon [Kansas] Criterion*, September 20, 1889. Reprinted in Meschter, *Sweetwater Sunset*, 218.

1. Rollinson, *Wyoming Cattle Trails*, 205–6.

2. Holt's New Map of Wyoming, 1885.

3. Beebe, *Reminiscing along the Sweetwater*, 77. Meschter, *Sweetwater Sunset*, 20–21.

4. Meschter, 21. The paper was the *Carbon County Journal* of April 5, 1884.

5. Meschter, 44–51.

6. Ibid., 39–42, 81–83, 105. Holt's New Map of Wyoming, 1885, also shows a Central Pacific Railroad survey paralleling the old emigrant route from Red Buttes to the Utah line, potential competition for the Union Pacific. Nothing came of it.

7. See, for example, Abbott and Smith, *We Pointed them North*, for cowboy Teddy Blue Abbott's take on his friendships with the prostitutes of Miles City, Montana, in the early 1880s. The women's take on those particular friendships, unfortunately, has not survived.

8. A three-part document survives in Lander, ninety miles away in Fremont County. Its first two sections, an application and the license, are filled out and

were notarized in Rawlins, and probably filed from there by mail. And Averell's bride to be changed her last name. She signed as Ellen Liddy *Andrews*, of Sweetwater, age twenty-four—the right place and age for Ella Watson. Averell signed with his own name. The final part of the document, the marriage certificate, is not filled out, however. Perhaps they delayed the ceremony, as they had not gotten word yet whether her divorce was final—though it was, only weeks before. Watson may not have used her real last name because, once she married, she could not take up land on her own behalf under the Homestead Act. Single—as Ellen Liddy *Watson*—she could, and using an alias on the marriage papers would have allowed her to keep that option open. See Meschter, *Sweetwater Sunset*, 30–33.

9. Meschter, 23–31, and, on the fact that she worked at the Rawlins House, John H. Fales, quoted in Hufsmith, *Wyoming Lynching*, 143.

10. Meschter, 118–19, 140, 192. The Wyoming Stock Growers' Association sued Lineberger and Cooper in the spring of 1884 for taking possession of unlawfully branded cattle, and the following spring appropriated thirty Spear H cattle at the roundup and sold them as mavericks. But the two men hired good lawyers. In 1886 the suit was dismissed and the association had to pay them back for the thirty cattle, plus costs. Meschter, 122.

11. Meschter, viii, 159–60, 206.

12. Ibid., 86–90.

13. Meschter, 86, 90, 157–62. Averell also built a ditch, as he was entitled to do, across Conner's claim to water land around his road ranch. Meschter, 97.

14. Ibid., 103–4, 130–39.

15. Ibid., 43, 69–71, 90–92, 104–5.

16. See the roundup list for 1889, American Heritage Center, Wyoming Stock Growers Association Collection, Box 243, Folder 3. Kathleen and Steve Sun, interview by author, June 27, 2004. Gaynell and Norman Park, interviews by author, July and August 2003. Kathleen Sun, widow of Tom Sun's grandson John Hugh Sun, heard the incriminating story of the twenty shot cows from Ruth Beebe. Beebe heard the story from her father, Joe Sharp, who was on the roundup in 1889. She left the story out of her 1973 book, *Reminiscing along the Sweetwater*, however. Beulah Belle Lake, where the roundup ended, is on the Dumbell Ranch; it was from Gaynell and Norman Park of the Dumbell that I learned the lynchers left from there on the day of the hanging. The rest of my version is drawn from the accounts in the *Carbon County Journal, Casper Weekly Mail*, and other papers, all usefully reprinted in Meschter's appendices, *Sweetwater Sunset*, pp. 207–32. Throughout, I kept in mind the compact version I heard from Kathleen's nephew, Dennis Sun: "Way my great grandfather told it, they went down there, they just wanted to scare them. But she got mouthy."

17. Owen Wister met one of the lynchers that month, before the grand jury dismissed the charges. He was on his third trip to Wyoming, by train to Rawlins and by stage to Fort Washakie, to hunt in the Wind River Mountains. Writing on a cold night as the stage headed north through Crook's Gap, the future author of *The*

*Virginian* noted: "Sat yesterday in smoking car with one of the gentlemen indicted for lynching the man and the woman. He seemed a good solid citizen, and I hope he'll get off. Sheriff Donnell said, 'All the good folks say it was a good job; it's only the wayward classes that complain.'" Wister, *Owen Wister Out West*, 90–91.

## Chapter 12: The Magic Touch of Water

*Epigraph*: James, *Reclaiming the Arid West*, 202–3.

1. Chittenden, *Western Epic*, 43–48; Pisani, *To Reclaim a Divided West*, 275–77, citing Warren's correspondence with Mead, Senator Joseph Carey, and others.

2. Chittenden includes this story in his section on Independence Rock in *The American Fur Trade of the Far West*, vol. 1, pp. 472–73. He attributes it to "one of the old residents still living in this locality"—which means Sun or Bothwell. But Bothwell seems the more likely raconteur.

3. Elwood Mead was chief engineer for the Bear River project, one of many business interests he maintained while also working as territorial and then state engineer for Wyoming. See Pisani, *To Reclaim a Divided West*, 235. It was the plans of the Bear River project which so alarmed Congress that it withdrew all public lands from entry while John Wesley Powell conducted his survey sorting irrigable from non-irrigable lands in the West. Pisani, 148–50.

4. Meschter, *Sweetwater Sunset*, 142–45. Natrona County land records show that John C. Davis of the Sweetwater Land and Irrigation Company was also one of Bothwell's principal creditors throughout this time, making frequent large loans to the rancher in the 1890s and early 1900s.

5. Pisani, *To Reclaim a Divided West*, 238–72. The dream was plain in the title of irrigation booster William Smythe's book: *The Conquest of Arid America*. New York: MacMillan, 1905, 1899.

6. *Natrona County Tribune*, February 12, 1903, citing the *Denver Post* for the phrase.

7. Chittenden, *Reservoir Sites*, 19. Much of the actual survey work for the report was done by F. R. Maltby, a government engineer who came through a few weeks after Chittenden and took more detailed measurements.

8. Chittenden, *Reservoir Sites*, 1–20, 63–64, and James, *Reclaiming the Arid West*, xvii–xx.

9. *Natrona County Tribune*, February 26, 1903. Four thousand new people would have tripled Natrona County's population. The U.S. Census Bureau counted 1,785 people in Natrona County in 1900.

10. Parshall's January 28, 1903, report is included in the appendices at the back of United States Reclamation Service, *History of the North Platte Project*, vol. 1, 100334, 100342–344. Newell's reply is on 100347. Parshall served as Wyoming state engineer from 1911 to 1915. A flume device he invented made it easy to measure water flow in ditches, so irrigators knew who got how much.

11. *Natrona County Tribune*, April 16, 1903; April 23, 1903; May 7, 1903.

12. Natrona County Land Records, including the deed showing the sale of the piece from Florence and her husband Lincoln Kelly to Bothwell, May 13, 1903, and the complaint *United States of America vs. The Bothwell Co. et al.*, Eighth Judicial Circuit, District of Wyoming, of the U.S. Circuit Court. For a copy of the complaint and judgment filed September 29, 1910, see p. 539 of Book 1, Miscellaneous.

13. Chittenden, *Reservoir Sites*, 20; USGS, *Second Annual Report*, 502–3.

14. *Natrona County Tribune*, August 27, 1903; October 1, 1903; October 15, 1903; USGS, *Second Annual Report, 505.*

15. U.S. Reclamation Service, *History of the North Platte Project*, 1913, vol. 1, p. 13: "Tradition says that Fremont, in the early part of the last century, passed through the 'Big Canon' in a boat, and that in so doing, he lost his surveying instruments in the river at some point near the present Pathfinder dam site."

16. *Natrona County Tribune*, November 5, 1903; December 17, 1903. Twenty years later, when he came to write his county history, Tribune Editor A.J. Mokler did not attempt to hide his resentment of the Reclamation Service for building a dam that provided huge benefits for Nebraska and very few, in the long run, for central Wyoming. See his *History of Natrona County*, 75-81.

17. James, *Reclaiming the Arid West*, 205; USRS, *History of the North Platte Project*, vol. 1, pp. 14–16, 32, 42. "Cyclopean rubble" comes from a letter from I. W. McConnell, cited in the 1908 Biennial Report of the Wyoming State Engineer, p. 45.

18. Meschter, *Sweetwater Sunset*, 146–49; *Natrona County Tribune*, August 6, 1903; Beebe, *Reminiscing along the Sweetwater*, 61.

19. USRS, *History of the North Platte Project*, vol. 1, 43–44.

20. This account is based on the Reclamation Service's records of the Bothwell land dispute, in boxes 747 and 748 of the files on the North Platte Project, Bureau of Reclamation General Administrative and Project Files, National Archives and Records Administration, Denver, Colorado. See in particular Bothwell to C. E. Wells, USRS supervising engineer, Casper, September 7, 1905; John C. Wallis to Wells, September 25, 1905; I. W. McConnell, supervising engineer, to the director, USRS, December 5, 1908; Secretary of the Interior James R. Garfield to Bothwell, January 26, 1909; Bothwell to Garfield, February 5, 1909; McConnell to director, USRS, March 16, 1909; Clark, Riner, and Clark, Cheyenne, to U.S. attorney general, June 16, 1909; McConnell to director, USRS, June 18, 1909; "Application for order for plaintiff to enter and occupy land," July 3, 1909; R. F. Walter, acting supervisor, USRS to director, USRS, November 27, 1909. It was Walter who called the verdict "a signal victory: and noted that state senators were Bothwell's "long suit." See also Clark, Riner, and Clark to AG, November 29, 1909; Clark, Riner, and Clark to Walter, December 16, 1909; Clark, Riner, and Clark to AG, December 29, 1909; J. R. Alexander, examiner, USRS, to director, USRS, February 5, 1910, on the difference between the defense and plaintiffs' witnesses.

21. North Platte Project file, NARA, Denver, Court of Claims complaint, *Bothwell and Bothwell Co. vs. United States*, June 9, 1915; Ottamar Hameles to chief

and district counsels [USRS], Mitchell, Nebraska, March 9, 1921; Meschter, *Sweetwater Sunset*, 202–3.

## Chapter 13: Story Spots

*Epigraph*: *Deseret News*, June 23, 1931, p. 2.

1. Meeker, *Kate Mulhall*, 71–75, 219–25.

2. Webber, *Ezra Meeker*, 72.

3. Underbrink, "Oregon Trail Memorial Half-Dollar." Only 203,000 of the six million half-dollars authorized were ever minted, and 61,000 of those were melted back down unsold. Congress finally rescinded the authorization in 1939.

4. Webber, *Ezra Meeker*, 7–72. See also, Meeker, *Busy Life of Eighty-Five Years*, 23–50, 235–41, 271–89. Meeker found the country along the Sweetwater in much better shape in 1906 than when he'd last seen it in 1852—but oppressively silent, empty as it was of the emigrant crowds and their livestock. At Devil's Gate, he stopped in at the post office, and asked Tom Sun about pioneer graves—hoping, perhaps, to find some sign of his brother's. Sun replied that there were many about, but all had been trampled smooth by the tread of stock along the trail— 225,000 eastbound cattle came over in 1882 alone, Sun said, and in some years, half a million sheep. Now they seldom saw more than five wagons a week. Misled perhaps by the trace of an accent in Sun's speech, Meeker believed he was a Swede, based on a story Sun's neighbor's told. "The story runs that when he first went to the bank, then as now sixty miles away, to deposit, the cashier asked his name and received the reply Thompson, emphasizing the last syllable pronounced with so much emphasis, that it was written Tom Sun, and from necessity a check had to be so signed, thus making that form of spelling generally known, and finally it was adopted as the name of the postoffice." Meeker, *Busy Life*, 279–80.

5. Billy Owen's mother was one of these. Her husband converted in Gloucestershire and she came with him and their infant daughter to Utah in 1854. No one had told her about polygamy before she arrived, however, and she refused to join the church. Billy's father left the family to go on a mission back to Europe when the boy was nine months old, and they never saw him again. In 1868, she finally left Utah with her three children and reached Laramie a few weeks before the Union Pacific tracks. She started a restaurant. Billy was eight. See his May 9, 1938, letter to his great-niece, Barbara Nelson. Owen Collection, Jackson Hole Historical Society.

6. *Who's Who in America*, vol. 28, 1954–55, 734. Driggs, *Old West Speaks*, 13, 19, 21.

7. *Casper Daily Tribune*, July 2, 1930, p. 1.

8. Jackson to Ellison, March 10, 1925 and Ellison to Jackson, March 21, 1925, cited in Hales, *William Henry Jackson*, 284. The Ellison papers are in the Western History Collection of the Denver Public Library.

9. Hales, 286–91. Particularly interesting is an exchange of letters that Hales cites, 286–87, between Ellison and Jackson about a painting of the 1865 Battle of Red Buttes. Ellison wanted more war bonnets on the Indians.

10. Merrill Mattes recalled decades later that Driggs "could wave the flag, bring the Oregon Trail cavalcade to life, and make the blood of his listeners boil in their ears." See Mattes, "Tribute to the Oregon Trail Memorial Association," 31.

11. Historical Landmark Commission, *Biennial Reports*, 1927–28, 1929–30. Ewig, "Give Them What They Want."

12. The centennial officially extended from the hundredth anniversary of the April 10, 1830, departure of the first wagon train from St. Louis, to December 29, the hundredth anniversary of Ezra Meeker's birth. The so-called wagon train was actually a fur-trade caravan with a few wheeled vehicles in it, bound for rendezvous on the tributaries of the Wind River, east of the Continental Divide. Its proprietors, Jedediah Smith, Dave Jackson, and William Sublette, had no intention of taking it to Oregon.

13. *New York Times*, June 15, 1930; *Casper Daily Tribune*, June 20, 1930, in Mokler Collection scrapbook A, Casper College Library Special Collections. In the actual battle of Red Buttes, July 26, 1865, two army wagons and twenty-one men under Sergeant Amos Custard were attacked by Lakota and Cheyenne warriors on a hill several miles west of Platte Bridge, and nearly all of them killed. This was the party that Caspar Collins had been sent to relieve when he, too, was killed. The Governor's Island reenactment involved sixty wagons, Governor's Island–based U.S. infantrymen dressed as Indians and more dressed as Civil War–era soldiers—and the "Indians" lost. The crowd was also entertained with an air show and songs by Rudy Vallee. On hand were Driggs, Jackson, General Pershing, Al Smith, Franklin Roosevelt, and Elizabeth Custer.

14. Martin, *Boy Scouts and the Oregon Trail*. G. P. Putnam's Sons also published several of Driggs's books.

15. Peterson, *Boy Scouts*, 17–112.

16. *Casper Daily Tribune*, July 2, 1930, p. 14; July 6, 1930, p. 8. Crawford and Kowalski did not know each other before they met in Casper.

17. Martin, *Boy Scouts*, 63, 75. The Pittsburgh scoutmaster was Edward Minister. Two or three photos of the 1930 gathering in the Dan Greenburg collection at the American Heritage Center at the University of Wyoming show two men in warbonnets and ceremonial garb striking dramatic poses on the Rock. One of these is probably Chief Tecumseh, but I've been unable to find out anything else about him.

18. *Casper Daily Tribune* and, on Sundays, *Casper Tribune-Herald*, July 2–6, 1930. Coverage was heavy. Also see Underbrink, "Covered Wagon Centennial at Independence Rock." *Overland Journal* 17:3 (fall 1999) 2–11, and the Historical Landmark Commission *Biennial Report* for 1928–29, 9–12.

19. *Deseret News*, June 28, 1930, p. 11. Brigham Young and the advance party of Saints nooned at Independence Rock on June 21, 1847, the paper reported. William Clayton noted in his journal that a few of the men climbed the Rock, and watched from the top as some Missourians buried a young woman. Lorenzo Young gathered a pailful of saleratus at one of the drying soda lakes nearby, and Harriet Young used it to raise her noontime bread. It worked well, and so the Saints filled many more pails.

20. Jenson, *Autobiography*, 12–27. The job of church historian went instead to one of Jenson's young assistants, Joseph Fielding Smith, who was the son of church President Joseph F. Smith and who late in his life would also become president. See http://www.media.utah.edu/UHE/j/JENSON%2CANDREW.html.

21. Roberts, *Autobiography of B. H. Roberts*, 31.

22. *Deseret News*, July 4, 1930. A beehive has long been a Mormon symbol of cooperation and industry.

23. Jones, *Forty Years among the Indians*, 69–70.

24. Burton noted only that most of the Martin Company moved to a place three miles away. See his journal entries in Hafen, *Handcarts to Zion*, 224.

### Chapter 14: Perfect Balance

*Epigraph*: *LDS Church News*, August 22, 1992, p. 3.

1. Scott Lorimer, interviews with author, December 10, 2004, and January 13, 2005. LDS *Church News*, October 19, 1991, and August 22, 1992. See also the Riverton Stake's web page on the subject at www.handcart.com.

2. The gate was famous. Lawrence Jamison, of Ervay, Wyoming, wrote a number of poems about his neighbors at midcentury, including this, from 1941:

The Gate of Perfect Balance

We've heard about the poets
And the stirring tales of old,
Imagine what this gate would say
If its story could be told.

It has balanced there for ages
Held in place by a strip of hide,
And a wealth of hospitality
Completes the charm of the home inside.

Well it knows of Bonny Earnest
And the elder Mr. Sun,
It's been wrapped in the dust of string teams
As they passed there one by one.

The balanced gate by the roadside
Has opened for "Old John Clay"
Many's the time Sam Johnson's hand
Pushed it back at close of day.

John Nolan, the Durbins, and Joe Sharp
Bothwell, Countryman, and P.J. Mac,
Jamerman, Fletcher, Sheehans, and Beaton
They have all pushed it back.

The old Gate of perfect balance
Has opened for all to come,
I wonder if the great gate up yonder
Has opened just the same.

I'll bet my horse and saddle
and throw in all the steers,
That the Golden Gate was in balance
When approached by those pioneers.

Do not pass the old gate unheeded
If you pass that way.
It has seen more of the old west
Than all of us folks today.

3. The changeover had some rough spots. According to Steve Sun, his grandfather Tom Sun, Jr., allowed Bill Grieve on the neighboring Dumbell Ranch to graze cattle on public land southwest of Independence Rock for three years, on sections the Suns had long considered their range. When the Taylor Grazing Act was passed, the new lease system was based on custom of the three previous years. Sun assumed the Grieves would tell the government that they were relatively new to the ground, but "Grieve never said boo," Steve said, and kept it as his lease. Steve and Kathleen Sun, interview with author, June 27, 2004. The families stopped talking to each other. Norman Park, who took over the Dumbell from the Grieves early in the 1970s, disputes this version.

4. Mr. N. D. Bucklin, who ranched alone, was pulling a cabin on skids with his tractor when something went wrong with the balance and flipped the tractor over backwards, pinning him under it. He took a week to die and slit his own throat at the end. Steve Sun, June 27, 2004. Beebe, *Reminiscing along the Sweeetwater*, 24.

5. The entire west side of the desert grazing allotments south of the mountains was never fenced, and Sun cattle have turned up from time to time as far away as Farson. The Suns share these allotments with other ranches, so the question of the ranch's precise size becomes gradually moot as you move farther west

into the Red Desert. More important is the number of cattle the land can support. On public land, the BLM gets to be the judge of that. I came to these conclusions after counting the sections on a BLM map of Sun allotments from about 1992.

6. If a new storm was coming in, wind and weather would blow out of the northeast, and the east-side gully would give the most shelter. If the wind was blowing from the southwest, as it does more or less all the rest of the time, the pocket on the other side would be more likely. Burton's journal of that desperate week in November 1856 says that after the first bad storm stopped, the weather turned very cold. When very cold, the wind is likely to stop completely. See Hafen, *Handcarts to Zion*, 224.

7. Hinckley by this time had been serving off and on as acting church president for several years, as Ezra Taft Benson's health declined. Benson died May 30, 1994, and was succeeded by Howard W. Hunter, who was also in poor health; he died and Hinckley succeeded him as president in March 1995. Since then Hinckley has been a relentless builder, more than quadrupling the number of Mormon temples around the world. The number has grown from 27 when he took office to 122 as of November 2005, with eleven more on the way, including temples planned or under construction in Kiev, Panama City, Helsinki, and Curitiba, Brazil.

## Epilogue

1. The fort consists of log buildings around a hollow *U*, with a stockade along one side of partly burnt planks, to remind visitors of the night the rescuers pulled logs out of the buildings to build big fires for the Martin handcarters as they straggled in. The foundation of the actual fort was discovered and excavated in 2001. The replica was built nearby on a new, concrete foundation.

2. Jack Kelly, manager, Lander Resource Area, BLM, personal interview, January 27, 2005. At least one BLM staffer feels his agency didn't fight hard enough for accuracy on the signs both at Martin's Cove and at the sites nearer South Pass. Gary Long, recreation coordinator at the time of the ranch sale for the Lander Office of the BLM, has now moved up to the state office of the BLM in Cheyenne. He has co-written a book, due soon from the University of Utah Press, tracing the Willie Company day by day on its journey, and feels the Mormons continue to cling to incorrect versions of events, especially concerning the Willie Company as it approached South Pass, despite clear documentary evidence that shows what really happened. "There's a simple elegance about the truth," he told me. "When you get it right, it seems to mean more. . . . Just making something up because it's a good story and it perpetuates a myth is not good enough. A lot of the so-called experts just blew it. Completely." Personal interview with Gary Long, January 28, 2005.

3. Interview with Jack Kelly, manager, BLM Lander Resource Area, January 29, 2005. See also *Casper Star-Tribune*, November 5, 2001; Hansen's letter to the editor on May 5, 2002; and *Star-Tribune* articles on May 5, 12, 14, 16, 17, 23, 29, 2002; June 7, 19, 2002; December 4, 2002; January 17, 2003; May 14, 2003; May 17, 2003; June 6, 2003; November 29, 2003; May 12, 2004; May 18, 2004; September 15, 2004; October 29, 2004. *Deseret News*, October 16, 2001. Christopher Smith, "Tragic Handcart Account Evolved Over Years," *Salt Lake Tribune*, June 30, 2002—a thoughtful article that helped me frame my own chapter 6; other *Salt Lake Tribune* stories appeared on September 17, 2003, and December 1, 2003. Interview with ACLU lawyer Mark Lopez, January 30, 2006; interview with Gary Long of the BLM, February 4, 2006.

# Bibliography

Abbott, E. C. ("Teddy Blue") and Helena Huntington Smith. *We Pointed Them North: Recollections of a Cowpuncher.* New York: Farrar & Rinehart, Inc., 1939.

*Annual Report of the Adjutant General of the State of Maine for the year ending December 31, 1862.* Augusta: Stevens & Sayward, 1863, 146–47.

Archambault, Amanda Z. "Historic Document Tells Early Day Drama of the West," *Annals of Wyoming* 15:3 (July 1943) 229–33.

Appelgate, Heidi. "A Traveler by Instinct." In *Hudson River School Visions: The Landscapes of Sanford R. Gifford,* edited by Kevin J. Avery and Franklin Kelly, 53–75. New York: Metropolitan Museum of Art, and New Haven: Yale University Press, 2003.

Athearn, Robert G. *The Mythic West in Twentieth-Century America.* Lawrence: University Press of Kansas, 1986.

Avery, Kevin J., and Franklin Kelly, eds. *Hudson River School Visions: The Landscapes of Sanford R. Gifford.* New York: Metropolitan Museum of Art and New Haven: Yale University Press, 2003.

Bagley, Will. *Blood of the Prophets: Bringham Young and the Massacre at Mountain Meadows.* Norman: University of Oklahoma Press, 2002.

Bancroft, Hubert Howe. *History of Nevada, California and Wyoming.* Vol. 25, *The Works of Hubert Howe Bancroft.* San Francisco: History Company, Publishers, 1890.

Barsh, Russell L. "The Substitution of Cattle for Bison on the Great Plains." In *The Struggle for the Land: Indigenous Insight and Industrial Empire in the Semiarid World,* edited by Paul A. Olson, 103–26. University of Nebraska Press, 1990.

Bartlett, Richard A. *Great Surveys of the American West.* Norman: University of Oklahoma Press, 1962.

Barry, Louise. *The Beginning of the West: Annals of the Kansas Gateway to the American West, 1540–1854.* Topeka: The Kansas State Historical Society, 1972, 447,

501. Mentions Descoteaux (Decoto) traveling down the Platte with Charles Lajeunesse, 1842; meets Fremont headed upstream.

Beebe, Ruth. *Reminiscing along the Sweetwater*. Casper, Wyo.: Westerner News, 1973.

Bennett, John W. "Human Adaptations to the Great Plains." In *The Struggle for the Land: Indigenous Insight and Industrial Empire in the Semiarid World*, edited by Paul A. Olson, 41–80. Lincoln, University of Nebraska Press, 1990.

Benton, Frank. *Cowboy Life on the Sidetrack*. Denver: Western Stories Syndicate, 1903.

Bitton, Davis. *The Ritualization of Mormon History and Other Essays*. Urbana: University of Illinois Press, 1994.

Blight, David W. *Beyond the Battlefield: Race, Memory, and the American Civil War*. Amherst: University of Massachusetts Press, 2002.

Brandhorst, L. Carl. "The North Platte Oasis: Notes on the Geography and History of an Irrigation District." *Agricultural History*, 51:1 (1977), 168–72.

Brown, Richard Maxwell. *Strain of Violence: Historical Studies of American Violence and Vigilantism*. New York: Oxford University Press, 1975.

Bryans, Bill. *Deer Creek: Frontiers Crossroad in Pre-Territorial Wyoming*. Glenrock, Wyo.: Glenrock Historical Commission, c. 1990.

Bryson, Michael A. *Visions of the Land: Science, Literature, and the American Environment from the Era of Exploration to the Age of Ecology*. Charlottesville: University Press of Virginia, 2002.

Burton, Richard F. *The City of the Saints, and Across the Rocky Mountains to California*. Edited, with an introduction and notes by Fawn M. Brodie. New York: Alfred A. Knopf, 1963.

*Carbon County Journal*. Rawlins, Wyoming. 1905, 1906.

Carter, Kate B., comp. *Heart Throbs of the West*. Salt Lake City: Daughters of the Utah Pioneers, 1939–1949. Ten volumes.

*Casper Daily Tribune* and *Casper Tribune-Herald*. Casper, Wyoming. July 1930; June 1931; April 1933.

Cassidy, James G. *Ferdinand V. Hayden: Entrepreneur of Science*. Lincoln: University of Nebraska Press, 2000.

Chaffin, Tom. *Pathfinder: John Charles Frémont and the Course of American Empire*. New York: Hill and Wang, 2002.

Chittenden, Hiram Martin. *The American Fur Trade of the Far West: a History of the Pioneer Trading Posts and Early Fur Companies of the Missouri Valley and the Rocky Mountains and of the Overland Commerce with Santa Fé*. 2 vols. 1902. Stanford, Calif.: Academic Reprints, 1954.

———. *Preliminary Examination of Reservoir Sites in Wyoming and Colorado*. House Document 141, 55th Cong., 2d sess., Dec. 10, 1897, referred to the Committee on Irrigation of Arid Lands and ordered to be published.

———. *A Western Epic: Being a Selection from His Unpublished Journals, Diaries and Reports*. Edited by Bruce Le Roy. Tacoma: Washington State Historical Society, 1961.

Clow, Richmond L. "Bison Ecology, Brulé and Yankton Winter Hunting, and the Starving Winter of 1832–33." *Great Plains Quarterly* 15 (1995): 259–70.

Cook, James H. *Longhorn Cowboy*. Edited with an introduction by Howard R. Driggs. New York: G. P. Putnam's Sons, 1942.

Cooke, Philip St. George. *Scenes and Adventures in the Army: or Romance of Military Life*. Philadelphia: Lindsay and Blakiston, 1857. Reprinted by Arno Press Inc., 1973.

Coutant, C. G. *The History of Wyoming from the Earliest Known Discoveries*, vol. 1. Laramie: Chaplin, Spafford & Mathison, 1899.

Craig, Nute [Newton N.] *Thrills, 1861 to 1887*. Oakland, California: N.N. Craig, ca. 1931.

Denton, Sally. "What Happened at Mountain Meadows?" *American Heritage* 52, no. 7 (October 2001).

———. *American Massacre: The Tragedy at Mountain Meadows, September 1857*. New York: Alfred A. Knopf, 2003.

*Deseret News*. Salt Lake City. June and July 1930. June 1931.

DeVoto, Bernard. *Across the Wide Missouri*. New York: Bonanza Books, 1972. Reprint of the 1947 Houghton Mifflin edition.

———. *The Year of Decision, 1846*. Boston: Little, Brown and Company, 1943.

Dippie, Brian W. "'Flying Buffaloes' Artists and the Buffalo Hunt." *Montana The Magazine of Western History* 51, no. 2 (Summer 2001): 2–17.

Dodds, Gordon B. *Hiram Martin Chittenden: His Public Career*. Lexington: University Press of Kentucky, 1973.

Dorn, Robert D. *The Wyoming Landscape, 1805–1878*. Cheyenne: Mountain West Publishing, 1986.

Driggs, Howard R. *Mormon Trail: Pathway of Pioneers Who Made the Deserts Blossom*. New York: American Pioneer Trails Association, 1947.

———. *The Old West Speaks*. Englewood Cliffs, N.J.: Prentice-Hall, Inc., 1956. With watercolor paintings by William Henry Jackson.

———. *Westward America*. New York: G. P. Putnam's sons, 1942. With reproductions of forty watercolor paintings by William H. Jackson.

Dunham, Harold H. "Some Crucial Years of the General Land Office, 1875–90." *Agricultural History* 11 (1937): 117–41.

Egan, Ferol. *Frémont: Explorer for a Restless Nation*. Garden City, N.Y.: Doubleday, 1977.

Ekins, Roger Robin, ed. *Defending Zion: George Q. Cannon and the California Mormon Newspaper Wars of 1856–1857*. Spokane, Wash: Arthur H. Clark Co., 2002. Vol. 5 of *Kingdom in the West: The Mormons and the American Frontier*, Will Bagley, series editor.

Ellison, Robert Spurrier. *William H. Jackson: Pioneer of the Yellowstone*. Casper, Wyo.: R. S. Ellison, 1925.

———. *Independence Rock, the great record of the desert*. Casper, Wyo.: Natrona County Historical Society, 1930.

Ewig, Rick. "Give Them What They Want: The Selling of Wyoming's Image between the World Wars." In *Readings in Wyoming History: Issues in the History of the Equality State*, edited by Phil Roberts, 110–24. 4th ed. Laramie: Skyline West Press, 2004.

Field, Matthew C. *Prairie and Mountain Sketches.* Edited by Kate L. Gregg and John Francis McDermott. Norman: University of Oklahoma Press, 1957.

Findholt, Scott L. "Population Status, Reproductive Success, Food Habits, Foraging Areas, Prey Availablitity, Movements, and some Management Considerations of American White Pelicans Nesting at Pathfinder Reservoir, Wyoming." Nongame Special Report, Biological Services, Wyoming Game and Fish Department, 1987.

Fowler, Loretta. *Arapahoe Politics, 1851–1978: Symbols in Crises of Authority.* Lincoln: University of Nebraska Press, 1982.

Franzwa, Gregory M. *The Oregon Trail Revisited.* St. Louis: Patrice Press, 1972.

Frémont, John Charles, *The Expeditions of John Charles Frémont.* Edited by Donald Jackson and Mary Lee Spence. Urbana: University of Illionis Press, 1970. In four volumes, of which the fourth is a map portfolio.

———. *The Exploring Expedition to the Rocky Mountains.* With an introduction by Herman J. Viola and Ralph E. Ehrenberg. Washington, D.C.: Smithsonian Institution Press, 1988.

———. *The life of Col. John Charles Fremont, and his narrative of explorations and adventures, in Kansas, Nebraska, Oregon and California. The memoir by Samuel M. Smucker.* New York: Auburn, Miller, Orton & Mulligan, 1856.

———. *Memoirs of My Life, with Sketches of the Life of Senator Benton by Jessie Benton Fremont.* Chicago: Belford, Clarke & Co., 1887.

Glass, Jefferson. "Crossing the North Platte River: A Brief History of 'Reshaw's' Bridge—1852–1866." *Annals of Wyoming* 74:3 (Summer 2002): 25–40.

Godfrey, Kenneth W., Audry M. Godfrey, and Jill Mulvay Derr. *Women's Voices: An Untold History of the Latter-day Saints, 1830–1900.* Salt Lake City: Deseret Book Company, 1982.

Goetzmann, William H. *Army Exploration in the American West, 1803–1863.* New Haven: Yale University Press, 1959.

———. *Exploration and Empire: The Explorer and the Scientist in the Winning of the West.* New York: W. W. Norton, 1966.

Graham, Bob. John Charles Frémont website, www.longcamp.com.

Hafen, Leroy, and Ann Hafen. *Handcarts to Zion: The Story of a Unique Western Migration, 1856–1860, with contemporary journals, accounts, reports; and rosters of members of the ten Handcart Companies.* Glendale, Calif.: Arthur H. Clark Company, 1960.

Hafen, Leroy R., ed. *French Fur Traders and Voyageurs in the American West.* Selected, with an introduction, by Janet LeCompte. Lincoln: University of Nebraska Press, 1997.

Hales, Peter B. *William Henry Jackson and the Transformation of American Landscape.* Philadelphia: Temple University Press, 1988.

Hammond, Andy. "Those Beautiful !#%X@$%&! Mules." *Overland Journal* 20 (Summer 2002): 74–78.

Harris, Edwin D. *John Charles Frémont and the Great Western Reconnaissance.* New York: Chelsea House Publishers, 1990.

Hargrove, Gene. "Why We Think Nature Is Beautiful." Website produced by University of North Texas philosophy department, online as of 5/19/06 at http://www.cep.unt.edu/show/

Hayden, F. V. *Preliminary report of the United States Geological Survey of Wyoming and portions of contiguous territories : (being a second annual report of progress) / conducted under the authority of the Secretary of the Interior.* Washington, [D.C., U.S. Dept. of the Interior], 1871.

———. *Eleventh annual report of the United States Geological and Geographical Survey of the Territories: embracing Idaho and Wyoming: being a report of progress of the exploration for the year 1877; conducted under the authority of the Secretary of the Interior.* Washington, D.C.: Government Printing Office, 1879.

———. "Arapohos." In "Contributions to the Ethnography and Philology of the Indian Tribes of the Missouri Valley," *Transactions of the American Philological Society*, n.s. 12 (1862): 321–39.

Hileman, Levida. "Archaeological Excavation near Devil's Gate," folio, August 2001, 24–27.

———. *In Tar, Paint, and Stone: The Inscriptions at Independence Rock and Devil's Gate.* Glendo, Wyo.: High Plains Press, 2001.

Hill, Burton S. "Thomas S. Twiss, Indian Agent." *Great Plains Journal* 6 (Spring 1967): 85–96.

Historical Landmark Commission of Wyoming. *Biennial Reports, 1927–1954.* Cheyenne: Historical Landmark Commission of Wyoming, 1928–1954.

Holmes, Kenneth L., ed. and comp. *Covered Wagon Women: Diaries and Letters from the Western Trails, 1840–1890.* Glendale, Calif.: Arthur H. Clark Company, 1988. 11 volumes. Sutton's 1854 diary, vol. 7, 15–77; Mousely's 1857 diary, vol. 7, 163–89.

Hooker, William Francis. *The Bullwhacker: Adventures of a Frontier Freighter.* Edited by Howard R. Driggs. Yonkers-on-Hudson, New York: World Book Company, 1925.

Hoopes, Alban W. "Thomas S. Twiss, Indian Agent on the Upper Platte, 1855–1861." *Mississippi Valley Historical Review* 20 (December 1933): 353–64.

Hogan, Linda. *The Woman Who Watches over the World: A Native Memoir.* New York: W. W. Norton, 2001.

Hufsmith, George W. *The Wyoming Lynching of Cattle Kate.* Glendo, Wyo.: High Plains Press, 1993.

Hyde, George. *Life of George Bent, Written from His Letters.* Edited by Savoie Lottinville. Norman: University of Oklahoma Press, 1968.

————. *Red Cloud's Folk: A History of the Oglala Sioux Indians.* Norman: University of Oklahoma Press, 1937. Third printing, 1967.

————. *Spotted Tail's Folk: A History of the Brulé Sioux.* Norman: University of Oklahoma Press, 1961.

Jackson, Clarence S. *Picture Maker of the Old West, William Henry Jackson.* New York: Charles Scribner's Sons, 1947.

Jackson, William Henry. *The Pioneer Photographer: Rocky Mountain Adventures with a Camera.* In collaboration with Howard R. Driggs. Yonkers-on-Hudson, N.Y.: World Book Company, 1929.

————. *Time Exposure: The Autobiography of William Henry Jackson.* New York: Cooper Square Publishers, 1970. First published 1940.

————. *The Diaries of William Henry Jackson, Frontier Photographer, to California and return, 1866–67; and with the Hayden Surveys to the Central Rockies, 1873, and to the Utes and Cliff Dwellings, 1874.* Edited by Leroy R. Hafen and Ann W. Hafen. Glendale, Calif.: Arthur H. Clark Company, 1959.

James, George Wharton. *Reclaiming the Arid West: The Story of the United States Reclamation Service.* New York: Dodd, Mead and Company, 1917.

Jenson, Andrew. *Autobiography of Andrew Jenson, Assistant Historian of the Church of Jesus Christ of Latter-day Saints.* Salt Lake City: Deseret News Press, 1938.

Johnson, Hervey. *Tending the Talking Wire: A Buck Soldier's View of Indian Country, 1863–1866.* Edited by William E. Unrau. Salt Lake City: University of Utah Press, 1979.

Johnson, Thomas Hoevet. *The Enos Family and Wind River Shoshone Society: A Historical Analysis.* Ph.D. diss., University of Illinois at Urbana–Champaign, 1975.

Jones, Daniel. *Forty Years among the Indians: A True Yet Thrilling Narrative of the Author's Experiences among the Natives.* Los Angeles: Westernlore Press, 1960. First published 1890 by the Juvenile Instructor's Office, Salt Lake City.

Kappler, Charles J., ed. and comp. *Indian Affairs: Laws and Treaties.* Vol. 2, *Treaties,* 594–96. "Treaty of Fort Laramie with Sioux, etc., 1851."

Kimball, Solomon F. "Our Pioneer Boys," *The Improvement Era* (July 1908): 679.

————. "Belated Emigrants of 1856," *The Improvement Era,* 12, nos. 1–4 (1914).

Knight, Mrs. Amelia Stewart. Diary, 1853. Starting from Monroe County, Iowa, Saturday, April 9, 1853, and Ending Near Millwaukie, Oregon Territory, September 17, 1853. As of 5/19/06, online at http://www.isu.edu/%7Etrinmich/00.ar.knight.html.

Knight, Dennis H. *Mountains and Plains: The Ecology of Wyoming Landscapes.* New Haven: Yale University Press, 1994.

Knight, Wilbur. "The Wyoming Fossil Fields Expedition of July, 1899." *National Geographic Magazine* 11:12 (December 1900): 458.

Lageson, David R., and Darwin R. Spearing. *Roadside Geology of Wyoming.* Missoula, Mont.: Mountain Press Publishing Company, 1988.

Leeming, David, and Jake Page. *The Mythology of Native North America.* Norman: University of Oklahoma Press. 1998.

Limerick, Patricia N. "Judging Western History: From the Battlefield to the Courtroom." *Western Legal History* 14 (Winter/Spring 2001): 9–18.

Linklater, Andro. *Measuring America: How an Untamed Wilderness Shaped the United States and Fulfilled the Promise of Democracy.* New York: Walker & Company, 2002.

Madsen, Brigham D. *Glory Hunter: A Biography of Patrick Edward Connor.* Salt Lake City: University of Utah Press, 1990.

———. *The Shoshoni Frontier and the Bear River Massacre.* Salt Lake City: University of Utah Press, 1985.

Marsden, Jason. "Why oh why does the Wyo wind blow?" *Casper Star-Tribune,* June 11, 1996.

Martin, Clinton S., ed. *Boy Scouts and the Oregon Trail: A Centenary Pilgrimage.* New York: G. P. Putnam's Sons, 1930.

Mattes, Merrill J. *Platte River Road Narratives: A Descriptive Bibliography of Travel over the Great Central Overland Route to Oregon, California, Utah, Colorado, Montana, and other Western States and Territories.* Urbana: University of Illinois Press, 1988.

———. *The Great Platte River Road: The Covered Wagon Mainline Via Fort Kearny to Fort Laramie.* Vol. 25 of Nebraska State Historical Society Publications. Lincoln: The Nebraska State Historical Society, 1969.

———. "Potholes in the Great Platte River Road: Misconceptions in Need of Repair." *Wyoming Annals* 6 (Summer/Fall 1993), 6–14.

———. "A Tribute to the Oregon Trail Memorial Association." *Overland Journal* (Winter 1984) 29–34.

McDermott, John D. *Frontier Crossroads: The History of Fort Caspar and the Upper Platte Crossing.* Casper: City of Casper, Wyoming, 1997.

McPhee, John. *Rising from the Plains.* New York: Farrar, Straus, Giroux, 1986.

Meeker, Ezra. *The Busy Life of Eighty-Five Years of Ezra Meeker.* Seattle: Published by the author, 1916.

———. *Kate Mulhall: A Romance of the Oregon Trail.* New York: Published by the author, 1926.

———. *Ox-Team Days on the Oregon Trail.* Revised and edited by Howard R. Driggs. Yonkers-on-Hudson, N.Y.: World Book Company, 1922.

———. *Story of the Lost Trail to Oregon.* Fairfield, Wash.: Ye Galleon Press, 1984. Originally published Seattle, 1915.

Meschter, Daniel Y. *Sweetwater Sunset: A History of the Lynching of James Averell and Ella Watson near Independence Rock, Wyoming on July 20, 1889.* Wenatchee, Wash., privately published, 1996.

———, comp. *A Carbon County Chronology, 1867–1879.* Cheyenne, Wyo.: privately published ca. 1970.

Mokler, Alfred James. *History of Natrona County, Wyoming, 1888–1922 : true portrayal of the yesterdays of a new county and a typical frontier town of the middle West: fortunes and misfortunes, tragedies and comedies, struggles and triumphs of the pioneers.* Chicago: R. R. Donnelley & Sons Co., 1923.

Morgan, Dale, ed. *Overland in 1846: Diaries and Letters of the California-Oregon Trail.* Two volumes. Georgetown, Calif.: Talisman Press, 1963.

Morgan, Dale L., and Eleanor Towles Harris, eds. *The Rocky Mountain Journals of William Marshall Anderson: The West in 1834.* San Marino, Calif.: Huntington Library, 1967.

Muir, John. *The Story of My Boyhood and Youth.* Madison: University of Wisconsin Press, 1985.

Munkres, Robert L. "Independence Rock and Devil's Gate." *Annals of Wyoming,* vol. 40, (April 1968), 23–43.

———. "The Plains Indian Threat on the Oregon Trail before 1860." *Annals of Wyoming* 40, no. 2 (1968): 193–221.

———. "Wives, Mothers, Daughters: Women's Life on the Road West." *Annals of Wyoming* 42 (October 1970): 23–43.

Nash, Gerald D. *The Federal Landscape: An Economic History of the Twentieth-Century West.* Tucson: University of Arizona Press, 1999.

*Natrona County Tribune.* Casper, Wyoming. Mokler brothers, proprietors. 1897, 1903.

Nevins, Allan. *Frémont: Pathmaker of the West.* 2 vols. New York: Frederick Ungar, 1961. First published 1939, reprinted 1955.

Osgood, Ernest Staples. *The Day of the Cattlemen.* Minneapolis: University of Minnesota Press, 1954.

Owen, William O. Unpublished autobiography, ca. 1930. American Heritage Center, University of Wyoming, William O. Owen Collection, #94. Box 1.

Paden, Irene D. *The Wake of the Prairie Schooner.* New York: Macmillan, 1943.

Palmer, Rosemary Gudmundson. *Children's Voices from the Trail: Narratives of the Platte River Road.* Spokane: Arthur H. Clark, 2002.

Parkman, Francis. *The Oregon Trail. The Conspiracy of Pontiac.* New York: Library of America, 1991. Published 1847 in serial form in *Knickerbocker,* first published as a book in 1849.

———. *The Journals of Francis Parkman.* Edited by Mason Wade. 2 vols. New York: Harper and Brothers, 1947.

Peterson, Robert W. *The Boy Scouts: An American Adventure.* New York: American Heritage Publishing Co., 1984.

Phillips, Catherine Coffin. *Jessie Benton Frémont: A Woman Who Made History.* San Francisco: J. H. Nash, 1935, 62–63.

Pisani, Donald J. *To Reclaim a Divided West: Water, Law, and Public Policy 1848-1902.* Albuquerque: University of New Mexico Press, 1992.

Preuss, Charles. *Exploring with Frémont: The Private Diaries of Charles Preuss, Cartographer for John C. Frémont on his First, Second and Fourth Expeditions to the Far West.* Translated and edited by Erwin G. and Elisabeth K. Gudde. Norman: University of Oklahoma Press, 1958.

*Rawlins Republican.* Rawlins, Wyoming. July 1930, June 1931.

Reisner, Marc. *Cadillac Desert: The American West and Its Disappearing Water.* New York: Penguin Books, 1986.

Roberts, B. H. (Brigham Henry). *The Autobiography of B. H. Roberts.* Edited by Gary James Bergera, foreword by Sterling M. McMurrin. Salt Lake City: Signature Books, 1990.

———. *Studies of the Book of Mormon.* Edited with an Introduction by Brigham D. Madsen. With a Biographical Essay by Sterling M. McMurrin. Urbana: University of Illinois Press, 1985.

Roberts, David. *A Newer World: John C. Frémont, Kit Carson and the Claiming of the American West.* New York: Simon and Schuster, 2000.

Rea, Tom. *Bone Wars: The Excavation and Celebrity of Andrew Carnegie's Dinosaur.* Pittsburgh: University of Pittsburgh Press, 2001.

Rolle, Andrew. *John Charles Frémont: Character as Destiny.* Norman: University of Oklahoma Press, 1991.

Rollinson, John K. *Wyoming Cattle Trails.* Edited and arranged by E. A. Brininstool. Caldwell, Idaho: Caxton Printers, 1948.

*Salt Lake Tribune.* Salt Lake City. June and July 1930, June 1931, June 2002, September and December 2003.

Sakolski, A. M. *The Great American Land Bubble: The Amazing Story of Land-Grabbing, Speculations, and Booms from Colonial Days to the Present Time.* New York: Harper & Brothers Publishers, 1932.

Schama, Simon. *Dead Certainties, Unwarranted Speculations.* New York: Knopf, 1991.

Scott, George C. "These God-Forsaken Dobie Hills: Land Law and Settlement of Bates Hole, Wyoming, 1880-1940. Master's thesis, University of Wyoming, 1978.

Shakespeare, Tom. *The Sky People.* New York: Vantage Press, 1971.

Shoumatoff, Alex. *The Mountain of Names: a History of the Human Family.* New York: Simon and Schuster, 1985.

Skogen, Larry C. *Indian Depredation Claims, 1796–1920.* Norman: University of Oklahoma Press, 1996.

Slack, Charles W. *Noble Obsession: Charles Goodyear, Thomas Hancock, and the Race to Unlock the Greatest Industrial Secret of the Nineteenth Century.* New York: Hyperion, 2002.

Smaby, Beverly P. "The Mormons and the Indians: Conflicting Ecological Systems in the Great Basin." *American Studies* 16 (Spring 1975): 35–48.

Smith, Christopher. "Tragic Handcart Accident Account Evolved Over Years." *Salt Lake Tribune,* June 30, 2002.

Smith, Helena Huntington. *The War on Powder River: The History of an Insurrection.* Lincoln: University of Nebraska Press, 1966.

Smith, Henry Nash. *Virgin Land: The American West as Symbol and Myth.* Cambridge: Harvard University Press, 1970. First published 1950.

Spring, Agnes Wright. *Caspar Collins: The Life and Exploits of an Indian Fighter of the Sixties.* New York: Columbia University, 1927.

Stegner, Wallace. *Beyond the Hundredth Meridian: John Wesley Powell and the Second Opening of the West.* Lincoln: University of Nebraska Press, 1982. First published by Houghton Mifflin, 1954.

————. *The Gathering of Zion: The Story of the Morman Trail.* Lincoln: University of Nebraska Press, c1964.

Stenhouse, T. B. H. *The Rocky Mountain Saints: A Full and Complete History of the Mormons, from the First Vision of Joseph Smith to the Last Courtship of Brigham Young.* Salt Lake City: Shepard Book Company, 1904. First published 1873, by D. Appleton & Co., New York.

Sturgis, T. H., WSGA secretary, speech to the National Stock Growers' Convention, Chicago, 1886, quoted in the *Cheyenne Daily Sun*, November 25, 1886.

Sun, Kathleen R. "Ranch Management of Streamside Zones." In *Wyoming Water 1986 and Streamside Zone Conference: Proceedings.* Laramie: University of Wyoming Water Research Center, 1986, 155–66.

Talbot, Theodore. *The Journals of Theodore Talbot, 1843 and 1849–52. With the Frémont Expedition of 1843 and with the First Military Company in Oregon Territory, 1849–1852.* Edited, with notes, by Charles H. Carey. Portland, Ore.: Metropolitan Press, 1931.

Trenholm, Virginia, and Maurine Carley. *The Shoshonis: Sentinels of the Rockies.* Norman: University of Oklahoma Press, 1964.

Trenton, Patricia, and Peter H. Hassrick. *The Rocky Mountains: A Vision for Artists in the Nineteenth Century.* Norman: University of Oklahoma Press, in association with the Buffalo Bill Historical Center, Cody, Wyoming, 1983.

Tyler, Ron. "Alfred Jacob Miller." In Alfred Jacob Miller. *Alfred Jacob Miller: Artist as Explorer; First Views of the American Frontier, with an Essay by Ron Tyler.* Santa Fe: Gerald Peters Gallery, 1999, 9–45.

Underbrink, Lee. "The Covered Wagon Centennial at Independence Rock." *Overland Journal* 17:3 (Fall 1999): 2–11.

————. "The Oregon Trail Memorial Half-Dollar." *Overland Journal* (Fall 2004): 118–21.

United States Geological Survey. *First Annual Report of the Reclamation Service, from June 17 to December 1, 1902.* F. H. Newell, Chief Engineer. House of Representatives Document 79. 57th Cong., 2d sess. Washington, D.C.: Government Printing Office, 1903.

————. *Second Annual Report of the Reclamation Service, 1902–1903.* F. H. Newell, Chief Engineer. House of Representatives Document 44, 58th Cong., 2d sess. Washington, D.C.: Government Printing Office, 1904.

United States Reclamation Service. *History of the North Platte Project, Nebraska-Wyoming, 1902–1913.* Vols. 1 and 9.

Unruh, John D., Jr. *The Plains Across: The Overland Emigrants and the Trans-Mississippi West, 1840–1860.* Urbana: University of Illinois Press, 1979.

Utley, Robert M. *Frontiersmen in Blue: The United States Army and the Indian, 1848–1865.* New York: MacMillan, 1967.

Webber, Bert, and Margie Webber. *Ezra Meeker; Champion of the Oregon Trail.* Medford, Ore.: Webb Research Group, 1992.

Wedel, Waldo R. "The Prehistoric Plains." Chapter 6 in *Ancient North Americans.* Edited by Jesse D. Jennings. San Francisco: W. H. Freeman and Company, 1983, 205–35.

West, Elliott. "Reconstructing Race." *Western Historical Quarterly* (Spring 2003).

Western, Samuel. *Pushed off the Mountain, Sold down the River: Wyoming's Search for Its Soul.* Moose, Wyo.: Homestead Publishing, 2002.

Whitney, Orson F. *History of Utah.* Vol. 1. Salt Lake City: George Q. Cannon and Sons, 1892.

*Who's Who in America.* Vol. 28, 1954–55. Chicago: Marquis Publishing Co.

Wilkinson, Norman B. *Lammot du Pont and the American Explosives Industry, 1850–1884.* Charlottesville: University Press of Virginia, 1984.

Williams, Roger L. *A Region of Astonishing Beauty: The Botanical Exploration of the Rocky Mountains.* Lanham, Md.: Roberts Rinehart, 2003.

Wilson, Elijah Nicholas. *The White Indian Boy: the story of Uncle Nick among the Shoshones.* In collaboration with Howard R. Driggs. Yonkers-on-Hudson, N.Y.: World Book Company, ca. 1919.

Wister, Fanny Kemble, ed. *Owen Wister Out West: His Journals and Letters.* Chicago: University of Chicago Press, 1958.

Worster, Donald. *Dust Bowl: The Southern Plains in the 1930s.* New York: Oxford University Press, 1979.

———. *Rivers of Empire: Water, Aridity and the Growth of the American West.* New York: Pantheon Books, 1985.

———. *A River Running West: The Life of John Wesley Powell.* New York: Oxford University Press, 2002.

# Index

Bancroft, Hubert Howe, 269n12
Barclay, Lorne W., 221
Bar Eleven Ranch. *See* Sun Ranch
Barometer, cistern, 34–36, 38–40, 42;
    repaired by Frémont, 43; breaks
    final time, 43
Bartlett (Hayden assistant), 118, *119*
Bates Creek, 40, 158
Bates Hole (Bates Park) 76, 158
Beaman (Hayden meteorologist), *119*,
    120, 129
Bear Hunter, 112
Bear River irrigation project, 196–97,
    271n3
Bear River Massacre, 112
Bear Robe, 29
Beausoleil, Thomas, 135, 259n12. *See
    also* Sun, Tom
Beauty, Francis Parkman's ideas of,
    24; Hervey Johnson's ideas of,
    267n14; Oregon Trail emigrants'
    ideas of, 58–59, 62; Richard
    Burton's racial hierarchies of,
    74; Sanford Robinson Gifford's
    paintings and, 128–29; Sarah
    Sutton's racial hierarchies of, 65;
    William Henry Jackson's ideas of,
    117–18, 125–26, 260n12
Beaver trade, 25–26. *See also* Fur trade
Beebe, Ruth, 11, 270n16
Beef Acre. *See* Sun Ranch
Benoît, Leonard, 47
Benson, Ezra Taft, 234, 277n7
Benton, Thomas Hart, 36, 45, 50
Bent's Fort, 24, 27
Bernier, Baptiste, 47
Berra, John, 169
Bessemer, Wyo. 183–84
Beulah Belle Lake, 186, 270n16
Big Horn Expedition, 139
Bighorn Mountains, 31, 113–14, 139,
    171
Bighorn River, 13
Bird Island, 6, 18
Bissonette, Joseph, 39, 65, 70, 100
Black Bear, 109, 112, 113; death of, 114

Black Coal, 114–16
Blackfeet Indians, 25–26
Blackfeet Lakota. *See* Lakota Indians,
    Blackfeet
Black Hawk (Oglala), 31, 113
Black Hills, 122
Black Kettle, 265n11
Black's Fork of the Green River, 27
Blue Water Creek, battle of, 70
*Book of Mormon*, 244
*Book of Mormon Difficulties: A Study*, by
    B.H. Roberts, 227
*A Book of Mormon Study*, by B. H.
    Roberts, 227
Bordeaux, James, 66, 70
Bothwell, Albert, 7, 179, 182, 201, 203,
    *209*, 271nn2, 3, 272n20; battles
    Reclamation Service 207–11; eyes
    Sweetwater Valley development,
    176–77; 196–97; helps lynch
    Averell and Watson, 186, 188–90;
    hosts Chittenden, 195–96,
    199–200
Bothwell, John, 176–77, 182, 196, 197
Bothwell, Margaretta, 195
Bothwell, Wyo. 183–84, 187, 189
Bothwell Railroad, 177. *See also*
    Wyoming, Yellowstone Park and
    Pacific Railroad Company
Bothwell Ranch, 208
*Boy Scouts and the Oregon Trail*, by
    Clinton S. Martin, 221
Boy Scouts of America, 221, 226, 228;
    at Independence Rock, 1930,
    221–24
Bozeman Trail, 113
Bridger, Jim, 27, 31, 51, 67, 103, 257n8;
    painted in conquistador armor by
    A. J. Miller, 59
Bridger Valley, 224
Brooks, Byrant B. (B. B.), 230
Brulé Lakota. *See* Lakota Indians, Brulé
Bryant, Edwin C. 30
Buchanan, Frank, 188–89
Buchanan, James, 71, 94
Bucklin, N. D., 276n4